THE KILLING SKIES

RAF BOMBER COMMAND AT WAR

by

Simon Read

'The Fighters are our salvation,
but the Bombers alone provide the means of victory.'

Winston Churchill, *3 September 1940*

SPELLMOUNT

British Library Cataloguing in Publication Data:
A catalogue record for this book is available
from the British Library

Copyright © Simon Read 2006

ISBN 1-86227-329-4

First published in the UK in 2006 by
Spellmount Limited
The Mill, Brimscombe Port
Stroud, Gloucestershire. GL5 2QG

Tel: 01453 883300
Fax: 01453 883233
E-mail: enquiries@spellmount.com
Website: www.spellmount.com

1 3 5 7 9 8 6 4 2

Printed in Great Britain by
Oaklands Book Services
Stonehouse, Gloucestershire GL10 3RQ

Then shall the right aiming thunderbolts go abroad; and from the clouds, as from a well-drawn bow, they shall fly to the mark

— Wisdom 5:21, Air Ministry's *Bomber Command Handbook*, 1941.

It made me burn with rage on Thursday night as we were going to Schweinfurt to see the raid on London going on. I thought of your folks and mine underneath it all and I would not have turned back had we caught fire. Of course, I hate the job, but idealism is not enough. I am fighting for the people I love and the boys who have already paid the full price. To give into matters on ideological grounds is to let them all down.

— From a letter written by George Hull, a 23-year-old navigator killed over Frankfurt.

In loving memory of my grandfather, Michael Elelman,
and for all others who served in Bomber Command — both living and
dead — to whom we owe so much.

Contents

Acknowledgements

I spent six years researching, writing and revising this book. Many people helped in the course of this somewhat daunting endeavour, but to name them all would border on the impossible. The most important source of information in *The Killing Skies* by far are the records at the National Archives, Kew. Research was also done at the Imperial War Museum and the RAF Museum in Hendon. To those who leant their time and assistance to me at these amazing institutions, many thanks. Two people in particular deserve to be named: Johnny Biggs and Jack Catford, both veterans of the British bomber war. Johnny —otherwise known as Biggsy — served alongside my grandfather. Throughout my research, Johnny proved to be an amazing source of information. From providing detailed descriptions of crew briefings and the interior layout of a Wellington, to providing copies of combat reports and recounting take-off and landing procedures in a Stirling, Johnny's assistance proved priceless. Likewise, Jack — who sadly passed away in 2005 — was kind enough to hand over private papers and spend hours answering incessant questions. Bomber Command veteran Gordon Hart provided wonderful details regarding operations over Berlin, while the family of Sid Brans and other veterans gave me kind permission to reprint letters and journal entries. Many veterans I spoke with were loath to discuss their experiences. Some were embarrassed to talk out of fear it might come across as bragging, while others saw nothing overly special in their wartime contribution to Great Britain — their stance being that everyone contributed something. But as we inevitably lose more and more veterans of the Second World War with each passing day, it is important those still with us share their stories with today's younger generation, so that people never forget the bloodshed and sacrifice of yesteryear.

There is one person without whom this book might not have been written — and that is my grandmother, Hazel Elelman. A woman of amazing strength and vitality, she did her part during World War II by serving in the Woman's Auxiliary Army. Her enthusiasm for the book and intense interest was a fantastic source of inspiration, as were her amazing home-cooked meals and brandy-laced coffees! Naturally, I have to thank my parents — Bill and Susan — who have always had the utmost faith in everything I do. And to my sister, Sarah, heartfelt thanks and love for everything.

Foreword

In my apartment hangs a modest homage to my grandfather, Michael Elelman, and his war. It's a framed collection of photographs, grainy black and white images of a young man — a flight sergeant — in uniform. Among them are pictures of him and wartime comrades smiling and hoisting pints at the Fort St George, a riverside pub in Cambridge not far from RAF Stradishall, the airfield from which he flew thirty-one operations between January and July 1941 with No. 214 Squadron of RAF Bomber Command. In one picture, the winged-bullet badge of an airgunner can clearly be seen above his left breast pocket. One image, taken in 1942, is a particular favourite. A breeze is blowing the flap of his jacket. His cap is perched at a precarious angle on the right side of his head. He is leaning against the rear turret of a Stirling, his right hand resting on the Perspex bauble, his left hand confidently placed on his hip. Not everything, however, is a reminder of such wartime joviality.

His log book and the combat reports folded between its pages tell a violent tale. He rarely spoke of his experiences with Bomber Command, nor did he attend squadron reunions after the war. There was, he said, little point in dwelling on the past, though he would frequently revisit the pages of his log book, pulling it off the bookshelf in his sitting room to review where he was flying on any given night. Not until after his death from cancer in 1989 did I take a serious interest in the little blue book's contents. When he started flying combat operations against Nazi Germany in 1941, he was 27 — five years younger than I am now. His six crewmates — all in their late teens and early twenties — often called him 'Dad.'

His first combat operation — flown in a Vickers Wellington (No. T2542) — was against industrial facilities in Bremen on the night of 1 January 1941. He was over Bremen again the following night, and then Mannheim three nights later. The target for the night of 29 January was the harbour at Wilhelmshaven, but he and his crew never made it. With 4,500 lbs of high explosives and incendiaries in its underbelly, the bomber plummeted to the ground just minutes after its wheels left the flarepath. Trailing flame in its wake, the aircraft smashed through the airfield's perimeter fence, skidded over a stretch of road and ploughed into a farmer's field on the other side. As the aircraft came to a grinding stop in the dirt, my grandfather rotated his rear turret — so that it was at a right angle to the burning fuselage — and fell out backwards onto the muddy field. All six crew members managed to escape with only minor injuries.

My grandfather recorded the incident in his log book in the understated style common with such documents: 'Ops Wilhelmshaven / Crashed on take off with full bomb load.' The notation in the squadron's Operation Records Book adds a few more details: 'This crew was just airborn [sic] when port engine cut out. Aircraft caught fire in the air and crashed. The entire crew escaped before the entire fuselage blazed up and several bombs detonated. The observer obtained a sprained ankle.'

In 1942 he began his second tour of duty, this time in the Stirlings of No. 7 Squadron, flying from RAF Oakington. Four operations in, on the night of 19 May, he was shot returning from Mannheim when his bomber was attacked by a Junkers JU-88 off the Dutch Coast at 8,000 feet. The enemy aircraft attacked from below dead astern, pumping machine-gun and cannon fire into the Stirling's underside from a range of fifty yards. Shells tore through the floor of the rear turret, passing through my grandfather's left foot. The Junkers continued its ascent, climbing dead astern above the Stirling. As it roared passed the rear turret, my grandfather again, along with the mid-upper gunner, opened fire. The .303 Browning shells pierced the belly of the Junkers, which rolled over in a sudden dive and spun violently into the darkness below, belching flame as it went. Notes the combat report filed by the crew: 'The only casualty was our rear gunner who was hit in the left foot. Our aircraft started diving when attacked . . . with machine gun and cannon shells exploding inside our a/c, very fortunately without injuring any other members of the crew.' A photograph tucked away inside the pages of my grandfather's log book shows the Stirling the morning after the attack, its body peppered with holes.

One month later, he was back in the air. He took part in the 1,000-bomber raid against Bremen on the night of 26 June 1942. His aircraft was attacked on the night of 26 July en route to Hamburg, this time by three Messerschmitt 110s. They came under fire again from a Messerschmitt the following night, returning from another operation over Hamburg. The Stirling was heavily damaged and the mid-upper gunner was severely wounded. With its hydraulics system crippled and fuel lines leaking, the bomber crashed on landing back at base. The following month, the navigator and pilot in his crew were injured by flak when their aircraft was ensnared by searchlights over Düsseldorf.

In total, my grandfather flew fifty-one operations over Nazi Germany and Occupied Europe. A personal reason for undertaking the writing of this book was to glean a better understanding of what it was he — and the more than 100,000 other British and Commonwealth airmen — went through in the killing skies of Europe. Of the 125,000 men who flew with Bomber Command, 55,573 were killed. Another 9,838 men were shot down and taken prisoner of war. An additional 8,403 were wounded. Thus, Bomber Command suffered a total of 73,814 casualties — a casualty rate of fifty-nine per cent. Despite these staggering figures, the veterans of the RAF's bomber offensive remain without a campaign medal.

Since the end of the war, the actions of Bomber Command and the men who flew the operations have been vilified by many, criticised for the perpetration of mere acts of terror and wanton destruction. It is impossible to argue that Bomber Command's actions were not brutal, but to categorise its campaign as a means of simply terrorising the German populace is to ignore the greater context of the times in which it was waged.

There is certainly no shortage of books on Bomber Command. However, many accounts either omit certain operations or are light on aircrew experiences. It was my intent with this effort to find a balance between the two; to shed a greater light on the human side of the story. It is hoped the following account might change the perception some have towards Bomber Command's campaign and the men who waged it.

Preamble

The red glow of fire climbed skyward on billowing clouds of black smoke and mists of dust and debris. A crimson dome rose from the city centre like a massive molten bubble, expanding upward and outward. From the inferno stretched beams of blue and white light, groping in the darkness for the bombers passing overhead. Burning incendiaries glistened like stars, while high explosives detonated in vibrant white flashes. Everything was bathed in a violent spectrum of colour. Tracer rocketed skyward in luminescent blurs of red and green. Black clouds of flak hung heavy in the glare of searchlights. British bombers burned in lurid shades of red and orange. One fell in a long, shallow dive and disintegrated in a ball of flame before it lost much height. Another struggled to maintain its heading as fire licked its starboard wing. The air reeked of cordite and throbbed with the rumble of two-engined Wellingtons and four-engined Lancasters, Stirlings and Halifaxes.

The thunderous drone over Bremen had commenced at airfields in Cambridgeshire, Lincolnshire, Yorkshire and East Anglia. The sound carried across the blacked-out and war-scarred landscape of England as the men and machines of RAF Bomber Command set course for the killing skies of Nazi Germany. They crossed the English coast at King's Lynn and Southwold. In the towns below, the serenity of night gave way to a noise that carried with it the promise of indiscriminate death and destruction. London had burned. The heart of Coventry had been gutted. Incendiary and high explosive had torn through Manchester, Liverpool, Portsmouth, Bristol, Birmingham, Leeds and Glasgow. Thousands had died. Upon those who had unleashed such brutality, it would be returned, declared Churchill, in 'ever-increasing measure.' Now land gave way to the churning grey and white of the North Sea, and in those quiet coastal towns, the rumble of mechanised thunder faded into the distance as young men hurtled toward some grim conclusion.

A solitary patch of cloud obscured a distant slither of moon. Suspended in space on their solitary vigil, rear gunners sat cramped in the tight confines of their Perspex turrets. The guns — .303 Brownings — loaded and cocked, were test fired into the sea. Magnesium burned bright, spearing the darkness in incandescent streaks of red, as tracer rounds fell away into the restless waste of water. The interiors of the aircraft were cold and dark, and there was the scent of oil and metal polish. Crews worked by the glow of dimmed flashlights. Wireless operators sat at their radios. Navigators made vital log entries in the weak illumination of an amber light. Their outward track would take them across the Dutch coast at Ijmuiden. Easy prey for the Luftwaffe night fighters operating out of Schipol, they would cross the Zuider Zee. Those who survived the initial enemy engagement would continue to the Dummer See — a large inland lake — then turn north for the forty-mile run to the target.

The map of Britain and Western Europe at the evening's briefing was detailed in half-million scale. Lengths of red ribbon, illustrating the outward journey, stretched across it and converged on 'the target for tonight.' Blue ribbon showed the return trip, a route that would take the survivors across the Dutch coast at Helder, but within range of night fighters based at Leeuwarden. The map was the centrepiece of a large cartographic display set atop a raised dais at one end of the briefing room. Model fighter planes hung from the ceiling in motionless flight, lost in thickening palls of grey tobacco smoke. On long wooden benches, men sat together as crews and listened to the briefing unfold in a series of short lectures. Watches were synchronised and routes were discussed.

The Intelligence Officer explained detailed infrared images of the target area taken by RAF Reconnaissance, pinpointing the whereabouts of known anti-aircraft batteries and the city's industrial complexes, particularly the Focke-Wulf factory. The Met Officer briefed them on the weather. Clouds would top out at 9,000 feet, with their base extending to 5,000 feet. Above the clouds, conditions would be moderately clear with a quarter moon. There would be no clouds over Bremen. The journey back would be made in a misty haze with light rain expected over England. The Signals Officer reviewed emergency frequencies and recognition colours. Navigators made note of the information on slips of edible rice paper. Reviewing the silhouette of the Junkers JU88, the Gunnery Leader briefed the men on expected enemy opposition. Any questions?

The station commander stood and wished them all good luck then strolled from the room. The briefing was over; the waiting had begun. As one pilot wrote in his journal: 'My heart rose, and I would have done anything to escape the horror and oblivion I knew the darkness would bring.'[1] Navigators conferred with their captains as they plotted routes on their Mercator projection charts. In the mess, crews dined on bacon, eggs and buttered toast. The meal finished, the cod liver oil capsules swallowed, it was time to prepare. There were good-luck rituals to be done and letters to write. Penning a letter to his father before his first operational flight, one young pilot wrote:

> As this letter will only be read after my death, it may seem a some-what macabre document, but I do not want you to look on it that way. I have always had a feeling that our stay on Earth, that thing we call 'Life,' is but a transitory stage in our development, and that the dreaded monosyllable 'Death' ought not to indicate anything to be feared.[2]

He would never return.

Flyers emptied their pockets of personal possessions. Over their uniforms, they pulled on their flying clothes. Heavy sweaters were worn to help combat the cold. Over this went the Irvine Jacket with its inflatable Mae West life preserver. To spare feet from the ravages of frostbite, flying boots lined with lamb's wool were pulled over woollen stockings and silk socks. Hands went into wool-lined gloves, then came the leather flying helmet with its oxygen mask. In their pockets they carried escape kits, a metal box containing silk maps of Germany and the Low Countries, water purifying tablets, a button-sized compass, a pocketknife and Horlicks tablets. In the crew room, flight rations were handed out in brown paper bags. 'The ideal ration,' noted the Air Ministry, 'consists of a few biscuits, an apple or an orange, some barley sugar, chewing gum, and raisins. Each member of the crew also carries a thermos flask of hot tea or coffee.'[3]

Parachutes tucked under their arms, burdened by the weight of multiple layers of clothing, they walked to dispersals, where the bombers stood in silhouette against the gathering gloom. The bomber, painted in 'its coat of dull black paint enlivened only by the code letters painted on it and by some fanciful device chosen by the squadron or by the individual captain — a bent bow with the arrow against the string, a large portrait of "Jane" of picture paper fame, a bird with spread wings, a kangaroo on a cloud.'[4] The crews spread out on damp grass. Some sat in quiet contemplation, nursing their cigarettes and pipes, others — prompted by nervous energy — discussed any available topic. The chief ground mechanic and pilot circled the plane, inspecting all moving parts. As the time for take off drew near, the station commander made the rounds, wishing all the crews well.

Pilots test fired their bombers' engines. The great Merlins came to life in a splutter of machinery and a dazzling shower of sparks. The engines screamed as throttle levers were pushed forward. Sitting in his bucket seat with his feet on the rudder pedals, the pilot moved his eyes over the cockpit's instrumentation, checking revs, boost, brake pressure, oil and air gauges, and magneto drop. Satisfied with the readings, he eased back the throttle and flashed his ground crew a thumbs up. Like a man renting a car, the pilot had to sign for the aircraft each night prior to takeoff. Now the rest of the men climbed aboard as ground engineers disconnected the battery cart from the engines. Inside the aircraft, metal closed in from all directions. The wireless operator and navigator made their way to the rear cabin, separated from the cockpit by an armoured bulkhead. The navigator's table — which would soon be covered in charts, maps, photographs and other tools of the trade — was on the port side. The wireless operator sat immediately behind him.

A bulkhead door opposite the one to the cockpit opened up on the main fuselage. A narrow catwalk stretched the length of the plane. It was along here the rear gunner made his way — past the flare chute and chemical toilet — remaining hunched at the shoulders so as not to knock his head. Near the back of the aircraft were four tanks, each containing 2,000 rounds of ammunition. A track — upon which incendiary, armour-piercing and tracer shells were fed into the rear guns — extended from each tank. Scrambling over the mainspar, he came to the aircraft's rear bulkhead. He opened the door and took hold of the grab handle above it, swinging himself feet-first into his turret. Because space was so restricted, he was forced to leave his parachute outside the bulkhead door. If the plane went down in a flaming spiral, his odds of escape were near zero. He would also be the first target in any night-fighter attack. At the opposite end of the aircraft, forward of the cockpit in the front turret, the front gunner was positioning himself in the nose of the aircraft

Oxygen lines were connected to face masks and wireless communications were checked. Chocks were pulled away from wheels, and aircraft moved about the perimeter track toward the runway controller's caravan. 'The aircraft,' stated the Air Ministry in 1941, 'are sent off at short intervals of between two and five minutes. The signal to take off is made to them by those in charge of the flarepath who flash a green or red light indicating whether the aircraft should, or should not, begin its run.'[5] With flaps set at 15 degrees and a green light flashing, the pilot slowly pushed the throttle levers forward. It was always a daunting moment, sitting atop thousands of pounds of aviation fuel, high explosives, incendiaries and ammunition as it hurtled down the runway. It did not always go smoothly, as one squadron intelligence officer recorded in 1941:

This crew was just airborne when the port engine went out. Aircraft caught fire in the air and crashed. The entire crew escaped before the entire fuselage blazed up and several bombs detonated. The observer obtained a sprained ankle.[6]

But when things went as they should, it made for an impressive spectacle. 'The air is full of the noise of engines,' read an article in the 4 October 1941 edition of The Sphere. 'The sky darkens and most of the bombers have gone. When the last of them disappears, the night seems strange and quiet again.' It was similarly strange for the men in the machines. Recalled one airgunner:

> At first, when only a few hundred feet up, we could just observe the dusk-shrouded rooftops of Downham Market. Then, quite quickly, the sight of the town disappeared into an opaque nothingness.[7]

The standard tour of duty was generally thirty operations. Flying through the darkness, each man knew the odds of survival were stacked against them at one in ten. The absence of familiar faces the morning after an operation was a constant reminder that death was always imminent. But even in the most violent of situations, each man harboured the unwavering belief that catastrophe would befall someone other than himself. Men held fast to that belief as they winged their way across the North Sea, waiting to hear the warning that signalled the true start of their ordeal: 'Enemy coast ahead.' In the near distance could be seen probing searchlights and the flash of exploding anti-aircraft fire. Writing in his diary after a torturous episode over Germany, a pilot with 218 Squadron described a scene that played out nightly:

> Red stars in the sky told of the flak bursting around the aircraft ahead as they probed the deep coastal defence system. Dead ahead came a sudden huge outburst of flame, which commenced to sweep lower and lower until it ended in a terrific flash and then was there no longer. They'd got someone, and his bombs had gone up.[8]

Pilots weaved patterns against the sky, hoping to avoid the searchlights. Once ensnared by a master beam the world outside was lost to a blinding glare. Satellite beams swung in from three opposite directions, effectively trapping the bomber in a cage of light, presenting an ideal target for the defenders on the ground. Anti-aircraft gunners worked furiously to find their range, buffeting the aircraft with a murderous volley of fire. Evasive manoeuvre or destruction were the only means of escape for the beleaguered bomber and its crew. Many airmen succumbed to the violent range of motion, throwing up in their face masks or being knocked unconscious as the pilot threw the machine about the sky in a desperate bid to break free of the searchlights' grasp. Witnessing the terrible episode unfold, other crews were thankful for the distraction as they made their way through the defences.

For the most part, the journey was made in silence. No casual chatter among the crew was allowed. The navigator fed the pilot course changes as the gunners kept their silent vigil. An airgunner might fly an entire tour of duty without once encountering an enemy fighter. Others weren't so fortunate. When the guns were fired, the sound permeated the entire aircraft, and with it came the overpowering smell of cordite. But Junkers and Messerschmitts weren't the only enemies aligned against the crew. There were the dangers of fatigue and the numbing bite of the savage temperatures at 10,000 feet. The latter was especially true for the airgunners. A large square portion of Perspex was removed from the gun turrets to improve the gunners' field of view. Many times, crews were flying in temperatures well below zero. One airgunner remembers a night the numbers dropped to minus 51 degrees:

> The cold was intense, and the air outlet on my oxygen mask was repeatedly gathering long icicles, which had repeatedly to be broken off. At one time I let it accumulate too much and before I realised what was happening, I had a spike 10 or 12 inches long protruding from the mask... Even more diabolical was the fact that my eyelashes began freezing together. I had to lift my goggles and put the palms of my heated gloves over my eyes to thaw my lids out.[9]

As the aircraft approached the target, the second pilot — whose main task was to assist on take offs and landings — took up position in the bomber's astrodome, a dome-shaped protrusion of Perspex sticking out of the aircraft's roof that provided an unobstructed view of the surrounding skies. Having reached the Dummer See, a course was set for the final forty-mile run to Bremen. The target was already visible in the distance. The sky ahead glowed red as great cones of light staggered back and forth. Men breathed heavily through their masks, their mouths tasting of damp rubber and spoiled air. 'As the aircraft draws nearer to the target, more flak becomes visible. It is of all kinds,' reported the Air Ministry. 'From high up it may look like the red eyes of beasts winking from the darkness of their lairs. Then, when the shells burst close at hand, they seem like great flakes and balls of fire.'[10]

At this point, the navigator came forward to assume the role of bomb aimer. He made his way through a hatch in the cockpit floor and descended to the nose of the aircraft. There he took up his position, lying on his stomach at full body length. Staring through the bombsight, he was privy to the best view in the house. He plugged in his intercom and began guiding the pilot, for now the bomb aimer was in true control of the aircraft, making sure the pilot got it just right. Below was a raging sea of fire. Tracer shot up from the flames, ascending at what seemed to be slowly at first, then rocketing past the bomber at lightning speed.

'Bomb doors open.'

The aircraft shook as the sky ruptured around it. Flak and searchlights burned the night away. The crew listened intently, hearing the words of the bomb aimer cut through the static in their headsets. 'Left, left… right… steady…. steady…' Everything now was noise and light as machine after machine descended upon the aiming point: the Focke-Wulf factory. The men knew what they were doing. They knew there were civilians down below. They knew women and children were dying, just as they had died in numerous British cities. 'We, too, had endured bombings and the destruction of our cities,' said one airgunner years later. 'This wasn't something we asked for or enjoyed. It was war, and you blocked the consequences from your mind. If you dwelled too long on it, you wouldn't be able to do your job.'

'Bombs gone!'

Incendiaries and high explosives fell to a burning earth. The crew felt the aircraft lift as it discharged the weight of its payload. The plane pitched in a sharp, diving turn to port as other aircraft came in behind it. The gauntlet of searchlights and flak would have to be run again on the journey home. Many bombers made the trek with dead or grotesquely wounded crew members on board. Some planes returned to base with whole sections torn away by enemy fire. Many aircraft, crippled over the target area, never made it to the coast. They were easy prey for the night fighters lurking along the return route. But there was no reprieve for those who returned to base safely. Indeed, those who survived only faced possible death again the next night.

The year was 1942. In their wake, bombers left vast areas of unimaginable destruction. The price paid on both sides was massive. Bomber Command was emerging as a devastating weapon of total war capable of razing entire cities in a single night.

It was a far cry from how it all started.

Blood and Water

Hard Lessons

Memories still lingered. A generation of British men wiped out in the mud-swamped, rat-infested trenches of the Western Front. A war not yet far removed by the passing of time. Now, on a Sunday morning, a mere two decades after the Great War's guns fell silent, the BBC carried the subdued tones of Prime Minister Neville Chamberlain, broadcasting from the Cabinet Room at 10 Downing Street:

> This morning, the British Ambassador in Berlin handed the German Government a final note, stating that, unless we heard from them by eleven o'clock that they were prepared at once to withdraw their troops from Poland, a state of war would exist between us. I have to tell you now that no such undertaking has been received, and that consequently this country is at war with Germany.'

The public received the news with quiet consternation.

At 1100 hours on 3 September 1939, as barrage balloons ascended above London, Big Ben tolled the hour of war. One minute later, Flying Officer A McPherson, a pilot with No. 139 Squadron at RAF Wyton, was ordered into the sky. McPherson and his crew, Commander Thompson, the naval observer, and wireless operator/air gunner Corporal V Arrowsmith, were to carry out RAF Bomber Command's first wartime operation. A minute past noon, their twin-engined Blenheim, number N6215, was airborne, climbing to 23,000 feet above the North Sea. The crew's objective was to photograph elements of the German Fleet. Notes No. 139 Squadron's Operations Record Book: 'Task successful. Seventy five photographs taken of German military objectives. This was the first aircraft of the Royal Air Force to cross the German frontier and the crew reported that the German fleet was just leaving Wilhelmshaven.'[1]

The freezing temperatures at 23,000 feet rendered the Blenheim's wireless radio unserviceable. Not until McPherson returned to base at 1650 hours did the Admiralty learn of the German Fleet's deployment. A belated attempt by fifteen Hampdens and nine Wellingtons to attack German warships on the move was thwarted by an early-evening thunderstorm. Not until the next day would British blood be shed.

Shadows of War

Prior to the onslaught of German bombs, Britain's landscape was drastically altered under the looming shadow of war. Earth-moving machinery levelled hills and bulldozed fields. Cement was poured, piping was laid, control towers, billets and mess halls went up and soon the stillness of rural life was assaulted by the arrival of the bombers. Britain went to war armed with twenty-three bomber squadrons — approximately 280 aircraft — dispersed amongst four bomber groups: Nos 2, 3, 4, 5. The Bristol Blenhiems, the 'medium' bomber of the day, was allocated to No. 2 Group and its six operational squadrons. The six squadrons of No. 3 Group were armed with the 'heavy' Vickers Wellington. In the north of England were based the five squadrons of No. 4 Group equipped with Armstrong-Whitworth Whitleys, also classified as a 'heavy' in the days prior to the four-engined machines. In Lincolnshire, south of No. 4 Group's Yorkshire location, were the airfields of No. 5 Group, also a 'heavy' bomber group boasting six squadrons of Handley Page Hampdens. But in what offensive capacity could .this arsenal be used?[2]

It was a question pondered by the British Air Staff in the wake of the Munich Crisis.

> It is impossible [states a report dated 27 September 1938] to define in any detail, in advance of the event, the course of action that will have to be adopted by the air striking force at the outset of a war with Germany. It must depend to a very great extent on the action taken by the German air forces, partly because they have the initiative owing to their superior strength, and partly owing to the policy of His Majesty's Government that we should not initiate air action which may cause heavy loss to the civil population.[3]

Objectives governing Britain's air offensive were drawn up by the Air Staff and presented to the Air Ministry in October 1937. Known as the Western Air Plans, they comprised thirteen objectives. The most vital were categorised in Group 1, Plans 1 to 5. The first plan envisaged damaging attacks on 'the German Air Striking Force and its maintenance organisation.' The second and third plans entailed a joint RAF and Royal Navy effort in safeguarding waters around the British Isles and protecting convoys in the Eastern Atlantic. 'Attacking the concentration areas of the German Army, and the interruption of its communications in an advance into Belgium, Holland and France' was Plan 4. Western Air Plan No. 5 targeted 'the enemy's manufacturing resources in the Ruhr, Rhineland and Saar.' Pertaining directly to Bomber Command were Plans 1, 4, and 5. But war does not abide by plans and, of these three, all but one crumbled under an intensive review of Bomber Command's capabilities.[4]

Hunting the Luftwaffe would entail a widespread search-and-destroy mission. The Germans had constructed numerous emergency air strips to which they could move their air forces upon the commencement of hostilities. It was not known where these airfields were. Bomber Command's Commander-in-Chief, Air Chief Marshal Sir Edgar Ludlow-Hewitt, a realist appointed to his command on 12 September 1937, argued that the undertaking of such operations would ultimately result in the complete annihilation of his medium- and heavy-bomber forces in less than two months. A disagreement over strategy hindered plans to attack the German Army and its communications in case of an advance on the Low Countries and France. The Air Staff favoured raiding railway stations and junctions. The British General Staff wanted to target bridges and viaducts. The French, who faced a graver threat from an advancing German onslaught, backed attacks on enemy troops and armoured columns. Regardless of what option was undertaken, RAF planners knew it would devour nearly all of Bomber Command, resulting in mass British casualties and questionable results.[5]

German industry remained the ideal target. The main brunt of force would fall upon the Ruhr: a geographical area 'smaller than that of Greater London,' yet housing '70 to 80 per cent of Germany's coal and coke supplies, and 67 per cent of her supplies of pig-iron, as well as 75 per cent of her steel capacity, and most of her basic chemical production.'[6] But this plan was complicated in June 1938 when, standing before the House of Commons, Chamberlain announced that the RAF would restrict its bombing to military targets and would do everything in its power to avoid civilian casualties. Subsequently, Bomber Command was ordered to focus its attacks on the Luftwaffe and German ground forces, regardless of the difficulties involved. In April the following year, a meeting between the French and British military staffs in London relegated the bomber to an army-supporting role, assisting with the battle on land when it came. Four months later, the Air Ministry issued its 'Instructions Governing Naval and Air Bombardment':

> Our policy in respect to air bombardment at the outset of a war was agreed with the French in the course of the Staff Conversations in London in April this year in the following terms. 'The Allies would not initiate air action against any but purely "military" objectives in the narrowest sense of the term, i.e. Naval, Army and Air Forces and establishments, and as far as possible would confine it to objectives on which attack would not involve loss of civil life.'[7]

'The intentional bombardment of civilian populations' was deemed illegal. It was a point further reinforced on 1 September. As German troops swept across the Polish border, President Roosevelt urged those nations on the precipice of war to refrain from bombing civilians. Britain and France offered their assurances. Hitler did too, promising to wage war in a manner as humane as the circumstances allowed.[8] But in the end, all assurances would be swept aside by the sheer brutality of the conflict. Germany would be reduced to smouldering ruins, Tokyo would be mercilessly firebombed and the United States would usher in the atomic age.

First Blood

Orders to attack the German Fleet were issued to Bomber Command on 4 September, the first full day of war. 'The greatest care is to be taken not to injure the civilian population,' they stated. 'The intention is to destroy the German Fleet. There is no alternative target.'[9] At 0835 hours that morning, McPherson and his crew were back in the air, again off to reconnoitre the North Sea. Heavy rain clouds seethed at 17,000 feet and forced McPherson to drop his Blenheim to 250 feet as he rocketed over the German naval bases at Wilhelmshaven, Brunsbuttel and the Schillig Roads. A large warship was spotted at Wilhelmshaven. Two were seen off Brunsbuttel. Again, not until McPherson returned to base was the presence of the warships made known. Thrown into action against the warship near Wilhelmshaven were fifteen Blenheims of Nos 107, 110 and 139 Squadrons. The two warships off Brunsbuttel would be targeted by fourteen Wellingtons of Nos 9 and 149 Squadrons.

The Blenheims flew in independent flights. The machines of 110 Squadron, led by Flight Lieutenant Ken Doran, took to the skies above RAF Wattisham at 1555 hours. Each Blenheim carried in its belly a 500-

lb. general purpose bomb fused with an 11-second delay to be dropped in a low-level attack. Cutting through the gloom, mist and rain swirling above the sea, the Blenheims were forced to fly no higher than 100 feet. Below them, violent water churned grey and unforgiving as England fell from view and the German coast loomed ever closer. As the Blenheims gained on their objective, the clouds began to lift. The planes swept into Wilhelmshaven Harbour a few miles north of their target and climbed to 500 feet. With cloud cover dissipating, the five aircraft broke into two sub-flights of two Blenheims each and one single Blenheim. Through their rain-splattered windscreens, the pilots could see their prey — the battleship *Admiral Scheer*. Drawn up astern was the cruiser *Emden*.

Doran flew over the ship at masthead height — cutting diagonally across the aft deck — releasing his two bombs 'bang amidships' which were seen to bounce harmlessly off the *Admiral Scheer's* armour-plated deck. Other bombs fell wide, exploding in the water as the ships' anti-aircraft batteries — and those on shore — opened fire. On the deck of the *Admiral Scheer*, sailors could be seen running to their battle stations, leaving their washing hanging out around the stern. The second Blenheim came in for its attack, dropping its bombs short of the target. They detonated in shallow water underneath the ships, as the third Blenheim, unable to make it in eleven seconds, veered off and dropped its bombs in open water. Tracer tore through one Blenheim, blasting it from the sky and sent it slamming into the *Emden's* fo'c's'le. A column of flame shot skyward, killing nine of the ship's crew.[20]

The five Blenheims of No. 107 Squadron swooped in for their attack only minutes later. As the aircraft came in low, both shore and ship defences threw heavy fire into the sky, destroying four of the five aircraft. Having failed to locate the targets, the men and machines of No. 139 Squadron were spared a similar massacre and returned to base without suffering any losses. Meanwhile, against the *Scharnhorst* and *Gneisenau* at Brunsbuttel, the Wellingtons fared little better. Bad weather forced a majority of the formation to turn back home. Six of the fourteen aircraft reached the target area and were torn into by a swarm of Messerschmitt Bf 109s of fighter Gruppe II JG/77. Wrote Squadron Leader Lamb, who led the first wave of No. 9 Squadron Wellingtons in the attack:

> Towards the end of a fighter attack carried out by 9 German fighters at approx. 18.35 hours on, I jettisoned my three bombs 'live and in stick' at 400 feet in the south side of the harbour. At the moment of bombing I felt sure there was no shipping in the vicinity, but having pressed the bomb release I saw a merchant ship, approx. 7,000 tons, athwartships. I climbed rapidly, still being attacked by fighters and succeeded in reaching cloud cover. It was necessary for the safety

of my crew that these bombs were jettisoned as the decreased load enabled the machine to successfully evade the attack.[21]

Two Wellingtons in this first wave of three were pulverised, but the merchant ship was blown apart in a crimson flash. The second wave of three Wellingtons was also forced into the clouds as anti-aircraft fire seared the formation. In his post-operation report, the formation's leader, Flight Lieutenant I P Grant, wrote:

> The expected error of my own bombs was 500 yards. On the north bank of the river two shore batteries were firing at us from positions about a mile and 1½ miles west of Brunsbuttel, respectively. These batteries had three or four guns and were firing with far less accuracy than the ships. Six or eight cruisers were firing at us as well as the battleship. We were hit three times. All three machines dropped their bombs at the same time.[22]

Thus, Bomber Command's first offensive action of the war failed in its objectives and cost the British seven of the twenty-nine aircraft dispatched. This was a casualty rate of twenty-four per cent and one that could not possibly be sustained. The RAF now found itself in the school of hard knocks, and the lessons would come fast and furious.[23]

The Nickel Run

A bomber's interior was a brutal environment — one where bare flesh stuck to metal and men nearly froze to death. It was not uncommon for guns to be rendered useless by the build-up of icicles, or ice in oxygen masks to slowly asphyxiate the wearer. It was in such conditions that Whitley and Hampden crews took Bomber Command's propaganda offensive to the German mainland. On the first night of war, ten Whitleys of Nos 51 and 58 Squadrons — carrying five million leaflets — flew to Hamburg, Bremen and the Ruhr. The leaflets, printed by the Ministry of Information, were placed in bundles of 1,500 and secured by a piece of string. Over the target, a crew member would cut the string and shove the bundles down the aircraft's flarechute. Caught in the bomber's slipstream, the leaflets would scatter and fall over a wide area below.

The operations, code-named Nickel, would be flown throughout the war. The British public was rightly doubtful that such operations would be of any consequence to the German war effort, the running joke being that bomber crews were ordered to make sure the bundles were untied so as not to harm anyone on the ground. Arthur Harris, then AOC-in-C of No. 5 Group, believed leaflet raids did nothing more than supply 'the Continent's requirements of toilet paper for the five long years of war.'[24] While he was undoubtedly right, nothing of jest could be derived from the punishment the crews endured on these nightly excursions.

On the night of 27 October, as Whitleys passed in the blackness overhead, leaflets descended upon Frankfurt. The temperature that night had dropped to a painful minus 32 Centigrade. Flying through thick cloud, one Whitley pilot was forced to cut his starboard engine when, after being ensconced in six inches of ice, it overheated and burst into flames. With one engine gone and thickening ice spreading across its wings, the plane lunged forward in a violent dive, dropping to 7,000 feet before both pilots, pulling with all their strength on the control column, were able to level her out. As the pilots struggled to maintain a level heading, the port engine cut out. Looking through the cockpit window, they could see four inches of ice protruding from inside the engine cowling and the crystallised blades of the propeller. The windscreen too was becoming more clouded as ice crept across it. The order was given to bail out, but was quickly cancelled as there was no response from either the front or rear gunner. In the aircraft's dive and subsequent recovery, both men had been knocked unconscious. Now ice had rendered the aircraft's rudder and elevators immobile. The plane was losing height at a rate of 2,000 feet per minute. Reported the crew afterwards:

> We opened the top hatch to see where we were going, and the second pilot, who was at the controls, opened the side window. The aircraft emerged from the clouds in heavy rain at about 200 feet above the ground. All we could see was a black forest with a grey patch in the middle, for which we were heading; the second pilot pulled the aircraft over the trees brushing their tops, and the aircraft dropped flat into a field, travelled through a wire fence, skidded broadside on and came to rest with the port wing against the trees on the further side of the clearing.[25]

The crew survived without injury, but were forced to spend the night in the bomber. They were found the next morning and aided in their return to England by local French residents. That same night, another Whitley suffered a failure in its oxygen-delivery system as ice slowly worked its way about the plane's construction. Chunks of ice could be heard flying off the spinning propellers and slamming into the side of the aircraft. The cold was crippling, and crew members were forced to bang their heads against the floor and on the navigator's table so as to inflict some other form of pain to distract them from the awful frost-bite and strangling lack of oxygen. Despite such conditions, the plane and crew returned safely.[26]

Later in the war, Nickel operations would be used to encourage the resistance movements in occupied countries. Though leaflet dropping had no impact on German morale, it did prove that Bomber Command was capable of flying deep penetration raids over the Reich, thus providing crews with night-flying and reconnaissance training. Of considerable note were the fewer casualties Bomber Command suffered by night as opposed to day. Between the nights of 4 September and 23 December, 113 leaflet sorties were flown. During these, only four aircraft were lost. It was a figure that appealed to Ludlow-Hewitt, a man greatly shocked by the grievous casualties suffered by Bomber Command so far during its daylight operations.[27] Perhaps, thought 'Ludlow' as he was commonly known, it would be wise to strike the enemy by night. There were, however, more hard lessons to be learned before that happened.

North Sea Fury

Eleven Hampdens, flying in two formations of five and six, skimmed across the North Sea on the morning of 29 September, reconnoitring the Heligoland area in search of German shipping. Bomber Command was now flying 'reconnaissance in strength' — dispatching ready-made attack forces to hunt and destroy German naval forces. It was a new policy derived in the wake of 3 and 4 September, when too much time had elapsed between the actual spotting and attacking of German warships. On this bleak morning, the Hampdens of Nos 61 and 144 Squadrons spotted two enemy destroyers and proceeded to attack.

Coming in from 300 feet, the first formation of six were torn into by heavy pom-pom fire. One shell ripped through the nose of the lead aircraft, hit the pilot and sent the bomber veering off track. All bombs fell wide of the target, exploding in the water — yet all six aircraft survived. The same cannot be said for the second formation. In the course of reconnoitring the area, the two formations had become separated. Pressing home its offensive, the formation from 144 Squadron was intercepted by 'a hornet's nest' of Bf 109s. The .303 Browning machine guns with which all Bomber Command aircraft were armed were no match against the Messerschmitt's 20-mm cannon. Incendiary shells tore through the Hampdens and their crews, destroying all but one aircraft. Of twenty four-aircrew, eighteen were killed, including the commander of 144 Squadron, Wing Commander J C Cunningham.

Bad weather greatly limited operations throughout October and November but, in December, conditions began to clear and the men and machines of Bomber Command were at it again. At this early stage of the war, the RAF believed in the self-defending bomber formation, relying on the collective fire of its airgunners to fend off a fighter attack. The events of 29 September had done little to discredit such faith, though it was decided Wellingtons were better suited for the task. So it was that on 3 December, twenty-four Wellingtons of Nos 115 and 149 Squadrons were dispatched to the Heligoland area.

At 10,000 feet, they flew in sections of three, with the lead section serving as a reconnaissance force. At 1126 hours they appeared over Heligoland and, through the clouds, spotted two German cruisers and attendant merchant ships. Using armour-piercing bombs, the Wellingtons attacked by sections from heights of 7,000-10,000 feet. The ships threw up a violent barrage of shell and shrapnel, peppering two bombers but failing to inflict any serious damage. Bombs fell, exploding in water, but a stick of three is believed to have struck a cruiser. As the Wellingtons pressed home their attack, they were intercepted by a force of Bf 109s and Bf 110s.

In the ensuing confrontation, the German fighters gave wide berth to the sting of the Wellingtons' rear armaments, breaking off their assaults at 400 to 600 yards. No bombers were lost, but one Bf 109 was shot down. If it seemed Bomber Command's policy was sound, and the belief in the self-defending bomber formation was justified, events eleven days later would rock the foundations of that belief when forty-two Wellingtons took part in another armed-reconnaissance operation.[28]

The force included twelve Wellingtons from No. 99 Squadron at RAF Newmarket. Taking off at 1143 hours, they set a course toward the coastal crossover point at Yarmouth. Flying conditions were foul. Visibility was only two miles and a heavy haze obscured the horizon. The bombers crossed the English Coast at 1,000 feet and cut their way through thickening cloud and rain, flying in two groups in line astern. As they swept across the North Sea, a descending cloud base forced them ever lower. By the time the Dutch coast was spotted at 1305 hours, the two formations were flying at a mere 600 feet.[29]

To deceive enemy patrol ships, Wing Commander Griffith, the formation's leader, veered the raiders towards Heligoland before steering them on track — at 1347 hours — toward the Schillig Roads north of Wilhelmshaven. By now, flying visibility had been reduced to a mere ½ mile and the sinking cloud base had forced the aircraft down to 200 feet. They proceeded on course through the gloom, turning on a north-easterly track at 1414 hours off the island of Wangerooge. Some eleven minutes later, two German cruisers were spotted heading south. To avoid flying directly over the enemy ships, the formation banked sharply to the north then swung round to the left to catch a better glimpse of their prey. As the bombers levelled out in their approach, the cruisers opened fire.[30]

Green tracer scorched the formation's airspace, as great plumes of water exploded beneath the aircraft. The concussion of the blasts and the buffeting of exploding pom-pom fire forced the bombers to veer evasively to the west. Everything was veiled in a grey shroud of mist through which the dark outline of Wangerooge loomed. From the island's silhouette and the lingering haze, three Bf 109s emerged and immediately set upon the formation.

The battle was joined minutes later by a second wave of Messerschmitts. They dived in from above, coming in line astern and brought their awesome firepower to bear before breaking away. All the while, the Wellingtons struggled to maintain formation and concentrate their return fire.

In their desperate plight, the bombers were ravaged by three Bf 110s, attacking off the formation's port beam and firing from below. A flurry of white tracer passed within two feet of Griffith's aircraft as three more twin-engined fighters appeared in line astern of the formation and an additional six joined the fray one minute later.[31]

Hopelessly outgunned, the young men in the Wellingtons' front and rear turrets fired frantically in a desperate bid for survival, states No. 99 Squadron's combat diary.

At 1456 a twin-engined fighter appeared about 20 feet behind and 50 feet above the leader's aircraft. The tail gunner of this machine, No. 565040 Cpl Bickerstaff, A., Metal Rigger/AG, brought the guns to bear and tracer was seen to pass directly through the aircraft in the pilot's position. The machine hovered momentarily and then burst into flame just inside the port engine. The flame spread very rapidly and the aircraft fell off to the left in a vertical dive, and struck the water in a sheet of flame.[32]

Fighters screeched about the sky. Fire from the enemy cruisers rocked the British formation, exploding in large, luminescent flashes of green. Bombers, trailing smoke and fire, plunged into the churning waters below. At 1501 hours, some twenty-seven minutes after the assault began, the Messerschmitts launched one last offensive action from astern before the Wellingtons were able to make their escape.

When the smoke cleared and the blazing embers of obliterated bombers had fallen away, only seven of the twelve Wellingtons remained as the beaten formation limped back to England. One bomber, which jettisoned its bombs in the North Sea, crashed shortly after crossing the English coast.[33]

Some within the Bomber Command hierarchy were hard pressed to admit that half a bomber formation had been obliterated by enemy fighters. Among the non-believers was Bomber Command's Senior Air Staff

Officer, Air Commodore N H Bottomley. In a report dated 28 December 1939, he wrote:

> It is now by no means certain that enemy fighters did in fact succeed in shooting down any of the Wellingtons. Considering that enemy aircraft made most determined and continuous attacks for twenty-six minutes on the formation, the failure of the enemy must be ascribed to good formation flying. The maintenance of tight, unshaken formations in the face of the most powerful enemy action is the test of bomber force fighting efficiency and morale. In our Service it is the equivalent of the old 'Thin Red Line' or the 'Shoulder to Shoulder' of Cromwell's Ironsides.[34]

One man who did not draw a correlation between 14 December and Great Britain's grand military legacies was Ludlow-Hewitt, who openly criticised the bombing leader's decision not to turn around once it became apparent the formation would not be able to bomb from 2,000 feet — the height authorised for the operation. It was a point of view shared by the commander of No. 3 Group, Air Vice-Marshal J E A Baldwin. The foundations upon which the faith of the self-defending bomber formation was built was beginning to crumble.[35]

The Longest Battle

Ludlow-Hewitt — who succeeded Air Chief Marshal Sir John Steel, Bomber Command's first C-in-C — 'was a man with a minute and detailed knowledge of every aspect of his job.'[36] Although commissioned into the Royal Irish Rifles in 1905, he spent the 1914-18 war airborne, having transferred to the Royal Flying Corps in August 1914. By the age of 21, he was a Brigadier General. The inter-war years saw him serving overseas as AOC Iraq Command, followed by AOC RAF India. Back in England he was made Director of Operations and Intelligence at the Air Ministry and served as Commandant of the RAF Staff College.

Assuming command of the RAF's fledgling bomber arm in September 1937, it did not take 'Ludlow' long to ascertain the force's many deficiencies. Over the next two years, he sent a succession of reports to the Air Ministry in which he detailed what he saw as Bomber Command's primary handicaps. Chief among them was the force's standards of air gunnery. In a memorandum to the Air Ministry dated 25 May 1939, Ludlow wrote that Bomber Command's gunners lacked the ability and training to fend off an attack by enemy aircraft. The demand for airgunners to remain calm under pressure and to operate in the most adverse conditions was, Ludlow wrote, 'almost superhuman.'[37]

Bomber Command was an evolving entity. The power-operated gun turrets with which the Wellingtons and Hampdens were now equipped were a vanguard of air combat technology — but the urgent haste and extent of pre-war expansion had left Bomber Command with an inadequate training scheme.

So it was that Ludlow campaigned for more bombing and navigation practice, night-flying exercises and the creation of an air-gunnery school. One month after the outbreak of war, the Central Gunnery School was established.[38] As the war progressed, Bomber Command would continue to evolve and adapt. By December 1943 there would be no fewer than twenty-two Operational Training Units — as opposed to eight at the outset of war.

As future Bomber Command chief Arthur Harris would later write: 'Any sustained campaign in the Autumn of 1939 would have very quickly brought us to the end of our small supply of trained crews.'[39] But in those dark days of early conflict, crews would go forth with the training they had and do the best they could. Sometimes with fatal consequences.

On the afternoon of Sunday 17 December 1939 orders from No. 3 Group HQ were dispatched to Squadrons 9, 37 and 149, placing them on two-hour notice for take-off anytime after 0730 hours the following morning.

Twenty-four Wellingtons would make up an armed-reconnaissance force and sweep the Wilhelmshaven area, attacking any element of the German Fleet they might encounter. The order came through the following morning. At 0940 hours six Wellingtons from No. 37 Squadron's 'A' Flight, led by Squadron Leader Hue-Williams, left RAF Feltwell. They would bring up the rear in a diamond formation of four flights, consisting of nine Wellingtons from 149 Squadron and nine from 9 Squadron. Each individual flight was made up of six aircraft as the bombers rendezvoused over the coastal town of King's Lynn and proceeded on their course at 14,000 feet.[40]

The sky was clear and blue, offering no cover whatsoever as the Wellingtons winged their way towards their objective. Four days earlier, snow and rain had made flying conditions horrible and severely limited visibility. Now, on the morning of 18 December, one could see as far as thirty miles. The formation, proceeding across the North Sea, presented, notes the *Luftwaffe War Diaries*, 'a spectacle of imperturbable morale and fighting power'[41] — despite the fact that two bombers were forced to turn back.

Still some twenty minutes from the enemy coast, the bombers tripped the German radar screen at 1350 hours and alerted the Luftwaffe to their presence. Unaware and maintaining formation, the Wellingtons, flying wing-tip to wing-tip, turned south off Heligoland and proceeded to the naval base at Wilhelmshaven.

The bombers flew over at 12,000 feet, photographing the *Tirpitz* and two other warships — the *Gneisenau* and *Deutschland* — in the harbour's inner basin. Because all three vessels were docked, bombing was prohibited lest they risk killing civilian workers. They flew over twice, the ground-defences throwing up a tempest of flak. The anti-aircraft fire failed to inflict any damage, but it did loosen the formation as it turned to the north-west for its return journey. 'After Wilhelmshaven,' notes 149 Squadron's Records Book, 'the formation was attacked by a large number of fighters, mostly Messerschmitts 109s and 110s — probably 60 or 70 were involved. The ensuing battle lasted 40 minutes and proved to be the biggest to date in the history of the Royal Air Force.'[42]

As the bombers cut their way through the shrapnel over Wilhelmshaven, German fighters loitered along the formation's flanks and waited for their chance to strike. The ensuing battle set a new standard of savagery in air combat.

A swarm of twin- and single-engined fighters beset the British on all sides, battering the ravaged bombers far out to sea.[43] 'Cromwell's Ironsides,' to use Bottomley's parlance, were beaten with an unrelenting brutality. 'The Squadron's casualties were seen to go down in flames during the action,' reads the entry in 149 Squadron's Records Book.

> One was forced down in the sea on the return journey through petrol shortage due to the tanks being damaged in the flight... Besides the fighter attacks, the enemy opposition included A/A fire from the land defenses around Heligoland Bight but this fire, although heavy, did not cause casualties.[44]

The sheer ferocity of the engagement is exemplified in the ordeal of Wellington N2983 of No. 9 Squadron. Great swaths of the aircraft's skin were torn away in a frenzy of cannon fire. The wings were nearly completely skinned, exposing the skeletal geodetic construction underneath. The rear turret was annihilated and the gunner was splattered within its cramped confines, his body torn through in a barrage of enemy fire. Bullets ripped through the inside of the aircraft, ricocheting off metal and striking the second pilot. The floor and side of the nose turret were completely peeled away, and the guns were sheared in two. The intercommunication system was put out of commission, and the wireless exploded in a flash of spark and flame. The surviving crew members were rescued and brought home by a passing trawler.[45]

Twelve of the twenty-two Wellingtons were shot down. Three more crashed on the desperate flight home. Seven bombers from the original force managed to land back at their bases. Only two of the nine bombers sent by 9 Squadron returned. Only one of 37 Squadron's aircraft made it back. The number of men flying that day was 114, the number lost was fifty-three. Fifty per cent of the force dispatched was destroyed. Nearly fifty-five per cent of the force engaged was wiped out. This was, says the Official History, 'at least ten times the casualty rate which Bomber Command could ever afford as a regular drain on its crews and aircraft.'[46]

For the Luftwaffe, though numerous aircraft returned to base severely damaged, only two Bf 109s were destroyed.

In the wake of such slaughter, there was much speculation at Bomber Command HQ as to how it was possible. For Captain Reinecke, commander of German fighter group I/ZG 76, the key factor was speed:

> The Me 110 is easily capable of catching and overtaking this English type [Vickers Wellington] even with the latter at full boost. This provides scope for multiple attacks from any quarter, including frontal beam. This attack can be very effective if the enemy is allowed to fly into the cone of fire. The Wellington is very flammable and burns easily.[47]

Back in England, concern, too, was voiced over the Wellington's flammability by AOC No. 3 Group, Air Vice-Marshal Baldwin, though, in his opinion, the battle was lost because of loose formation flying. On 24 December he wrote to Ludlow-Hewitt:

> I am afraid there is no doubt that the heavy casualties experienced by 9 and 37 Squadrons were due to poor leadership and consequent poor formation flying. Squadron-Leader Guthrie is reported as being almost a mile ahead of his formation. For some unknown reason, Hue-Williams, who, I thought, was a very sound leader, appears to have done the same thing…
>
> There is every reason to believe that a very close formation of six Wellington aircraft will emerge from a long and heavy attack by enemy fighters with very few, if any, casualties to its own aircraft. A loose formation is however liable to suffer heavy casualties under the same conditions.[48]

As they were both dead, neither Guthrie nor Hue-Williams could argue their case. And in spite of the bitter experience to be garnered over the following years, in 1943 the Americans would foster the same faith in the self-defending bomber formation. They, too, would suffer grievously.

In any event, Bomber Command was not yet ready to scrap its pre-war policy. It still held on to the belief 'The bomber will always get through!'

Standing by this mantra was Harris, who, on 2 January 1940, shared his opinion that as long as 'three bombers were in company in daylight the pilots considered themselves capable of taking on anything.'

Such belief would further be put to the test in the year ahead.

II

Blood and Snow

A Cold Dawning

'We can create for ourselves a world of our own,' wrote 25-year-old Pilot Officer Michael Andrew Scott before dying on his first operational flight:

> . . . a world of fancy, where the only things that matter are the things of the spirit, such as music and poetry, the food of the spirit. But such a world would be lonely and desolate without anyone to share in it, and sooner or later the noise of the outer world would interrupt this dream of ours and bring us back to reality, the reality of sirens and air raids, of slaughter and destruction, which is the Autumn of 1940.[49]

In 1940, the first full year of war, radical events were at hand: Hitler's onslaught through Western Europe and the Low Countries; the fall of the British government under the leadership of Prime Minister Neville Chamberlain and the appointment of a new man to the office of No. 10 Downing Street; the capitulation of France and the deliverance from Dunkirk. Mussolini's Italy, holding off until sure of a German victory, would join the fray on the side of Hitler. Germany would turn towards Britain with a plan for invasion. It would be the year of the German Blitzkrieg and Britain's Finest Hour.

It was a year that dawned cold and bleak. Frost swept the fields and capitals of Europe from Britain to Italy. During the opening months of 1940, weather conditions greatly limited major air operations. At night, the pointless leaflet campaign carried on and, during the day, Blenheims — because of their speed — swept the North Sea in search of enemy shipping. All the while, Bomber Command still licked the wounds suffered in December.

Ludlow-Hewitt was distraught by the outcome of 18 December. For him, the cold dawning of 1940 was a period of contemplation as he pondered the future of Bomber Command and how it would wage an offensive war. He aired his concerns in a letter to the Air Ministry on 28 January. In it, he stressed 'the urgent necessity' to scrap plans to attack the Ruhr and to instead align Britain's bomber force against targets without exposing it to the threat of heavy losses.[50] The Air Ministry agreed the following month and relegated the Ruhr Plan to an extreme measure, only to be undertaken in the event of a German invasion of the west. On 19 March, Bomber Command launched its first assault on a land target.

The target was the German seaplane base at Hornum on the island of Sylt, several miles off the Dutch coast. Three days prior, German bombers had attacked the British Home Fleet at its base in Scapa Flow. Although the raid inflicted only minor damage on two ships, three civilians were killed, thus fuelling a demand for retaliation. So it was that thirty Whitleys of No. 4 Group and twenty Hampdens of No. 5 Group were tasked with bombarding the base at Hornum. It was Bomber Command's first air strike by night. Over the objective, flak and tracer lit a deadly tangled web against the black, ensnaring one Whitley and sending it crashing to the ground. Two others were damaged. Twenty tons of high explosives and more than 1,000 incendiary bombs were dropped. Crews reported good bombing results, claiming hangars and runways had sustained much damage. Such claims, however, were cast in doubt when photo reconnaissance in the coming weeks showed the base had taken only a few knocks. It was a foretaste of the difficulties Bomber Command would face in attacking targets by night.

That same month, Ludlow-Hewitt was relieved of his command and assigned to the post of RAF Inspector-General. While there is no official documentation chronicling the reason for Ludlow's dismissal, historians have ventured to guess at the factors behind the move. Age may have been one. Ludlow was 54 at the time — only four years older than Harris was when he assumed command two years later. Perhaps it was his insistence on forming more Operational Training Units instead of combat squadrons, as was desired by the Air Ministry — or his lack of faith in his force's abilities. Whatever the reason, Ludlow was out, and Air Marshal Charles Frederick Algernon Portal was in.[51]

Conquest in Norway

Amidst the blacked-out German landscape could be seen the blur of fast-moving headlights darting along the Autobahn between Hamburg and Lübeck on the night of 6 April. British bomber crews dropping leaflets that night reported seeing what they believed to be a vast motor convoy flowing between the two port cities. While at Kiel, 'there was great activity among shipping under the glare of brilliant arc lamps. The Germans made no pretence of concealment. When all is on the hazard they rarely do, believing that speed is more important that secrecy.'[52] That afternoon, a naval force consisting of the battle cruisers *Scharnhorst* and *Gneisenau* was photographed anchored off Wilhelmshaven. Two days prior, RAF reconnaissance reported a frenzy of German naval activity in the Elbe Estuary when sixty German merchant ships were spotted heading northward in formations of five. On the morning of 7 April, the *Scharnhorst*, *Gneisenau* and their accompanying flotilla had put to sea.

That same morning, fourteen aircraft of No. 107 Squadron at RAF Wattisham 'stood by for striking duties.' According to the squadron's Operation Records Book: 'At 1045 hours information was received that an enemy cruiser accompanied by six destroyers was in a position DKRU 1848 steaming at 350 and instructions were received that these ships were to be attacked.' At 1130 hours twelve Blenheims led by Wing Commander Basil Embry took off to intercept the German vessels. The aircraft flew in two formations of six.

> The weather for the greater part of the outward journey was fine with no clouds and a visibility of thirty miles. On reaching a position about twenty miles off the estimated point of interception, however, the visibility deteriorated to approximately five miles and clouds formed to 10/10ths at 7,000 feet. On arrival at the estimated point of interception both formations turned on to a course of 350 and after four minutes flying located seventeen ships of the German navy including the 'Gneisenau' and 'Scharnhorst.'[53]

With the glare of the sun behind them, the Blenheims attacked the ships in sections of three from a height of 6,000 feet and from their underbellies fell sticks of 12 x 250-lb. bombs. Great plumes of water erupted across the paths of the *Scharnhorst* and *Gneisenau*, 'but no direct hits were observed, although it was possible that some may have been obtained.' The first section attacked before the ships returned any retaliatory fire. But as the remaining two formations swooped in, they did so against a thunderous barrage of flak and pom-pom fire. Shells rocketed between individual aircraft with only inches to spare, as the Blenheims zeroed in.

Although no aircraft received direct hits, the fire was sufficiently accurate to force one section to break formation. An attack report and a message giving the composition, disposition and estimated speed of the fleet was dispatched by W/T during the homeward journey. All aircraft returned to base safely.[54]

The fleet continued cutting a swath towards neutral Norway, through which vast amounts of iron-ore mined in Sweden passed en route to Germany. German merchant ships — carrying this lifeblood of the nation's war effort — sailed from the Norwegian port of Narvik and always travelled close to the Scandinavian coast, thus gaining not only calmer seas but also neutral waters.[55] For some time it had been Allied intention to put a stranglehold on the deliveries. Winston Churchill, then First Lord of the Admiralty, had been urging the War Cabinet — since the beginning of the year — to allow the Royal Navy to mine Norwegian waters. The War Cabinet approved Churchill's scheme on 3 April. Five days later, a flotilla of British destroyers laid mines across the approaches to Narvik. This was to be followed by British and French landings at Narvik, Trondheim, Bergen and Stavanger — but the Germans pre-empted the Allied assault.

In the early morning hours of 9 April, German sea, land and airborne forces descended upon Norway. To shorten lines of communication and establish further bases for the Luftwaffe, the Wehrmacht simultaneously stormed into Denmark and smashed the opposition.[56]

The British War Cabinet met in urgent session that morning and approved an emergency plan to counter Hitler's aggression. By mid-morning, the Royal Navy was poised to strike less than 100 miles off the Norwegian coast. Seven destroyers would attack German forces at Trondheim and Bergen under the protective fire of four cruisers, knocking out enemy forces ready to oppose Allied landings. But the offensive went to the Luftwaffe. Eighty-eight Heinkel 111s and Junker 88s set upon the British warships with fire and bombs for three unrelenting hours. One destroyer went to the bottom and three cruisers were damaged.

Within two days the Germans were well entrenched. The aerodromes at Stavanger, Vaernes — near Trondheim — and the airport at Oslo were the secured domain of the Luftwaffe. The Germans had free range of the Scandinavian skies.

At 1810 hours six Wellingtons of 115 Squadron left for Norway to attack the airfield at Stavanger. Their objective was to bomb 'runways, aircraft and aerodrome installations.' In their bomb bays they carried 500-lb. explosives. Two Blenheims of 254 Squadron Coastal Command flew in ahead of the heavies and laid down a field of machine-gun fire. Hangars and runways were strafed, as were German fighters caught unaware on the ground in prologue to the main assault. As snow and ice resettled in the wake of the barrage, the Wellingtons roared over at low-level, dumping their explosive cargo. Though a massive conflagration was reported, the true extent of the damage could only be guessed. The next day, the prime objectives were elements of the German fleet, including the *Scharnhorst* and *Gneisenau*. It was the largest bombing operation of the war thus far. Eighty-three Wellingtons and Hampdens swept the icy grey waters in search of their prey. It was not long before the 'Wellingtons and Hampdens detailed for the operation… found themselves heavily engaged by a swarm of Me 109s and 110s, which pursued them 200 miles out to sea.'[57] Cannon fire ravaged the British raiders as they fought a desperate action. Six Hampdens and three Wellingtons were blasted from the skies for a loss of only five German fighters.[58]

For Portal, it was a defining moment. The next day, April 13, he restricted Wellingtons and Hampdens to night operations.[59] A Hampden pilot with 83 Squadron during the Norwegian campaign, Wing Commander Guy Gibson recalled in his memoirs *Enemy Coast Ahead:*

> When these Hampden squadrons were given the chance and did get to Norway in daylight, it was pretty fierce slaughter. Their orders were to fly in a very tight box so as to bring as much defensive armament as possible to bear on oncoming fighters, but the Germans were no fools; they had found a weak spot in the Hampdens, for at that time there was a blind area on either side, and the Huns made the best of their knowledge.[60]

'The Hampden,' wrote Harris after the war, 'was cold meat for any determined enemy fighter in daylight.'[61] Its feeble armaments were no match against the Messerschmitt, as Gibson explained:

> The Germans were flying in Messerschmitt 110 fighters, which have one gun which can fire sideways. Their mode of attack was to fly in formation with the Hampdens perhaps fifty yards out and slightly to the front, and pick off the outside man with their one gun, aiming with no-deflection shot at the pilot. The bomber boys could do nothing about it: they just had to sit there and wait to be shot down. If they broke away they were immediately pounced on by three Messerschmitt 109s waiting in the background. If they stayed, the pilot received a machine-gun serenade in his face. One by one they were hacked down by the wing man inwards… It was a terrible sight

to see them bursting into flames at about twenty feet, then cartwheeling one wing into the cold sea.[62]

The cold sea was its own field of battle — one that Bomber Command would continually traverse throughout the war. On the evening of 13 April, fifteen Hampdens of No. 5 Group flew low over the waters off the Danish coast and dropped mines as they winged their way through the chilled night. The 1,500-lb. mines were magnetic and dropped by parachute at a height not exceeding 600 feet. The process was code-named Gardening. The mines were referred to as 'vegetables.' Flying such operations was a tedious undertaking. 'It is not unusual for a mine-laying aircraft to fly round and round and up and down for a very considerable time, occasionally even for as long as an hour, in order to make quite sure that the mine is laid exactly in the correct place,' reported the Air Ministry in 1941. 'When opposition in the form of anti-aircraft fire or night-fighters is met with, the difficulties attending such an operation are obvious. It calls for great skill and resolution.'[63] 'Gardening' would become a mainstay of Bomber Command's offensive. As one airgunner, Flight Sergeant Sid Brans of 97 Squadron, would write home in 1942:

> Last Friday we were mining enemy waters but I'm afraid I can't tell you where we went, although both the route and the destination would prove very interesting. It's the longest trip I've had so far, involving a round-trip journey of 2,000 miles and taking over 9 ½ hours. Compared with normal 'ops' these mining trips are very dull and monotonous, but it has its compensations. We missed the usual flak, of course, but personally, I found it quite exciting enough creeping into an enemy harbour at 500ft, especially when there was quite a lot of shipping about. We were in and out before the defences really woke up, in fact I think our height, or rather lack of it, messed them up temporarily.[64]

From April 1940 until the end of the war, Bomber Command would 'plant' 47,152 'vegetables' and lose 467 aircraft in the process. Throughout the course of the Norwegian campaign, 'Gardening' operations would account for the destruction of twelve German ships. Between 1942 and 1945, such operations would sink or damage 900 enemy vessels.[65]

Norway Lost

Allied plans to assist the beleaguered Norwegian Army on land were underway. A British brigade and three battalions of French Chasseurs landed at Namsos — eighty miles north of Trondheim — on 14 April. Three days later, the British landed a second force south of Trondheim at Andalsnes. The Allied armies were to advance from the north and south on Trondheim and capture its harbour and neighbouring airfields. Once in Allied hands, it would allow the British and French to land a force of 50,000 men and block Germany's northern advance. But operating with only scant Allied air cover, the British and French soon found themselves mercilessly strafed and blasted from above.

Gladiator fighters of Fighter Command, trying to operate from a makeshift base on the ice of Lake Lesjaskog, were wiped out on 25 April by a wave of Heinkel 111s. Bombs and machine-gun fire devastated the antiquated aircraft and split open the lake's frozen surface. Many aircraft fell through the chasms in the ice and sank beneath the frigid waters.[66]

'Stavanger was bombed sixteen times by aircraft of Bomber Command between 11th and 24th April. It was also heavily shelled by HMS *Suffolk* at dawn on the 17th besides being repeatedly attacked by aircraft of Coastal Command and by the Fleet Air Arm.'[67] Twelve Blenheims of 107 Squadron — armed with 2 x 250-lb. general purpose bombs and 12 x 40-lb. general purpose bombs — took off for a raid on Stavanger at 0958 hours on 17 April. Records the squadron's Operation Records Book:

> The aircraft flew in two box formations of six aircraft each. En route to the target and at a point about 70 miles from the Norwegian coast at 1125 hours, from a height of 10,000 feet, an attack on a British cruiser and 4 destroyers by 7 Heinkels was observed. The leader of the formation circled with the object of giving the impression that his formation were fighters, whereupon the Heinkels dispersed into the clouds. The formation then proceeded on its course for the objective.[68]

The Blenheims executed a dual-level attack. One formation dropped fire from 18,000 feet, the other simultaneously attacked from 1,500 feet. Runways were cratered and hangars went up in flames. 'Hits were scored... on the aircraft dispersed around the edge of the aerodrome and considerable damage was done.' Enemy fire was intense and there followed a fierce engagement with a number of single-engined Messerschmitts. Two Blenheims were shot down, and the remaining ten all returned severely damaged. Nevertheless, it was the most successful action Bomber Command prosecuted against this specific target.[69]

Though the Allies succeeded in capturing Narvik on 28 May — their sole victory in Norway — plans for evacuation were already afoot. The Allies withdrew from Narvik between 4 June and 8 June, leaving the Norwegian Army to surrender on 9 June. On the last day of the evacuation, the *Scharnhorst* infiltrated the evacuation routes off Norway and confronted the carrier HMS *Glorious*. The battle was short and violent. In less than an hour, *Glorious* — swathed in flame — slipped beneath the waves and took 1,474 men of the Royal Navy and forty-one of the RAF with her. It was a disastrous end to a disastrous campaign. The Norwegian fiasco cost Bomber Command thirty-one aircraft and failed to strangle the flow of iron-ore into Germany.[70]

The Command was still far from peak strength. By April, the number of available frontline aircraft and crews hovered at around 200 and the myth of the self-defending bomber formation had been shattered once and for all.[71] It was in this diminished capacity that Bomber Command was thrust into the battle for Western Europe.

III

The Blitzkrieg Unleashed

A Government Falls

The collapse of Norway was a prelude to the collapse of the British government under the leadership of Conservative Prime Minister Neville Chamberlain. The Opposition, distraught by the catastrophes suffered in the brief campaign, called for a debate in the House of Commons on the conduct of the war. From 7 May to the evening of 8 May, recalled Churchill, both sides of the House lambasted Chamberlain and mercilessly assaulted the Government with one verbal jibe after another. It was Conservative MP Leo Amery who summed up the feelings of the House, quoting Oliver Cromwell's bitter recrimination of the Long Parliament: 'You have sat too long here for any good you have been doing. Depart, I say, and let us have done with you. In the name of God, go!' Chamberlain's downfall was engineered by his own party. In a Vote of Censure on 8 May, the House was divided. Forty-one Conservatives voted with the Opposition and sixty abstained. In a crushing blow, Chamberlain witnessed his party's majority fall from 240 to eighty-one. The debate and its final outcome was astounding testament to the lack of faith in Chamberlain's abilities.[72]

Two days later, on 10 May, Winston Churchill — at the behest of King George VI — ascended to the office of prime minister. That same day, Hitler unleashed his Blitzkrieg on the west.

Assault on the West

The German offensive commenced in the pre-dawn hours with an airborne assault on the Belgian fortress at Eben Emael — a frontier strong-
hold defending the Albert Canal on the Belgian-Dutch border — and
the Albert Canal bridges to the north-west. With the bridges in German
hands, the iron fist of General von Bock's Army Group B began blasting
their way into Belgium and Holland. As German forces advanced on land,
a storm broke in the skies above. Luftwaffe bomber formations swarmed
over Holland, bombing the aerodrome at Schipol. German bombs and
paratroops descended upon the airbase at Waalhaven on the outskirts of
Rotterdam. Further airborne assaults were carried out against other key
positions near The Hague, Eindhoven, Dordrecht, Ymuiden, the Hook of
Holland and Zandvoord. To achieve tactical surprise, the German attack
was made from the direction of England — but the Dutch were not fooled,
and set about a determined defence.[73]

As the armies of Britain and France moved north to counter the German
surge along the Dyle and Meuse rivers, the RAF was thrust into action.
Waging war by air against the German monolith was the RAF's Advanced
Air Striking Force (AASF), one component of the British Air Forces in
France (BAFF) under the overall command of Air Marshal Sir Arthur
'Ugly' Barratt. The AASF arrived in France the day before Britain's declaration of war, and comprised of ten Fairey Battle squadrons. By the time
blood and fire was again engulfing Europe, the Battle was already considered out of date with its fixed .303 machine gun in the starboard wing
and sole Vickers 'K' gun protruding from the back of its canopy. Built to
meet a 1932 Air Ministry specification, the Battle first came into service in
1937. With its crew of three, it carried a meagre bomb load of 1,000 lb.s and
boasted a top speed of 241 mph. Within days of the German advance in
the west, the Battle and the men who flew it would suffer indiscriminate
slaughter at the hands of superior German fighter technology.

In December 1939 Fairey Battle Squadrons Nos 15 and 40 of the AASF
were withdrawn to England and replaced by the Blenheims of Nos 114
and 139 Squadrons. By then, the Battle's inferiority in combat had already
been established. On 20 September a formation of three Battles from
88 Squadron was set upon by Bf 109s while flying reconnaissance. Two
Battles were lost. Another daylight reconnaissance ten days later by five
Battles of 150 Squadron ended in disaster when all five were wiped out by
a formation of German fighters. It signalled the end of the Battle's role in
daylight reconnaissance. When the 'Phoney War' came to its abrupt end

on 10 May, the AASF consisted of eight light bomber (Battle) squadrons, two squadrons of medium (Blenheim) bombers, two Hurricane fighter squadrons and a photo reconnaissance unit. Its role would be to assist Allied ground forces by attacking advancing German columns and lines of communication. To assist with this task, and also under the command of Barratt, were the seven Bomber Command Blenheim squadrons of No. 2 Group and two Whitley squadrons of No 4. Group back in England.

By 'the afternoon of 10 May four major aerodromes in Fortress Holland, those at Waalhaven, Ypenburg, Ockenburg and Walkenbrug were in German hands, despite the measures taken to deny their use to the invader.'[74] As the Dutch fought their brave but futile defence, German columns were quickly slicing their way through Luxembourg and the Ardennes. This, then, was the first offensive target for the Battles of the AASF. Four waves of eight were dispatched to stem the German advance. They took off at mid-day and flew low to avoid German fighters. At 250 feet they prosecuted their attack, thundering over the German armour and infantry to drop their fuse-delayed bombs. But the enemy column bristled with 20-mm and 37-mm anti-aircraft guns that threw up an inferno of flak. German troops ran for cover, firing at the aircraft with their machine guns and pistols. As the bombers rocketed overhead, they were cut to pieces in the hail of enemy fire. Thirteen of the thirty-two Battles were lost and the remaining nineteen all suffered various degrees of damage. A second attack followed later that afternoon. Again, thirty-two Battles attacking in four waves of eight zoomed in over the German troops at 250 feet — only to encounter a squadron of Bf 109s. In the ensuing melee, ten Battles were knocked from the sky.

The following day — 11 May — dawned with an urgent plea from the Belgian government, asking the RAF to bomb the bridges over the Albert Canal near Maastricht on the Dutch-Belgian border and slow the German advance in the north. Barratt tasked one of his Blenheim squadrons — No. 114 based at Conde-Vraux airfield on the north bank of the Aisne near Soissons — with the operation. The planes were loaded with bombs and fuelled in preparation for an 0600 takeoff. At 0545 hours, in the predawn light, as the crews went about their final preparations, there came the sound of bombers approaching from the Marne River. Twelve Dornier 17s emerged over the tree line and fanned out in formation over the airfield. For the next ten minutes, a flail of bombs rained down on the field, destroying six Blenheims and damaging the rest beyond repair. The Luftwaffe had wiped out half of Barratt's medium-bomber force in one lethal swoop. Eight Battles took off into bad weather that same day to attack the German spearhead at Luxembourg. Seven were shot down and one, riddled with gunfire, crashed on its return to base. Further, there was no evidence to suggest the bombers had even reached their target.[75]

May 12: The Battle for the Bridges

While the Germans continued their advance in the south through Luxembourg, the French became increasingly concerned with the German spearhead in the north. It was from Maastricht — where German armour, troops and transports were flowing freely over two unbroken bridges to the west of the small town into the Low Countries — that the French feared the Germans would launch the main thrust of their offensive. To stifle the German thrust in the north, Barratt sent nine Blenheims of No. 139 Squadron to attack the advancing column. They took off from their airfield at Plivot, with orders to attack from 6,000 feet but were intercepted by a formation of Bf 109s. Only two of the Blenheims survived.[76] Barratt had lost nearly his entire force of medium bombers in only two days. The bridges the Belgians were so desperate to destroy bristled with defences. Along the banks of the river, covering the aerial approaches to the targets, the barrels of 37-mm and quadruple 20-mm anti-aircraft guns pointed skyward.[77] Both the Belgian and French air forces had been horribly mauled flying against the bridges. Once again it was the RAF's turn, paving the way for a desperate action by Battles of No. 12 Squadron.

The crews were briefed at 0800 hours: the bridges were to be destroyed at all costs. Volunteers were called for, but the entire squadron stepped forward forcing the commanding officer to pick six crews by lot. The objectives were the bridges at Veldwezelt and Vroenhoven. It was a suicide mission from which one crew was spared when their aircraft suffered a hydraulics failure prior to takeoff.[78]

Two Battles — those of A-Flight led by Flying Officer N M Thomas — would attack the bridge at Vroenhoven. The three aircraft of B-Flight, led by Flying Officer Donald 'Judy' Garland, would bomb the Veldwezelt crossing. That afternoon, the two Battles of A-Flight, with their three-men crews of pilot, navigator and gunner, trundled along the airfield and took to the skies. Climbing to 7,000 feet, they flew through patchy cloud and covered the 120-mile distance to the bridge in an hour. Arriving over the concrete expanse, the A-Flight's other Battle, piloted by Pilot Officer T D H Davy, was set upon by a German fighter. As the two aircraft weaved desperate patterns about the sky, Thomas took advantage of the diversion and went in for his attack.[79]

He threw his Battle into a violent dive, dropping through a maelstrom of flak thrown up by the bridge's defenders. The plane shuddered violently under the stress of the manoeuvre and the blasts of anti-aircraft fire. In its belly were four 250-lb. bombs that Thomas began to release at

3,000 feet, dropping them one by one until he was less than 500 feet from the ground. As he levelled out through palls of rising smoke, a burst of shells buffeted the beleaguered aircraft. Unable to gain altitude, the Battle limped along before crashing in a nearby field where Thomas and his crew, free of injury, were taken prisoner. Davy, meanwhile, had succeeded in ditching the Messerschmitt, though his Battle, badly shot up, was now trailing smoke and flame. He dropped his bombs as close to the bridge as possible, then made a desperate bid for home. Though his aircraft was leaking fuel at an alarming rate, Davys succeeded in piloting his Battle back to base where it crashed on landing. Davys and his crew would be the only ones to return from the operation.[80]

Over the metal bridge at Veldwezelt, Garland and the men of B-Flight were living out the last desperate moments of their lives. The sky was a seething cauldron of enemy fire and fighter activity. One Battle, piloted by Flying Officer I A McIntosh, was raked through by cannon fire and burst into flames. McIntosh jettisoned his bombs and was forced to ditch in a nearby field. He and his crew, like Thomas, were to spend the rest of the war in a German POW camp. They would be the only survivors of B-Flight. Sergeant Fred Marland and his crew were vaporised in a massive fireball when their Battle, pulverised by flak, plunged nose-first into the ground. Garland's plane was hit as he came in on his attack run. In a final attempt to destroy the bridge, Garland guided his stricken aircraft — still carrying its full bomb load — into the bridge. The explosion engulfed the structure and ultimately severed it. Of the fifteen men tasked with the bridges' destruction, six were killed, six were taken prisoner and all five aircraft were lost.[81]

For their effort, Garland and his navigator, Sergeant Tom Gray, were posthumously-awarded the Victoria Cross — the first to be awarded to the RAF during the Second World War. Strangely, Garland's airgunner, Leading Aircraftman Roy Reynold's legacy was not awarded such an honour. Meanwhile, that same day, twenty-four Blenheims from two squadrons of Bomber Command's No. 2 Group attacked German columns near Maastricht. Almost half the bombers were wiped out and only ten returned. Blood was flowing freely. On 10 May the Battles suffered a horrendous forty per cent casualty rate. The situation worsened the following day when every Battle that took to the sky was annihilated. Casualty rates on 12 May exceeded sixty per cent.[82] In the course of two torturous days, Barratt saw his number of serviceable bombers drop from 135 to seventy-two.[83]

By the end of 12 May, the Ardennes was a raging field of battle and the Belgian Army was being forced back from Tongres — pulling back another twenty miles the following day. By 14 May, the British Expeditionary Force had taken up a position to the right of the Belgian line with the French armies in the north, but the cause was lost. The night before, the French

Ninth Army, defending the Meuse, collapsed and the Germans began crossing the river, punching a hole in the Allied lines and threatening to cut off Allied forces in eastern Belgium. The French turned to the British, pleading for an all out air assault against the German bridgeheads. For the AASF it would be the climactic massacre. Of the seventy-two bombers at Barratt's command, sixty-three were Battles. On 14 May, Barratt threw them all against the German river positions north of Sedan. Forty-three of the seventy-one aircraft were lost. An attack by twenty-eight Blenheims of No. 2 Group against the bridgeheads that evening was an unmitigated bloodbath when only seven of the bombers returned to base in the fading twilight of evening. Some damage was done to several pontoon bridges, yet any hindrance this caused the enemy was not long in the lasting.[84]

Rout and Ruin

By 13 May, the French Ninth Army was in a state of utter chaos. German armour had punched a hole some fifty miles wide in the Allied line through which a vast mass of enemy men and machinery now poured virtually unobstructed. By the evening of 15 May, German troops were reported sixty miles behind the fractured Allied front.[85] That same morning, Holland capitulated. For nearly five days, Dutch forces had fought a valiant struggle against the German invader. It all came to an end at 1500 hours on the afternoon of 14 May when fifty-seven He 111s appeared over Rotterdam. A torrent of high explosives fell upon the inner city, razing 20,000 buildings and killing 1,000 people. The following day, the War Cabinet gave Portal permission to commence operations against military targets inside Germany east of the Rhine.

Up until now, squadrons of Whitleys had floundered through the night skies, restricted to bombing lines of communication and marshalling yards to the west of the River in a vain attempt to assist the Allied land battle. That night, ninety-nine aircraft — thirty-nine Wellingtons, thirty-six Hampdens and twenty-four Whitleys — flew to sixteen different targets throughout the Ruhr Valley intent on destroying factories and railways. They accomplished little. Bombs fell off the mark and caused little damage. One report in Cologne stated that a man switched on a light while making his way to the outhouse and was promptly blasted by a stick of high explosive. In the end, however, both the man and the outhouse survived. Anti-aircraft guns and searchlights failed to claim a single bomber. But one Wellington crew was killed when their aircraft slammed into a hillside in France. They were the night's only casualties — and the first casualties of the RAF's strategic bomber offensive.[86]

As the sun rose on 16 May, the Germans were busy exploiting the success of their Meuse crossing, attacking Avesnes and Vervins more than forty miles west of the river and sending in troops and armour through a wide gap to the west of the beleaguered First French Army. British and Belgian forces were fighting for survival along the Dyle River. As the apparatus of Germany's war machine devoured great sects of the French countryside, Bomber Command — at the behest of Barratt, the French and Lord Gort, Commander-in-Chief of the British Expeditionary Force — were tasked with stemming the German tide, attacking troop and armour columns and transport convoys. On 17 May, twelve Blenheims from 82 Squadron were dispatched from England to attack enemy troops at Gembloux.[87]

Flying in two formations of six, they encountered heavy flak near the target area. As the Blenheims loosened formation to avoid the lingering clouds of shrapnel, they were ravaged by Bf 109s covering the German advance near the target area. Eleven of the twelve bombers were wiped out. Only one pilot succeeded in bringing back his aircraft and crew.[88] Meanwhile, heavy bombers continued to strike German industrial targets by night and frontline positions by day — but it was of little use. France was rapidly being swallowed by the German tide. The First French Army and the British Expeditionary Force had been completely severed by 21 May. A British counter-attack at Arras had failed to stall the German onslaught, which had now reached the mouth of the Somme at Abbeville. British survival and the means to continue the war now meant evacuation.

The evacuation of the BEF from Dunkirk began on 27 May. As the Royal Navy and the men on the beaches struggled against heavy air bombardment and artillery fire, the French were fighting a last desperate action on a contracting front at Lille. The final pocket of French resistance collapsed four days later. Between 27 May and 4 June, 338,226 men of the British Army and much of the French northern forces were spirited away across the Channel under murderous enemy fire. By night, Wellingtons pounded the German positions around the besieged port while Blenheims attacked by day. Since the opening of the German offensive, Blenheims had flown 956 operations for a loss of fifty-seven aircraft. The loss was equivalent to the complete destruction of four squadrons.[89]

So desperate had the situation become, the crippled Battle squadrons of the AASF were once again called into action. The Germans struck south across the Somme on 5 June. Battles and Blenheims were thrown against the advancing German columns in a futile action. They strafed and blasted concentrations of infantry and motorised vehicles and flew in support of the British 51st Highland Division still fighting at St Valéry. Heavy bombers dumped high explosives on lines of communication by night. Within a week, airfields of the AASF were under German threat, forcing the surviving men and machines to withdraw to the tightly crammed airfields around Nantes and Saumur. On 15 June, the handful of remaining Battles were withdrawn to England. Two days later, the French sued for peace.[90] The struggle for France was over. Bomber Command lost nearly half of its front-line strength and had achieved nothing. The AASF lost 174 bombers, 137 of which were the long-suffering Battles. Ninety-eight Blenheims of No. 2 Group were shot down. Twenty-six Wellingtons had succumbed to enemy fire, as had the same number of Whitleys. In the aerial field of battle, the RAF lost more than 1,300 men. The Luftwaffe lost 1,279 aircraft. For the British Army, casualties exceeded 68,000. The armies of the Continent had been smashed.[91]

As France sank ever deeper beneath the swarming grey tide of Hitler's hordes, Italy declared war on the already-defeated nation and Britain on 10 June. Mussolini — with his visions of a new Roman Empire in the Mediterranean and a share of Hitler's European conquests — thus brought his nation to bear in Bomber Command's crosshairs. The following night, thirty-six Whitleys took off from England. Their objectives were the Fiat works in Turin and factories in Genoa. The crews faced a 1,350-mile round trip and were forced to refuel on the Channel Islands off England's southern coast. Crossing the Alps on the outward trek was an arduous task. Storms and low cloud buffeted the aircraft. The lightning was constant and icing was severe, forcing twenty-three of the Whitleys to abort the operation. Of those that carried on, nine aircraft bombed Turin, but failed to hit the Fiat works. Their bombs slammed into some railway yards and killed forty people. Two aircraft bombed Genoa with unknown results. One Whitley was hit by heavy flak over Turin and crashed near Le Mans on the return flight. All on board were killed.

The British had expected Mussolini's siding with Hitler. One week prior to the Italian declaration, orders were issued for 'the immediate creation of a British bombing force to operate against Italy.'[92] The force — comprising of a small number of Wellingtons — was to operate from an airfield at Salon, near Marseilles, and arrived at the aerodrome on the afternoon of 12 June. They were readied for an attack on Milan that night, but plans were thrown into disarray when the French — who had originally agreed to the attacks — sought to prevent them out of fear of Italian reprisals. This argument between the French Government and the headquarters of the British Air Force in France 'lasted from about half-past seven until late in the night.' The RAF officer in charge, however, eventually disregarded French concerns and ordered the operation to go ahead, knowing he had the backing of the War Cabinet.[93]

Shortly after midnight, the Wellingtons began taxiing to their take-off points. As they did so, a number of blackened silhouettes moved across the airfield and onto the runway. They were French military trucks, strategically placed to prevent the bombers from taking off. In order to maintain some aspect of civility with the French, the British cancelled the raid. Not until three nights later, on June 15, did the French rescind their restrictions. In light of the hassle involved in getting the go ahead, the raid — code-named Operation Haddock — was remarkably ineffective. Eight Wellingtons took off into thunderous weather for the Piaggio and Anseldo works in Genoa. Only one aircraft succeeded in dropping its bombs. The weather remained foul the following night, but a number of Wellingtons made it through to Milan, though their actions were of little consequence.

Two days later, the French asked for an armistice and the bomber force was called back to England. Britain readied herself for the onslaught of a lonely war.

IV

Their Darkest Hour

An Exterminating Attack

In September 1940 'London can take it!' became the battle cry for a city under siege as the Luftwaffe laid great swaths of the metropolis to waste. On 8 July, two months prior to London burning, Winston Churchill sent a memorandum to Lord Beaverbrook, Minister of Aircraft Production. In it, he outlined Britain's bleak war prospects. The nation had no army on the continent to counter German military might. Hitler had the resources of Europe — and, if he so decided — Asia and Africa to draw from. If German forces decided to thrust east into Russia, the British had nothing to stop him. In Churchill's mind, the only thing capable of bringing Germany down was an 'absolutely devastating' attack by heavy bombers. The key to British survival, Churchill wrote, lay in the ability to set the Nazi homeland ablaze. Britain should strive for nothing less than total air supremacy. When, the Prime Minister wanted to know, could this aim be achieved?[94]

The answer would be nearly three years coming.

Alone

In the wake of the French collapse, Hitler's grasp extended along Europe's coast from the north of Holland to the south-west of France. Between the German Army and its last remaining adversary stood twenty miles of unpredictable and merciless water.[95] On 16 July, less than one month after the French armistice, Hitler issued his Füehrer Directive No. 16:

Since England in spite of her militarily hopeless position shows no signs of coming to terms, I have decided to prepare a landing operation against England, and if necessary to carry out a landing operation against her. The aim of this operation is to eliminate the English motherland as a base from which war against Germany can be continued and, if necessary, to occupy completely.

The British, meanwhile, were busy issuing their own memorandum. On 20 June a directive instructed Portal to direct Bomber Command's efforts 'towards objectives which will have the most immediate effect on reducing the scale of air attack on this country.' The German aircraft industry and all related ventures were given top priority. These were targets to which Portal's 'heavies'— the Wellingtons, Hampdens and Whitleys — would be dispatched by night. Lines of communication were also targeted, with the marshalling yard at Hamm — Germany's largest — taking precedence along with similar objectives in the Ruhr and Cologne. Aqueducts were listed as were oil refineries. The directive also called for incendiary raids on crops and forests. The Blenheims would harry occupied airfields in France and the Low Countries, while the Hampdens of No. 5 Group would continue mining operations commenced during the Norwegian campaign.[96]

The final days of June saw Bomber Command lashing out against a hectic myriad of targets — sometimes attacking nearly two dozen objectives in one night. The Blenheims surveyed and attacked occupied airfields by day, while the heavies bombed industrial plants by night. These operations were of little consequence to the German war machine. The British bombers were fighting on a widely-scattered front, blindly searching their way through inhospitable darkness and savage cold. Bombing by night was a new science, one for which methods of navigation and accurate bombing had yet to be fully developed. Additionally, Bomber Command's numbers limited any substantial forces from being dispatched against a single target. German night defences, meanwhile, were far from their zenith. In a two-week period in which Britain's heavy bombers flew nearly 1,200 sorties, only seventeen were lost.

The 20 June directive was just one of a rapid-fire succession of orders. On 4 July, another Air Ministry directive crossed Portal's desk. German shipping was the new priority, with heavy emphasis on German warships and the invasion ports along the occupied coast. The Germans had commenced preparations for their cross-Channel invasion and were scouring the rivers and waterways of conquered Europe in search of barges. Reported the Air Ministry in 1941:

The word 'barge' conjures up a pleasant picture of a bluff-nosed wooden craft with a gaily-painted stern supporting a cabin in which a fat and comfortable woman can be perceived while, forward, the bargee exchanges back-chat with the lock-keeper. The barges collecting against us in the invasion ports were very different. German, Dutch, Belgian and French barges are all sizes up to 3,000 tons carrying capacity, although the largest are few in number and limited to special trades. The most common type can carry between 300 and 400 tons and if self-propelled has a speed of about eight knots.[97]

From Rotterdam to Boulogne, German shipping came under fire as Portal threw man and machine into the new campaign. From this would emerge a long, violent struggle between Bomber Command and two of Germany's most formidable warships: the *Scharnhorst* and *Gneisenau*. Against the *Scharnhorst*, docked in the harbour at Kiel, Guy Gibson dropped the first 2,000-lb. armour-piercing bomb of the war on the night of 1 July. Gibson made his attack from 6,000 feet, diving on the target six times before dropping his deadly cargo. But the great explosive missed the warship and slammed into the town of Kiel. 'This, of course, may have killed some civilians,' Gibson later wrote, 'but it was purely an accident, as we had been told carefully to avoid the town.'[98] The shrill of air raid sirens became regular happenstance in the ports of Hamburg and Bremen as each suffered minor beatings, though primary targets such as the troop ships *Europa* and *Bremen* remained afloat. July was a busy time. Recalled Gibson:

> Every night between 100 and 150 bombers would leave England bent on bombing missions over Germany. Their course would take them over separate areas far and wide, from Denmark to Southern France. For these were the days when raids were spread over a period of the whole night, so that the sirens would blow everywhere all night long, causing as much disruption to war production as possible.[99]

Such a wide dispersion of force led the Air Ministry to refocus operations with its 13 July directive, ordering Portal and Bomber Command to zero in on fifteen selected targets. Ten of these targets were within the German aircraft industry; the remainder were oil related. Portal protested, arguing on 16 July — the same day Hitler ordered preparations for the invasion of Britain — that of the selected targets, his crews, on average, could only find three of them, assuming conditions were ideal. Furthermore, the majority of targets listed were located in such isolated regions that the high percentage of bombs that missed the target would hit nothing of any consequence and cause no collateral damage.[100] Penned in the heat of frustration, Portal's argument predestined Bomber Command's future war against the German populace.

Two months earlier, with the Allies on the brink of defeat in France, Churchill ordered a review of Britain's ability to prosecute the war alone pending a 'certain eventuality.' Various ministers, under the guidance of former Prime Minister Neville Chamberlain, were asked to ascertain the situation. In their final report, delivered to Churchill at the end of May, one of the greatest concerns expressed was that of German air attack on British industry. The Luftwaffe would bomb factories by day or night, the report stated, concluding that large-scale area bombardment by the enemy would cause much devastation and eliminate the need for precision raids.[101]

This last point was the very one Portal was trying to make in relation to British air attacks on Germany. But his minute to the Air Staff was received with a great lack of enthusiasm from minds who did not approve of what it was he was insinuating — not least of all Sir Richard Peirse, Vice Chief of the Air Staff and an early proponent of precision bombing. Obediently, Portal followed orders, pitting his crews throughout July and August against Cologne, Hamm, and the Ruhr. In total, the Whitleys, Hampdens and Wellingtons of Bomber Command flew more than 1,800 sorties against German industry that July. And in a blatant disregard for Bomber Command's efforts, the Nazi war machine thundered on.

The Day of Eagles

August 12 was *Adlertag* — Eagle Day — the commencement of the Luftwaffe's assault on Great Britain. It dawned damp and overcast. A fine drizzle hung over the occupied airfields of northern France, and the English Channel lay obscured beneath a rolling fog, leaving Goering no choice but to push back zero hour to that afternoon. The order, however, did not make it down the ranks and fifty-five Dornier 17s of Luftlotte 2 took to the grim skies at 0500. Over southern England they swarmed, concentrating their attack on the airfield at Eastchurch on the south bank of the Thames estuary. Runways and hangars were blasted as the bombers thundered over the airfield and let loose their cargos of high explosive. Five Blenheims exploded on the ground, and more than four dozen craters were left on the fields and runways.[102]

Despite the worsening weather, the assault resumed that afternoon. An advanced echelon of Bf 110s rocketed across southern England in a bid to lure RAF Fighter Command into combat and clear the way for the

German bombers that would soon appear in the skies. On the ground, the alarm was sounded. At Exeter, Warmwell and Tangmere young men ran for their Spitfires and Hurricanes. There was the cough and sputter of machinery coming to life and the powerful reverberation of Rolls Royce engines as the fighters shot down grassy fields and up into the clouds. Within minutes the battle was joined. The Battle of Britain had begun.[103]

Two days prior to the German onslaught in the west, Portal had written to the Air Ministry and voiced his concern regarding the deployment of Blenheims. On 8 May, Portal wrote a strongly worded letter in which he argued that the use of Blenheims in daylight bombing raids could prove catastrophic.[104] The words had only served to prophesy the fate of 82 Squadron. An entire formation of its Blenheims had already been massacred over France. A similar bloody episode unfolded in an operation against Hamstede airfield in Holland on 13 August. Twelve Blenheims were attacked en route to their objective by single-engined Messerschmitts. The formation was blasted from the air and from guns on the ground. When the firing stopped, all but one of the bombers lay in smouldering heaps scattered across the Dutch countryside.

Bomber Command continued its campaign against German oil production and aircraft factories. Milan and Turin again found themselves on the receiving end when bombed by thirty-five Whitleys on the night of 13 August. German railways and lines of communication were continually harried and waters off the enemy coast were constantly mined. The Luftwaffe continued to fight by day, bombing and strafing and tangling with Spitfires and Hurricanes. Minor operations against British military depots and airfields were also being prosecuted by night. Oil tanks along the Thames estuary were the targets of German bombers on the night of 24 August. But some bombs fell wide of the mark and landed within the congested confines of London and its southern suburbs. It was the unfortunate consequence of an error in navigation. An outraged Churchill demanded immediate retaliation and turned to Bomber Command. He wanted Berlin to burn. The Air Staff was reluctant, for it saw no military value in such an operation — but they ultimately bowed to Churchill's demands on 25 August.

The trip to Berlin and back was some 1,200 miles, and was made by eighty Hampdens and Wellingtons. The bombers reached their objective unmolested, but found the German capital shrouded in heavy cloud through which a handful of crews dropped their bombs over a scattered area. Nothing of consequence was hit. Only two people on the ground were wounded when a bomb landed on their summer cottage in a Berlin suburb. It was, nevertheless, a propaganda victory. Goering had assured the populace that not one bomber would molest Berlin.

It was an assurance that now rang alarmingly hollow. Hitler saw British determination and the willpower of its people as Germany's most formidable threat, Churchill later wrote, insinuating that the Fuehrer was actually a secret admirer of British verve. Nevertheless, in the RAF's assaults on Berlin, Hitler saw the chance to publicly declare the German aim of reducing London and other British cities to smoking ruins.[105] Hitler, in fact, abandoned all restraint. 'If they bomb one of our cities,' he publicly ranted on 4 September, 'we will simply erase theirs!'[106]

Air raid sirens echoed through the blacked-out streets of London the following night. The first explosions ripped through London's docks at 2100 hours and continued until the break of day. Sixty tons of bombs ravaged the city's ports and surrounding areas, sending them up in a massive conflagration. Two days later, on 7 September, Hitler issued a directive from Supreme Headquarters: London was to be wiped off the map. That same afternoon, Goering stood on the coastal cliffs of Cap Blanc Nez with Field Marshal Albert Kesselring, commander of Luftwaffe forces engaged in southern England, and watched German formations fly overhead en route for London. Nearly 1,000 aircraft — a third of these bombers — clouded the skies above the Channel. The mechanized thunderhead covered 800 square miles and reached two miles high.[107] Flying escort were 648 single- and twin-engined German fighters.

In their approach they achieved complete tactical surprise, descending upon the city from a direction not anticipated by the RAF. More than 300 tons of bombs fell on London's East End and its docks in less than ninety minutes. Great columns of flame and acrid smoke blackened the sun and provided targets for the Luftwaffe raiders who returned that night. It was the beginning of London's ordeal and, for the RAF, it was their saving grace. The clash of wings above England had reached a feverish pitch in the final weeks of August. The month had seen RAF Fighter Command lose 390 Spitfires and Hurricanes, to the Luftwaffe's 231 Bf 109s. Wrote Major Freiherr von Falkenstein, of the Luftwaffe general staff:

> The British fighter arm has been severely hit. If, during September, we seize the opportunity of favorable weather to keep up the pressure one can assume that the enemy's fighter defence will be so weakened that our air assault on his production centres and harbour installations can be greatly stepped up.[108]

But it was at this stage in the Battle of Britain that the Luftwaffe was ordered to switch tactics.

Kesselring believed attacking London would force the RAF to throw up its last reserves of Spitfires and Hurricanes. In the sky, they would be devoured by the Luftwaffe. In this line of thinking lay the means to

Fighter Command's victory. Airfields were spared as London absorbed bomb blast after bomb blast and RAF numbers were rejuvenated as factories, now unmolested, replaced those machines lost in Britain's desperate struggle.

Battle of the Barges

While London and other British cities suffered, the Germans amassed barges and ships in the invasion ports along Europe's occupied coast. It was surmised by the Air Ministry in 1941:

> The 3,000 barges gradually collected in ports and harbours from Amsterdam to Cherbourg had a potential carrying capacity of some 1,000,000 tons, while that of the ships amounted to 4,000,000. They were a direct and immediate threat; but they were also a large and important target.[109]

In September the intensity of Bomber Command's attacks on the ports and assembling invasion craft reached a fiery frenzy. Antwerp, Flushing, Ostend, Dunkirk, Calais and Le Havre were all set aflame. On the night of 7 September, as London burned bright, ninety-two bombers of all types — including the Fairey Battle, which was back on operations — were thrown against targets along the occupied coast. That same day the British Government issued its invasion warning, believing the bombing of London signalled the start of the Nazi invasion. The Royal Navy and RAF were placed on their highest alert and the army was ordered to battle stations along England's southern coast. The following night more than 100 aircraft were dispatched to Hamburg, Bremen, Emden, Ostend and Boulogne — with forty-nine Hampdens attacking the Blohm and Voss shipyard at Hamburg. On the nights of 9 and 11 September 182 aircraft bombed the invasion ports — guided by the raging fires of previous attacks — and targets in Germany, including a power station in Berlin.

Despite their close proximity to airfields in England, the invasion ports were formidable targets, heavily defended by anti-aircraft guns and within easy range of German fighters. A Hampden of No. 83 Squadron was brutalised by enemy fire above the port of Antwerp on the night of 15 September as the pilot, Pilot Officer C A Connor, brought the plane in for an attack at 2,000 feet. Flak tore through the length of the aircraft, smashing through the petrol tanks and bomb bay. Within seconds the plane's interior was engulfed in flames so severe it began to melt. Great globs of molten metal peeled away from the floor and blew backwards, splattering against the rear bulkhead and walls of the plane. The navigator and airgunner quickly bailed out, but the wireless operator — 18-year-old Sergeant John Hannah — opted to stay on board and fight the flames. Struggling against the inferno, Hannah caught fire, but continued to beat at the conflagration with his log book as ammunition exploded around him.

It was an excruciating ordeal. Flames blew up through the aircraft's floor from the bomb bay with the intensity of a 'blow torch,'[110] but Hannah succeeded in beating them out. Severely burnt, he crawled forward to report the damage to Connor. The pilot was horrified at what he saw. The face and hands of his young wireless operator were scorched black — the skin blistered and peeling — and the eyes nearly swollen shut. In spite of his wounds, Hannah stayed up front, handing Connor maps as the pilot struggled to bring the stricken aircraft home. This Connor did despite there being 'a hole in the fuselage large enough for a man to crawl through. The rear gunner's cockpit and half the interior of the fuselage were charred ruins. There were holes in the wings and the petrol tanks.'[111] For his courage and sacrifice, Hannah was awarded the Victoria Cross. At 18, he was the youngest airman to be awarded Britain's highest military honour. Connor received the Distinguished Flying Cross, but died a few weeks later on operations. Hannah was invalided out of the RAF in 1942 and died shortly after Germany's surrender. He was only in his 20s and left behind a wife and three young children.[112]

The Turning Point

Sunday 15 September was the turning point. By 1330 hours that afternoon the 'skies over the whole of south-east England, from the Channel coast to London, were aflame with battle, and not a single German bomber formation reached its target unmolested.'[113] Against the sky the fierce combats unfolded in frantic swirls of contrail as 300 Spitfires and Hurricanes raged against the Luftwaffe menace. The German bombers — 148 of them — that succeeded in reaching London found the city obscured by cloud. Fighter Command was operating at maximum strength, every available Spitfire and Hurricane available was airborne. On this day, the Luftwaffe suffered its gravest single-day loss as the rampant 'Few' tore into the German formations and shot down fifty-eight aircraft. Reported Hellmuth Ostermann, a German fighter pilot with III/JG 54:

We clung to the bomber formation in pairs — and it was a damned awkward feeling. From below we looked up at the bright blue bellies of the Tommy planes... They would swoop down, pull briefly out, fire their guns and at once dive on down. All we could do was shoot off short nuisance bursts... and could only watch as the Tommies knocked hell out of one of the bombers...[114]

The British fighter arm, though desperately stretched, was not yet defeated. Domination of the air was yet to be wholly decided as the Luftwaffe would continue operations over England. The Germans would launch small raids in daylight pending favourable weather and strong fighter escort, while the main brunt of the German air offensive would now befall Britain by night. The Germans, echoing the British, had now abandoned large-scale daylight operations. To continue such attacks by day meant the Luftwaffe would die a violent death over England.[115] Two days later, a secret radio message was intercepted by British Intelligence. Hitler had ordered air-transport facilities in Holland to be dismantled. With the RAF still posing a threat to his invasion plans and the approach of autumn and rough waters in the Channel, Hitler postponed his invasion plans indefinitely.

This had little bearing on Bomber Command's operations. On the night of 18 September more than 170 aircraft raided the invasion ports. In the midst of its anti-invasion campaign, Bomber Command was diverted back to Berlin — its second operation against the German capital since the retaliatory strike of 25 August. For this endeavour, Portal mustered a force of 129 aircraft — Hampdens, Wellingtons and Whitleys — and sent them to eighteen different objectives throughout the city. Railway yards, power stations, aircraft factories and gasworks were targeted. The bombers scoured the skies above the fog-shrouded city for more than three hours, trying to locate their specific targets. Searchlights chased them through the darkness and clouds of flak threatened their path, but 112 aircraft reported a successful operation. Whether the intended targets were actually hit was never determined. Three aircraft failed to return.

The makeshift armada Hitler had assembled for his cross-Channel conquest was badly burned and battered by the end of September. Bomber Command had destroyed nearly thirteen per cent of the barges gathered in the invasion ports. 'The very severe bombing,' read a report by the German naval staff on 18 September, 'makes it necessary to disperse the naval and transport vessels already concentrated to stop further movement of shipping to the invasion ports.'[116] The Battle of Britain was effectively over and the threat of invasion was subdued — but the Blitz would continue. The moment ultimately belonged to the men of Fighter Command, though Bomber Command, in its battle against the barges, had paid a heavy price in blood and lost 718 men. The sacrifice spurred the Air Ministry to proclaim: 'The crews of Bomber Command are following the precedent set by Sir Francis Drake even though they are singeing the moustache of a bloodthirsty guttersnipe, not the beard of a Spanish King.'[117]

Night Moves

'Total war,' wrote the author J B Priestley in 1940, 'is war right inside the home itself, emptying the clothes cupboards and the larder, scream-ing its threats through the radio at the hearth, burning and bombing its way from roof to cellar.'[118] Every night — from 7 September to 3 November — an average of 300 German bombers swarmed over London, dumping maximum loads of incendiaries and high explosives. The air raid sirens always foreshadowed their arrival, sending London's weary masses underground into the tube with monotonous regularity. By mid-October, it was decided to refocus Bomber Command's efforts on Germany. But first there was a change at the top. On 25 October, Air Chief Marshal Sir Charles Portal replaced Air Chief Marshal Sir Cyril Newall as Chief of Air Staff, essentially becoming head of the entire RAF. Into Portal's place stepped Air Marshal Sir Richard Peirse — an air veteran of the First World War — as AOC-in-C Bomber Command.

Five days after assuming command — and following an Air Staff review of bombing policy for the approaching winter — Peirse received his first directive. The order was wide-ranging, calling for precision attacks on chosen industrial targets with German oil taking priority. Attacks on invasion barges would continue well into the winter, but efforts were also to be directed against industrial plants in Italy. There was another facet to the directive. When weather and moonlight con-ditions were not conducive to precision bombing, Bomber Command was to focus on

> regular concentrated attacks on objectives in large towns and centres of industry, with the primary aim of causing very heavy material destruction which will demonstrate to the enemy the power and severity of air bombardment and the hardship and dislocation which will result from it.[119]

Such wording echoed the desired strategy Portal had sought back in July: attacking industrial centres in populated areas, allowing bombs that missed to hit something of consequence. It was the first major step towards an area-bombing campaign.

Now in the hot seat, Peirse protested, arguing he was being asked to stretch his forces too thin. The directive was revised to bring concentration to bear mainly on synthetic oil plants. Other objectives were to be attacked when convenient. What Peirse did not protest was the implied stance towards area bombing. He was a man who believed in the virtue of precision attack, but was aware of the situation's realities, concluding that only one in three crews dispatched on short-range operations actually found the target. On long-distance raids, this number dropped to one in five. German oil plants were a worthy target, but would crews be able to hit them? Meanwhile, with Britain's cities being pounded relentlessly, Churchill was demanding action. He wrote to Air Chief Marshall Sir Cyril Newall on 20 October, asking whether it was possible to create a 'Second Line Bomber Force,' which would operate from high altitudes on moonless nights and above largely built-up areas of Germany rife with military targets. He went on, urging the RAF to make a 'whole-hearted effort' to create such a force that would enable as many bombs as possible to be dumped on Germany with little regard to accuracy.[120]

Bomber Command's front-line force was to maintain its campaign of 'accurate bombing' against German military targets deep within enemy territory.[121] Churchill wanted Bomber Command to wage two campaigns: one against German morale, the other being a precision-based battle against Nazi industry. Bomber Command did what it could, flying all over Germany throughout November and December. Targets ranged far and wide: Hamburg, Berlin, Munich, Kiel, Essen, Bremen, Duisburg, Düsseldorf and Cologne. On the night of 14 November, Bomber Command suffered its heaviest night loss yet with dual attacks on Berlin and Hamburg. Of the eighty-two bombers dispatched, ten were lost. Other targets throughout this period included airfields in the occupied countries and war factories in Italy.[122]

The same night Hamburg and Berlin devoured nearly a dozen British bombers, thermite and explosive devoured the heart of Coventry — a major munitions centre for Britain's military machine. The brilliant luminescence of Luftwaffe marker flares exploded over the city at 1915 hours as some 300 hundred enemy aircraft zeroed in on their objective. Coventry's big guns roared into the night. The German bombers kept high to avoid the barrage, but it did little to save the city. More than 500 tons of bombs fell on Coventry, destroying more than 60,000 buildings. Up in flames went the city's medieval cathedral and fifty per cent of the city centre's residential housing. The number of dead and injured reached 1,700. 'Coventry,' states The Luftwaffe War Diaries, 'became a monument to the terror of war by bombing, the peak of which had still to be reached.'[123]

An outraged public — and a furious Prime Minister — demanded retaliation of the most ruthless kind. Plans, under the code-name Abigail, were devised to select a German city and destroy as much of it as possible. Suggested targets included Bremen, Düsseldorf and Mannheim. The War Cabinet approved the plan on 13 December, with the date for the raid being set for 16 December.

It was decided Düsseldorf — code-named Abigail Delilah — would suffer for Coventry's ordeal and be made to burn under the aegis of Bomber Command's first intentional area attack. But late in the afternoon of 16 December, the meteorological forecast brought news of a violent weather front moving over the city. So it was that Düsseldorf was spared and Mannheim was bombed. For the operation, Bomber Command mustered 134 Wellingtons, Whitleys, Hampdens and Blenheims — the largest number yet assembled for any raid. Conditions over the target were clear and a full moon lit the bombers' way. Flown by the most experienced crews available, eight Wellingtons of No. 3 Group commenced the attack, dropping maximum loads of incendiaries on the town centre. Using the fires as guides, proceeding crews were to bomb with the sole intent of causing as much destruction as possible. Fires burned bright as aircraft after aircraft unburdened themselves of their devastating payloads. But the attacks were scattered — with residential areas taking the main shock of the assault — and not on the city centre. Two Hampdens and one Blenheim were destroyed, and four additional aircraft crashed on their return to England. In Mannheim, nearly 120 people were either killed or wounded. Five hundred buildings were obliterated, including thirteen commercial complexes. A railway station was wiped out, and 1,200 people were bombed out of their homes. Despite the carnage, Bomber Command failed in its primary objective: the destruction of Mannheim's centre.

Against their top priority, Germany's synthetic oil supplies, Peirse's crews fared little better. Two oil plants in the Ruhr town of Gilsenkirchen were attacked in late December by 265 aircraft loaded with 262 tons of incendiaries. The notion that the attacks had delivered a devastating blow was shattered on Christmas Eve when Spitfires of the RAF Reconnaissance Photographic Unit reconnoitered the target area. The images they brought back revealed neither plant had suffered any severe damage. The oil campaign was proving a failure. Between November 1940 and the following March, only 1,200 sorties would be flown against synthetic oil plants and many of those aircraft would fail to find the targets.[124] Perhaps the Command would fare better against the industrial and urban centres of Hitler's Third Reich.

V

A Return to Troubled Waters

Flawed Thinking

British bombers thundered over Bremen on the first night of the new year — 1941 — and blasted the Focke-Wulf factory in the city's southern suburb of Hemelingen. Though the raid was a moderate success, oil remained Bomber Command's primary objective — a point reinstated on 15 January when Peirse was informed, via another directive, 'that the sole primary aim of your bomber offensive, until further orders, should be the destruction of German synthetic oil plants.'[125] Behind this order was a report released by the intelligence branch of the Ministry of Economic Warfare in December. It incorrectly asserted that Germany had suffered a fifteen-per cent reduction in its synthetic oil output 'by the expenditure of only 539 tons of bombs or, in other words, no more than 6.7 per cent of the total effort expended by Bomber Command against industrial targets, communications or invasion ports.'[126] It suggested that Germany was in a desperate state, and that a final thrust by Bomber Command against this specific industry would cripple her war-making capacity.

The Air Staff, under Portal, drafted a plan calling for Bomber Command to destroy seventeen synthetic oil plants by mid-1941, inflicting upon Germany a loss of more than 1,000,000 tons of oil. Such devastating results could only be achieved, Portal believed, with an average of nine clear nights a month and the deployment of no fewer than ninety-five aircraft on these nights. Specifically, he was looking for 855 sorties per month against synthetic oil plants over a four-month period. The scheme was accepted by the Chiefs of Staff on 7 January and, eight days later, the order crossed Peirse's desk. But 1941 dawned in much the same fashion as 1940 under dark and violent skies. In the first three months of the year, only 221 sorties would be flown against German oil.[127]

On another front, the RAF began to engage the Luftwaffe in a war of attrition. It was a new method of assault, code-named 'Circus.' Blenheims would swoop over northern France and the occupied coast under an umbrella of fighter protection, baiting the Luftwaffe into combat. These joint operations between Bomber and Fighter Commands commenced on 10 January when six Blenheims of 114 Squadron, accompanied by seventy-two Spitfires and Hurricanes, attacked a German ammunitions depot in the Fôret de Guines, south of Calais. Following the German invasion of Russia in June, Circus operations would be stepped up in earnest with the partial intent of keeping Luftwaffe fighter forces away from the Eastern Front. Such operations proved unsuccessful. Between 14 June and 3 September, the RAF would lose 208 aircraft —fourteen of which were Blenheims — to the Luftwaffe's 128.

But the Blenheims of No. 2 Group maintained their daylight offensive, waging a fierce campaign against enemy convoys bringing iron ore and oil into German ports from Norway and Spain. The ships kept inshore, sailing under the protective fire of German coastal batteries and Luftwaffe fighter patrols. The bombers, painted sea green, would fly no more than a few hundred feet above the water to avoid the holocaust of enemy fire. At times they were flown so low, the aircraft's underbelly skimmed the crests of the waves. The impact of the propellers slicing through the water would sometimes bend the blades.[128] In the face of such fierce enemy opposition, thirteen per cent of the Blenheims that actually engaged German shipping were lost between April and June.

In March, however, all of Bomber Command was diverted to the war at sea, as the stranglehold on Britain's lifelines was tightened.

A Clash of Titans

The *Scharnhorst*. She was 26,000 destructive tons of cold steel, armed with nine 11-inch guns and mighty Krupps armament. Capable of cruising at 29 knots, she could outrun all the Royal Navy had to offer, as could her sister ship, the *Gneisenau*. In January, the two battle cruisers broke into the North Atlantic, skirting the British blockade and sailing north through the Denmark Straight. Within two months, they had sunk twenty-seven ships. Churchill had long demanded the destruction of these vessels, for the war at sea was rapidly deteriorating. The Royal Navy was heavily engaged in

the Mediterranean against both German and Italian forces, while struggling for supremacy in the Atlantic. By March, the 56,000-ton German
battleship *Bismarck* was preparing to sail and the dreaded Focke-Wulf
Kondor was ranging widely over the seas.

On 9 March, as per Churchill's orders, a new directive signed by Vice-
Chief of the Air Staff, Air Chief Marshal Sir Wilfrid Freeman, reached
Peirse's desk. Over the next four months, Bomber Command was to focus
on 'defeating the attempt of the enemy to strangle our food supplies and
connection with the United States.' The directive's wording made use of a
memo written by Churchill himself:

> We must take the offensive against the U-boat and Focke-Wulf wher-
> ever we can and whenever we can. The U-boat at sea must be hunted,
> the U-boat in the building yard or dock must be bombed. The Focke-
> Wulf, and other bombers employed against our shipping, must be
> attacked in the air and in their nests.[129]

Attached was a list of targets connected with the U-boat and long-range
aircraft menace: the shipyards of Hamburg, Kiel, Bremen and Vegesack, the
marine diesel-engine plants of Mannheim and Augsburg, aircraft factories
at Dassau and U-boat pens along the French coast. Added Freeman:

> Priority of selection should be given to those in Germany which lie
> in congested areas where the greatest moral effect is likely to result.
> You will appreciate that once a target has been selected it is particu-
> larly desirable that it should be subjected to a succession of heavy
> attacks.[130]

It was another step on the path towards area bombing.

Bomber Command had already attacked many of the listed objectives
— including ports along the French coast — numerous times. Wrote a
Daily Telegraph reporter in early 1941 who, from the Kent coast, watched
Bomber Command raid targets along the French sea border:

> For an hour I watched the huge flashes of bombs as they fell at the
> rate of between 30 and 40 a minute. A fire lighted the faintly moonlit
> sky and the dull thunder of the bombs occasionally rumbled across
> the Channel. A faint dull glow, apparently caused by fires, lit a sec-
> tion of the French Coast through the mist.

Now, Bomber Command's war at sea began with the targeting of the
Scharnhorst and *Gneisenau*.

In a memorandum to Portal on 17 April, Churchill referred to both
German cruisers as two of the war's most dangerous vessels as the Royal

Navy lacked the speed and firepower to catch and destroy them.[131] On 28 March, following an alert from the French Resistance, a Spitfire flying reconnaissance photographed the two ships in the French port of Brest. They had just put in for repairs following their devastating Atlantic run. Peirse sent more than 100 aircraft to Brest two nights later, but all bombs missed. Fifty-four aircraft returned on the night of 4 April. One bomb landed near the *Gneisenau* in its dry dock, while others slammed into the Continental Hotel nearby just as guests were sitting down for their evening dinner.

In the immediate wake of the attack, the *Gneisenau* was moved into the harbour where her captain believed she would be better protected. The ship was anchored along a wall on the north shore of the harbor. Rising up behind it were the surrounding hills peppered with anti-aircraft batteries. Further defences were secured along two arms of land encircling the outer harbour in which three anti-aircraft gunships were moored in a defensive line around the cruiser. It was into this, on the morning of 6 April, a lone Bristol Beaufort bomber of Coastal Command, piloted by 23-year-old Flying Officer Kenneth Campbell, dived and pressed home a daring attack.

Campbell flew in at sea level, thundering past the anti-aircraft gunships below mast-height — their guns roaring as the Beaufort rocketed towards the *Gneisenau*. Surrounding the cruiser was a stone mole, bending around it from the west. Over this skimmed Campbell's aircraft, dropping a torpedo at point-blank range and inflicting massive damage beneath the *Gneisenau's* waterline. Having penetrated the formidable defences, Campbell could not escape the rising ground beyond the harbour. Blasted by enemy fire, the Beaufort smashed into the raised ground. All on board were killed. The *Gneisenau* was moved back into the dry dock whence she had come the day before. With its starboard propeller shaft destroyed, the cruiser would remain there for the next six months. For his uncommon valour, Campbell was posthumously awarded the Victoria Cross.

That night Bomber Command returned to Brest and bombed through bad weather with no visible results. But four bombs found their mark on the night of 10 April, killing a number of the *Gneisenau's* crew. The harbor at Brest was a formidable target — one the crews of Bomber Command would return to both by day and night. The hazards of attacking the ships in the French port were described in 1941:

> The difficulties of an attack on Brest are not always realised. The Germans have done their utmost since it fell into their hands to make it immune from air attack. In this they have not succeeded, but an assault on it by bomber aircraft is a hazardous operation. Brest is protected by a very heavy concentration of A.A. guns, by a balloon barrage and a formidable array of searchlights. There are also

patrols of fighters on the watch to intercept our bombers. When weather conditions are suitable a smoke screen is laid over the targets in order to make the task of our bomb-aimers yet more difficult. It is not uncommon for a pilot to report that his aircraft has been held in a cone of searchlights for more than five minutes while he was over the target. Brest has been attacked sixty-nine times up to 10th July.[132]

Bomber Command would rage against Brest and the two cruisers — code-named Salmon (*Scharnhorst*) and Gluck (*Gneisenau*) — for the next ten months. The *Prinz Eugen* would be hunted and the *Tirpitz* would come to be continually harried. Hamburg, Bremen, Mannheim, Cologne, Düsseldorf and Kiel all suffered repeated attacks as Bomber Command waged war against the U-boat and Focke-Wulf. Blenheims continued their daylight sweeps over the North Sea, attacking enemy shipping and raiding fringe targets along and off the occupied coast. The gruelling nature of the work was all too evident, and squadrons engaged in such operations were often withdrawn from frontline service to recuperate from their catastrophic losses. Meanwhile, in the wake of the German thrust into Russia, several Luftwaffe fighter wings were withdrawn from the west to assist the Wehrmacht in its eastern advance. The Air Staff thus turned their attention to possible daylight raids over enemy territory with attacks by twenty-eight Blenheims and six Halifaxes on Bremen, Kiel, Norderney and Sylt.

On the afternoon of 4 July, twelve Blenheims of 105 Squadron, led by Wing Commander Hughie Edwards, targeted the Port of Bremen, Germany's second largest after Hamburg. Flying fifty miles inland to the target, the formation shot across Germany at a mere fifty feet, passing under high-tension cables and carrying away telegraph wires before smashing through a balloon barrage on the final approach to the target. Prosecuting their attack, the Blenheims stormed through a holocaust of flak. Enemy fire from 105mm and 88mm gun emplacements tore through all twelve aircraft and destroyed four of them. One Blenheim was last seen making its bombing run when its starboard engine suddenly vaporised in a ball of flame. The plane veered uncontrollably towards the ground and slammed into a factory, exploding on impact. Despite the heavy losses, much damage was done to railway lines, storage and vehicle depots and goods warehouses. The Dyckhoff & Widmann Factory was bombed, as was the Weserflung Aircraft Factory. Its hangar went up in flames and several Ju-88s were destroyed on the ground. Pieces of wreckage were blasted some 700 feet into the air. All bombs gone, the remaining eight Blenheims, still led by Edwards, turned and made it for home without further losses. For his planning and leadership, Edwards received the Victoria Cross. The achievement was made all the more remarkable by the fact that Edwards was handicapped by a physical disability suffered in a previous flying accident.[133]

Primary amongst Churchill's North Atlantic concerns was the *Bismarck*. Her 56,000 tons cast a long shadow over the war at sea. On 18 May, she left the shelter of Norwegian waters and — accompanied by the heavy cruiser *Prinz Eugen* — broke into the North Atlantic. The Royal Navy's response was immediate. Britain's mightiest warship, HMS *Hood*, armed with eight 15-inch guns, gave chase. The two titans brought their guns to bear on one another on May 22. The confrontation was short and intense in its ferocity. Built two decades earlier, *Hood* fell victim to the advances in naval technology that made the *Bismarck* such a formidable force. Within minutes, the *Hood* was devastated, exploding and sinking beneath the waves with all but three of her 1,400 sailors still on board. She was avenged on 27 May, when a massive Royal Navy taskforce sent *Bismarck* and 2,000 of her crew to the ocean's floor. The *Prinz Eugen* managed to escape, and joined the *Scharnhorst* and *Gneisenau* in the port at Brest in early June.

On the night of 1 July, fifty-two Wellingtons were sent to the French port to again engage Bomber Command's two old adversaries and the new arrival. Three bombers were lost. One slammed into the dry dock alongside the *Prinz Eugen*, exploding in a brilliant column of flame. The concussion of the blast catapulted from the wreckage one bomb that tore through the *Prinz Eugen*, detonating inside the ship and killing sixty of her crew. But what damage, if any, had been inflicted upon the cruisers in Brest through these countless attacks was not yet known. There was enough difficulty involved in hitting a factory, let alone a warship veiled by smoke screens and a canopy of heavy flak. Reported the Air Ministry in 1941:

> To inflict these hurts upon the enemy warships, an enormous weight of bombs has been dropped. The great majority of them have not hit the ships...
>
> Whatever maybe the amount of damage which has been inflicted on the 'Scharnhorst,' 'Gneisenau' and 'Prinz Eugen,' one broad fact is patent for all to see. Not one of these three ships, vital elements as they are in the battle of the Atlantic, has taken any part in it for a long time, the 'Gneisenau' and 'Scharnhorst' since the end of March, the 'Prinz Eugen' since the beginning of June. Hitler has been forced during the five critical months from April to August of this year, to fight the battle without three naval units of great power, which might, had they been on the high seas, have added enormously to the shipping casualties which German submarines and aircraft have been able to cause.[134]

In June the Secretary of State received a memo from the Air Ministry explaining the destruction of heavily guarded ships in dock was a near impossibility. They could not be sunk or made vulnerable to water damage, and immediate repairs could be rendered to whatever bomb damage was inflicted.[135] Nevertheless, by July the efforts of Bomber Command had helped stabilise Britain's precarious position in the Battle of the Atlantic with shipping losses that month at only 120,000 tons. This was down from 197,674 tons in May and June and more than 400,000 tons the month before.

A Growing Arsenal and Change of Strategy

By now, three new aircraft — albeit in small numbers — were appearing in the night skies over Germany. The Short Stirling, the Handley Page Halifax and the Avro Manchester were three of the new generation of four-engined heavy bombers specified in an Air Staff requirement dating back to 1936. Despite their increased payload, the performance of all three would prove to be a liability in varying degrees to the crews who flew them. The Short Stirling made its operational debut against Rotterdam on the night of 10 February. In its design, the engineers at Short faced a challenge in the restriction of its wingspan which was to be kept at 100 feet so it could fit in existing RAF hangars. This immediately inflicted upon the Stirling a low operational ceiling — something that would prove costly with the intensification of German defences in the coming years.

Another design flaw lay in its bomb bay which, although it carried 14,000-lbs of explosives, was divided into separate compartments, preventing it from carrying anything bigger than the RAF's 2,000-lbs bomb. In its defences it boasted eight to ten .303 Browning machine guns in front, rear and mid-upper positions and had a top speed of 270 mph, faster than any of the previously existing heavies. In January 1941 No. 7 Squadron — the first to be equipped with the new aircraft five years after it was ordered — moved from RAF Leeming in Yorkshire, south to RAF Oakington near Cambridge, having completed its conversion from Hampdens. Despite its flaws, the Stirling would prove a valiant and rugged machine loved by the men who flew it. It would be withdrawn from the bomber offensive's front line in 1943, during the Battle of Berlin, but go on to assist airborne forces in operations such as the drop into Arnhem.

The grim honour of being the first four-engined bomber to attack Germany would fall to the Handley Page Halifax. With a maximum bomb load of 13,000lb.s, it flew its first operational sortie on the night of 11 March against the fringe target of Le Havre. Although destined to become an exceptional aircraft second only to the mighty Avro

Lancaster, in its earlier incarnation, the Halifax proved to be a bomber in much need of improvement. In October 1942 Bomber Command's Operational Research Section would investigate why Halifax squadrons were suffering the highest casualty rate. The following year, blame would be placed on the aircraft's instability during hard manoeuvres. Over the next twelve months, the squadrons of No. 4 Group would begin converting to Halifaxes as the aircraft gradually joined the forefront of the bombing offensive.[136]

Loathed by all who were doomed to fly it, the Avro Manchester was an abysmal failure. Despite its appearance as a twin-engined bomber, the Manchester was a four-engined aircraft. A pair of Rolls Royce Kestrels conjoined with a shared crankcase was mounted under each wing. Its operational life was short. Its underpowered engines, called Vultures, were prone to all sorts of failures. Its operational debut was against Brest on the night of 24 February. A mere ten months later, Avro ceased production of the Manchester. The plane spent the majority of its time grounded, riddled with technical faults. Avro, meanwhile, had been experimenting with a variation of the Manchester design. Conceptualised by Roy Chadwick, the aircraft, called the Mk III, was powered by four Merlin engines and boasted a wider wingspan. The prototype flew on 9 January 1941 and the Lancaster was born.

By mid-year, the Chiefs of Staff were calling for a long-term strategic bombing policy. On 11 June, they sent Churchill a minute stating they were 'of the opinion that, in order to obtain the maximum offensive value from our Bomber Force, it is of the highest importance that its operations should not be conducted in a hand-to-mouth manner, but in accordance with a definite strategic aim.'[137] The minute went on to outline a plan to target German communications, transportation systems and the morale of the enemy's industrial workers. German military advancement into Greece, Yugoslavia and Crete, the Chiefs of Staff asserted, was straining lines of communication and transportation. It was the ideal time to strike. It was then proposed that German morale be Bomber Command's secondary aim. The communications and transportation targets 'lie among workers dwellings in congested industrial areas, and their attack will have a direct effect on a considerable section of the German people. The interruption of supplies will influence to some extent the morale of the whole of Germany.'[138]

Oil was out. Against the refineries, British bombers had accomplished nothing. The Chiefs of Staff felt it was about time Bomber Command emerged as a presence hard felt by the Germans. In these words sent to Churchill lay the foreshadowing of Bomber Command's city-busting campaign.

VI

Germany Under Fire

In the Hole

'The Hole' was the underground operations room at Bomber Command HQ in the Buckinghamshire town of Walter's Ash. Specifically built for Bomber Command prior to the outbreak of war, 'The Hole' lay protected, sheltered by deep layers of concrete beneath a large grassy mound. The room was large and oblong with a rubber floor and could only be accessed by one door which was constantly manned by an armed sentry — as was the staircase leading to it. The walls were festooned with charts, boards and maps. Three blackboards — each 30 feet by 10 feet and displaying the Order of Battle — occupied one whole wall. On these were listed current operations: Groups and squadron activities and the details of the previous nights' raids.[139]

A large meteorological map covered the room's right-hand wall and was updated every eight hours. Next to it was a lunar chart denoting the current month's phases of the moon. A quarter-inch map of northern Europe hung on the left-hand wall. In it were stuck pins with coloured labels marking enemy targets. A similar map of Italian objectives hung on the back wall. To the left of the door were desks for the controllers and duty officers. Phones on the desks provided a direct link to the various bomber groups and the Air Ministry. As Bomber Command was to be kept abreast of all naval matters, there was a desk for the Command's naval liaison and one for the army officer who was to report all Home Forces developments.[140]

In the left centre of the room was Peirse's desk, surrounded by three charts: one being a photographic mosaic of the Ruhr; the other a large map of Europe illustrating outward and return routes to various targets and the locations of night-fighter bases. This map was updated every twenty-four hours. The third chart was a display graph showing how many times certain targets had been attacked. A map of Berlin was accompanied by an enlarged visual representation of Bomber Command's more vital objectives.[141]

From this room, Peirse would direct Bomber Command's new campaign, the details of which were laid out in yet another directive on 9 July 1941. Following a 'comprehensive review of the enemy's present political, economic and military situation' it was determined that Germany's greatest weakness lay 'in the morale of the civil population and in his inland transportation system.' It continued:

> The wide extension of his military activities is placing an ever-increasing strain on the German transportation system and there are many signs that our recent attacks on industrial towns are having great effect on the morale of the civil population... You will direct the main effort of the bomber force, until further instructions, towards dislocating the German transportation system and to destroying the morale of the civil population as a whole and of the industrial workers in particular.[142]

Partially opposing this policy were members of a committee formed in 1939 called the Committee of Preventing Oil from Reaching Enemy Powers. A mere six days after this latest directive reached Peirse, Lord Hankey head of the committee, wrote to the Chiefs of Staff. He argued that aligning Britain's bombers against German synthetic oil would be of much greater consequence to Britain's new ally, the Soviet Union, which was currently being ravaged on the Eastern Front. Portal, however, was not swayed. He knew Bomber Command's track record against pinpoint targets. For now, the plan was to isolate the Ruhr and Rhineland and strangle the outward flow of war materials to Germany's war fronts.

During moonlit nights, Bomber Command was to strike at the railway installations of Cologne, Duisburg, Düsseldorf, Hamm, Osnabrück, Schwerte and Soest, all of which lay on the outward fringes of the Ruhr Valley. Attacks on German morale was to be the Command's secondary objective, with the populated areas of Cologne, Düsseldorf and Duisburg to be battered with high explosives and incendiaries on moonless nights. Hamburg, Bremen, Hannover and Munich would also be blasted. But the fact was, as with all previous operations, morale would be continually attacked as bombs fell wide and short of industrial targets and slammed into the surrounding populated areas. For the task at hand, Peirse now had forty-five operational squadrons with a front-line strength of 450 aircraft and crew. The new heavies — Stirlings, Halifaxes and Manchesters — made up six squadrons, while twenty-one squadrons still relied on the dependable Wellington. No. 4 Group still retained six squadrons of Whitleys, while No. 5 Group held on to its six Hampden squadrons. The plan for the eight Blenheim squadrons of No. 2 Group was to replace them with the faster American-made Boston at the end of the year.[143]

In the first week of Bomber Command's new campaign, Peirse took aim at Hamm, Munster, Aachen, Osnabrück, Cologne, Wilhelmshaven, Bremen, Hannover, Duisburg and Hamburg with varying degrees of success. The attack on Aachen by eighty-two aircraft on the night of 9 July was a general area attack. Suffering its first major raid of the war, Aachen's town centre was reduced to rubble. The destruction of 1,698 houses and apartment units left more than 3,000 people bombed out. Twenty commercial premises were hit and the town hall was severely damaged. Only two aircraft were lost, while German deaths numbered sixty.

The last six months of 1941 saw Bomber Command drop nearly 14,000 tons of bombs in its attempt to destroy German transportation and lines of communication. Against the *Scharnhorst* and *Gneisenau* — and other naval targets — it would dump more than 45,000 tons of high explosives. On the afternoon of 16 July, thirty-six Blenheims of No. 2 Group — flying in V-shaped formations — swept over Holland and stormed the harbour at Rotterdam. They flew in two waves of eighteen aircraft, all primed with 250-pounders fused with eleven-second delays. They infiltrated the harbour from the south-east, flying in below mast height. As they commenced their attack, the flak ships opened fire. Four aircraft were blasted from the sky, including one that smashed into the centre of Rotterdam. In the harbour, twenty-two German ships were left smouldering.

Daylight Assault

Bomber Command launched a massive daylight assault against Brest and the other French port of La Pallice on 24 July. Three days earlier, RAF reconnaissance confirmed the presence of the *Scharnhorst, Gneisenau* and *Prinz Eugen* at Brest. But at noon the following day — 22 July — a Coastal Command aircraft reconnoitreing the area reported that the *Scharnhorst* was missing. In her old berth, the Germans had placed a tanker and covered it with the same camouflage netting used to conceal the cruisers. A frantic search operation commenced. At 8:30 on the morning of 23 July, she was discovered at La Pallice some 240 miles south of Brest. Amidst fears that the cruiser was preparing for another Atlantic run, Bomber Command was immediately ordered to attack. Six Stirlings from No. 7 Squadron, dispatched on a daylight raid, were forced to fight through heavy fighter opposition as they struggled to reach their objective. One Stirling was shot down, and the German cruisers escaped unscathed.[144]

That night, thirty Whitleys and aircraft from Coastal Command followed up the attack, starting numerous fires in the docks area. The next day, Bomber Command launched its dual assault. A force of 100 Wellingtons, Hampdens and the American-built Flying Fortress — Bomber Command's newest edition — went to Brest, while fifteen Halifaxes targeted the *Scharnhorst* at La Pallice. A diversionary raid by Blenheims and Spitfires fell on the docks at Cherbourg but failed to draw the attention of German fighters protecting the three cruisers. Three American Flying Fortresses, reflecting the sun at 32,000 feet, commenced the attack on Brest, dropping their 1,100-lbs payloads. Explosions straddled the *Prinz Eugen*, bursting on her quayside and dry dock, buffetting the ship with plumes of water, concrete and flame. The raid's planners hoped this advanced echelon of the main attack force would draw the German fighters up prematurely. As the blasts echoed through the port, eighteen Hampdens swooped in low for the kill. They sky was dirtied by black clouds of shrapnel and the phosphorescent colours of tracer. The enemy fire loosened the Hampden formation. As the aircraft lost their cohesion, they were set upon by enemy fighters. Now the once clear skies above the port were a raging field of battle as more Luftwaffe fighters flew up to intercept the main force of seventy-eight Wellingtons. Although the *Gneisenau* was hit six times, ten Wellingtons and two Hampdens were lost in the struggle.

Meanwhile, above La Pallice, enemy fire was tearing into the Halifaxes of 35 and 76 Squadrons. The nine aircraft of 35 Squadron took off from their base at RAF Linton-on-Ouse at 1035 hours. They flew in three sections of three and crossed the English coast at 1,000 feet before beginning their climb to a bombing height of 15,000 feet. Notes the squadron's Operations Record Book:

> The weather was excellent, brilliant sunshine and no cloud, with perfect visibility. An enemy destroy was passed in the proximity of the Isle D'Yeo, which, apparently, believing itself about to be attacked, commenced evasive action and opened fire, but did no damage.

The Halifaxes' cover was now blown, as the destroyer alerted the German defenses to the approaching bombers. 'On approach to target area, a very heavy barrage of A.A. fire was immediately put up, and some thirty enemy fighters were observed, some in the air, others taking off from aerodromes in and about La Rochelle.' The Halifaxes attacked in echelon as planned, cutting through the clouds of flak and sustaining heavy damage.

One aircraft, piloted by Flight Sergeant Godwin, 'was seen to go down in a slow spiral with smoke coming from two of its engines.'[145]
Enemy fighters swarmed about the bombers, disregarding the possible consequences of flying amidst their side's own anti-aircraft fire. The air combat was fierce, as squadron records note:

> SGT. Bolton, the first operator of the Leader's aircraft, was killed, and the second pilot injured; P/O Stone, tail gunner of another aircraft, was killed by cannon fire which went to rake the aircraft and injure both beam gunners. Another Wireless Operator was wounded, seriously, and another tail gunner was slightly wounded, but all kept to their posts, and with the tail gunners, displayed the very highest standard of coolness and skill and not only successfully defended their aircraft throughout all attacks, but came away with the score of five enemy aircraft confirmed shot down and three probables. Many others damaged.[146]

All but one aircraft succeeded in dropping its bombs. Evasive action, however, made it impossible to view the results. One direct hit was observed, though the bomber responsible — that of Captain Flight Sergeant Greaves — failed to return. Squadron Nos 35 and 76 lost five of fifteen Halifaxes between them. Eight of the ten surviving aircraft returned to their bases with twenty-one dead or wounded men on board. In the event, five direct hits were scored on the *Scharnhorst*, causing extensive damage and putting her out of action for the next four months. That night, with 3,000 tons of water inside her, the *Scharnhorst* limped back up the coast to rejoin the *Gneisenau* and *Prinz Eugen* in Brest.[147]

The early incarnation of the Flying Fortress used at Brest would, in due time, prove a disappointment. The B-17C — an early incarnation of the later models that would deliver fire on behalf of the US Army Eighth Air Force — arrived in England in the spring of 1941. Twenty were delivered in May, but, by July, only seven were operational owing to the numerous modifications required. Its automatic bombsight was prone to malfunction above 20,000 feet. Its armour was too thin. The engines left vapour trails against the sky. Baubles had to be opened to fire the bomber's beam machine guns, thus sometimes reducing the temperature inside the aircraft to a point well below zero. Its range of operations was an inadequate 500 miles, and its oxygen system was unreliable.[148]

The Fortress flew its last bombing operation under RAF colours on 25 September against Bremen. On its outward track, the aircraft produced vapour trails at 27,000 feet, revealing its position against the clear sky, forcing the operation to be abandoned. In all, the Fortress flew fifty-one sorties with Bomber Command before a detachment of 90 Squadron — the squadron specifically formed to fly the aircraft — was sent to the

Middle East where Fortresses flew a handful of night operations over North Africa. In October the following year, the aircraft was transferred to Coastal Command to be used for reconnaissance.[149]

Night Defences

Bomber Command ranged far and wide in the Reich's night skies. In the last six months of 1941, seventy per cent of Bomber Command's efforts were geared towards setting Germany alight.[150] The first major raid on Kassel on the night of 8 September resulted in major damage being done to a railway-wagon works and an optical instrument factory. The city's main railway station was also hit, but attempts to sever lines of transportation in and out of the Ruhr were continually thwarted by the thick haze which hung over Germany's industrial heart. As British and Commonwealth crews struggled to cripple Germany, German defences in the west were being strengthened and reorganised to counter the increasing threat of fire from the sky. The German night-fighter arm was growing. The 'Kammhuber Line' was evolving.

Between July and November 1941, Bomber Command lost 526 aircraft over enemy territory — 414 of which were shot down on night operations. Statistically, this represented Bomber Command's entire front-line strength. The night skies were becoming an increasingly violent environment. The flak was fierce, and searchlights were throwing up ever greater walls of illumination. Vivid streams of tracer scorched the sky, and more and more could be seen the crimson glow of British bombers burning and dropping to the ground. The German night fighter too was a growing menace. The first British bomber torn through and destroyed by a night fighter was a Whitley, shot from the skies over northern Germany on 20 July 1940. It was a clear night, free of cloud and tinged silver by the light of a full moon, casting the landscape of the lower Rhine below in gentle shades of white and silver.[151]

Winging its way through the glistening night at 12,000 feet was a Bf 110, piloted by First Lieutenant Werner Streib. Behind him sat his radio operator, Colonel Lingen. In the early days of night-fighter operations, the majority of Luftwaffe pilots would return from operations without having seen a single bomber. But at 0200 hours on the night in question, Streib and Lingen saw what they thought to be another Bf 110 flying 300 yards off starboard. To confirm the other aircraft's identity, Streib moved his fighter alongside the shadowy craft, its crew unaware of Streib's presence. In the soft glow of the moon, Streib saw the unmistakable reflection of light on a gun turret and the faint colours of an RAF roundel. It was a Whitley. As Streib positioned himself for an attack, the bomber's rear gunner was alerted to the German fighter and opened fire. Streib, who returned with two short bursts of cannon and machine-gun fire, saw the starboard engine burst into flame and watched two men leap from the bomber's silhouette. Parachutes open, they drifted away in the darkness. Now Streib aimed for the port wing and engine and let loose a burst of cannon fire. The engine erupted in flames, and fire quickly engulfed the wing. There was no return fire from the bomber.[152]

The stricken aircraft flew on for several more minutes before plunging to the ground and vaporising in a violent flash. The Whitley's fate marked the beginning of a deadly phenomenon. It was one that would emerge from the darkness of the Reich and eventually stretch to Sicily and Africa. Its defensive arsenal would boast six searchlight regiments, nearly 2,000 radar stations and 700 specially equipped fighters.[153] Not until the promotion and appointment of Colonel Josef Kammhuber to General of Night Fighters in October 1940 did Germany's night defences begin their staggering evolution.

It began as a belt of searchlights and sound locators stretching west from Munster, growing throughout the winter of 1940-41, branching out north and south and gradually encompassing the entire Ruhr. This was the Kammhuber Line — a series of zones twenty miles long by twelve miles wide that would, by the end of 1941, extend across northern Germany and the Low Countries from Denmark to France. Each overlapping zone was the domain of a single Me 110 or Ju 88 and was equipped with radar-controlled searchlights that automatically locked onto the approaching bomber, illuminating it like a beacon in the night onto which the roving night fighter would zero in. This would evolve, in the summer of 1941, into the more lethal *Himmelbett* system with its radar-guided fighters. With a range of up to 100 miles, *Freya* radar was the system's first line of defence, detecting a bomber's course as it crossed the North Sea. *Freya* was supplemented by two *Wurburg* radar apparatus — one to track the bomber as it entered the zone, the other to monitor the fighter sent up to intercept. For each zone there was a ground s tation — Jaguar, Delphin, Lowe, Eisbar, Seidler and others[154] — each equipped with a glass-topped Seeburg evaluation table on which the fighter and bomber were monitored. Red and green points of light were projected onto the glass tabletop. Red represented the British 'terror flier,' green its German nemesis. Controllers monitored the progress of the deadly cat and mouse chase unfolding in the dark void above, radioing the German pilot as he desperately scoured the black expanse for his prey.[155]

In August 1941 Bf 110s of Nacht-Jagdeschwader 2 took to the night skies equipped with a new interception system: Lichtenstein Air Interception Radar. Without assistance from ground control, German pilots could now track and monitor British bombers from up to two miles away, closing in on the lumbering silhouettes as the bombers' exhaust ports belched flame in the darkness. The Line's effectiveness was further advanced in 1942 with the development of Giant Wurzburg, extending the length of each zone to nearly fifty miles.

Attacking from below, a Bf 110 tore into a Wellington of No. 75(NZ) Squadron on the night of 7 July 1941. The bomber, piloted by Squadron Leader R P Widdowson, was returning from a raid on Munster. It was attacked at 13,000 feet as it passed over the Zuider Zee in Holland. Cannon fire and incendiary bullets ripped through the Wellington's underbelly and blasted the starboard wing and engine. The rear gunner was shot in the foot, but managed to return fire, striking the German fighter and sending it hurtling uncontrollably into the dark below. But the damage was already done. Fuelled by petrol from a split pipe, flames quickly took hold of the damaged engine and threatened to incinerate the entire starboard wing. The crew tore a hole in the fuselage and, with fire extinguishers and the coffee from their flasks, made a desperate, yet unsuccessful, attempt to douse the flames. At that moment, Sergeant James Ward, the 22-year-old second pilot, stepped forward and perpetrated what was, arguably, one of the greatest single acts of bravery in the Second World War.

The episode was recorded in the squadron's Operation Records Book:

As a last resort, Sergeant Ward volunteered to make an attempt to smother the fire with an engine cover, which happened to be in use as a cushion. At first he proposed to discard his parachute to reduce wind resistance, but was finally persuaded to take it. A rope was tied to him, though this was of little help and might have become a danger had he been blown off the aircraft. With the help of the navigator, he climbed through the narrow astro-hatch, and put on his parachute. The bomber was flying at reduced speed, but the wind pressure must have been sufficient to render the operation one of extreme difficulty.

Breaking the aircraft's outer fabric to make hand and footholds where necessary, and also taking advantage of existing holes in the fabric, Sergeant Ward descended three feet down the fuselage to the wing, and proceeded another three feet to a position behind the engine, where the slipstream from the airscrew nearly blew him off the wing. Lying in this precarious position, he smothered the fire and tried to push the cover into the hole in the wing and block the leaking pipe from where the fire came...[156]

Positioning himself behind the wing, Ward smothered the fire with the engine cover. Badly battered by the wind and exhausted from the sheer effort involved, Ward clawed his way back along the wing, up the fuse-lage and, again with the navigator's help, back through the astro-hatch. Despite the damage, Widdowson succeeded in landing the aircraft safely on its return home — a return made possible through Ward's amazing actions. For his gallantry, Ward was honoured with the Victoria Cross. Immediate awards of the Distinguished Flying Cross and Distinguished Flying Medal were made to Widdowson and Sgt Box, the rear gunner, respectively.[157] A mere ten weeks later, on the night of 15 September, Ward was killed when his aircraft was shot down over Hamburg. He never lived to see his Victoria Cross.

The merciless alchemy of searchlights, flak and night fighters would inflict an ever more devastating toll on the British raiders as the technol-ogy of anti-bomber defence evolved. But not until 1943 would it reach its destructive zenith.

Night and Day

Bomber Command continued to hammer away at Germany by night, targeting the Ruhr and Rhineland. The village of Lauingen was reduced to a burning mass on the night of 12 October. Situated on the Danube, Lauingen lay some sixty-five miles from what was Bomber Command's primary objective that night: Nuremberg. For four hours, bombs rained down on the village and surrounding countryside, destroying forty-four houses and killing four people. Like Nuremberg, Lauingen sat on the banks of a wide river and was thus mistaken for the metropolis by crews who were attempting to navigate by dead reckoning and had no idea where they were.[158] It was a most severe example of the navigational prob-lems from which Bomber Command continued to suffer.[159] Navigation by night was a rough science. The navigator sat in the forward cabin at his small table, his charts and log book spread out before him. Pencils and erasers were the tools of his trade, along with a ruler course, speed calculator and a set square. As the pilot winged the aircraft through the night, the navigator worked feverishly to maintain a fix on the bomber's position. The wind could be as important a factor as the pilot's sense of direction. The job required the navigator to work ahead of the plane's progress: calculating air speed and ground speed — sometimes relying on the stars or landmarks below for guidance — and estimating the amount of time to the next turning point. One mistake and the wrong town could go up in flames.

Peirse, meanwhile, turned his attention to further daylight operations, targeting the Knapsack and Quadrath power-stations near Cologne on

12 August. It was another attempt to relieve the Red Army by drawing German fighter forces to the west. Fifty-four Blenheims were to take part in the operation — thirty-eight being dispatched to Knapsack and sixteen to Quadrath. Flying against the power station at Knapsack was Sergeant B F Brooks, a navigator with 107 Squadron. He recorded the day's events in his Diary of Operations that evening:

> We eventually took off at 0930 hrs., and after picking up our whirlwind fighter escort set course at sea level over the coast at 10.08 hrs. We crossed the Dutch coast at the estuary of the River Scheldt and set course for Duren approx. 20 miles down the river. Here our escort left us and we flew on in boxes of six, at ground level. I found map reading almost impossible, but as we progressed, I was able to pick out road-rail junctions and found that the whole formation was flying south of our track.

> I could see no flak of any description during the first part of the trip overland. Frequently, however, I saw groups of people in villages waving at us, while others in the fields panicked and hurried for shelter. The weather gradually deteriorated and we occasionally passed through showers while the cloud base came lower.

> On reaching Duren we turned N.E. map reading on to the target and climbing to 800 ft. We approached the station in a S.W. direction when light flak began to open fire. We were hit in both wings and the fuselage, but not seriously. I thought the flak was very accurate for height and amidst all the excitement and panic, I forgot to switch on my Camera. We followed our formation leader with gentle evasive action and passed slightly to the left of the centre of the target. I released the bombs [2 x 500lb.] slightly late perhaps, but I think they all went on to part of the target, which seemed to be a mass of smoke. As we came on, an Me 109 passed overhead and to port but did not close in. This, incidentally, was the only fighter I saw around the target area.

> After giving 'Bombs Gone,' Peter put the nose down and quickly we flew down into a quarry below at ground level where I failed to see any ack-ack at all. Ace [rear gunner Sgt Frank Burrell] however, told me afterwards that he thought he saw a machine gun post. When we came up out of the quarry we were still roughly in formation, but the boxes in front seemed to be rather spread out. We flew back at 50 ft. in a large 'Vic' of fourteen planes, and by a terrific piece of luck and good work on Peter's part, we just missed another plane which appeared to me to be crossing to port and slightly climbing.

Showery weather was frequently encountered but I did not see any more flak or fighters. However, Ju. 52 passed across us about 200 ft. up. I yelled through the inter-Com to Ace, but he did not hear. I don't believe one of our formation opened fire, but according to reports from planes following, it was fired at and last seen descending, believed destroyed. Later on, an He 111 crossed over about 500 ft. above, but this was left alone.

I again found map reading extremely difficult until we reached the River Scheldt. Here we should have met some Spitfires but I only saw two. As we proceeded out to sea, six Me 109 Fs attempted to attack five planes flying about a mile in front, but they appeared to me to be very half hearted, and I think all our planes were o.k.

No further events occurred as we gradually flew out to sea with the Spitfires still in company. We crossed the coast at Southwold and landed back at base about half an hour later. I must confess that I was very glad to get back again especially after looking round at the damage and noticing a hole in the fuselage only just in front of Peter.[160]

Total Bomber Command sorties for the day numbered seventy-eight, of which twelve aircraft — ten against Knapsack and Quadrath and two on diversionary raids against airfields and shipyards in France and Germany — were lost. This represented a casualty rate of more than fifteen per cent. It was a high price to pay for the minor damage inflicted upon the stations, the output of which was reduced by ten per cent for little more than a week. Blenheims again suffered heavy losses on 26 August, prosecuting coastal sweeps and attacks on enemy shipping. Of thirty-six Blenheims dispatched, seven were lost. Nearly half an entire attack force was wiped out during a daylight raid against the Rotterdam docks on 28 August. Seven out of eighteen Blenheims were destroyed. It was enough to garner a reaction from Churchill. He wrote to Portal the following day, expressing his dismay that such casualties should be suffered over a target of minimal importance. Were the Blenheims attacking the likes of the *Tirpitz*, Churchill wrote, such losses would be acceptable. While the Prime Minister expressed his admiration for the bravery of British pilots, he suggested Bomber Command focus on 'easier targets' yielding a higher return of damage. This would allow Bomber Command the chance to expand, while suffering fewer losses. [161]

Easier targets could be found in Italy and were attacked sporadically throughout 1940 and 1941 — the largest of which fell on Turin on the night of 10 September 1941. A force of seventy-six bombers — including thirteen Stirlings and seven Halifaxes — caused some damage to the city's marshalling yards, railway station and the Fiat steelworks. A vast majority of the bombing, however, fell short of its mark and landed in residential areas. Compared to operations over Germany, bombing Italy was a pushover. The Italian skies were not raked by searchlights or scorched with flak and tracer to such a severe extent. For the British crews, the biggest challenge lay in the 1,400-mile roundtrip and the flight over the Alps. Unless held in the violent throes of a storm, the Alps offered a mesmerising display of snow and moonlight. But the aesthetic beauty belied the torturous severity of temperatures exceeding twenty-five below zero.

Bomber casualties over Turin that night were light with a loss of only five aircraft. It was a far cry from the fifteen destroyed over Berlin three nights earlier. Having returned from their nightly venture over enemy territory, crews were taken by truck or bus to the operations room for debriefing and questioning by an intelligence officer. Such interrogations were long and searching, covering all aspects of the operation: time over target, weather conditions, positions of anti-aircraft defences, altitude at which bombs were dropped, where the bombs fell and what effect they had. Crews sat at tables, sipping from cups of tea, or coffee spiked with a dollop of rum. Large maps were spread out before them, perhaps a plate of half-eaten sandwiches held down one curled corner, as the intelligence officer read through the questionnaire — standard issue to all stations — and the pilots, navigators, wireless operators and air gunners answered to the best of their ability:[162] 'I dropped the incendiaries immediately north of the dry dock...fires looked like a heath fire to me...Over Berlin there were so many searchlights they lit up the entire sky...two rows of very vivid fire...there was very heavy flak...fired a 10-second burst...saw a bright orange glow through the clouds...'[163]

During 1940 the Blenheims of No. 2 Group were tasked with post-raid reconnaissance, flying over targets and photographing the carnage inflicted by Bomber Command. But more often than not, the images they brought back were inconclusive as Blenheims lacked the speed, range and operational ceiling for the task at hand. So it was that the reports made by crews were taken in good faith. Not until the end of 1940, with the advent of highly-modified Spitfires, capable of flying at 35,000 feet and zooming to Italy and back, did photographic reconnaissance begin to offer worthwhile results — results which conflicted directly with the claims of many aircrew.[164]

It was decided that by the end of April 1941 693 aircraft would be equipped with night cameras. Instead, only 165 had been fitted.[165] The cameras were automatic, taking exposures from the moment the bombs were released until the calculated moment of bomb impact. The bombing run was a relentless strain — one not relieved by repetition. Air Gunner Jack Catford:

Three minutes to go and by now it was like subdued daylight. Harry had reported a very large explosion and one enormous fire in the target area. These fires and searchlights were responsible for the very light conditions in which we were flying. Looking at the raging fires below, my mind went back to my earlier wartime experiences, particularly in the winter of 1940 as a firefighter during the major raids on London. I knew firsthand what the civil defence below was going through, as well as the population. Sadly, pity was not on any of my thoughts, for I, too, had had to endure being on top of a ladder as German bombs were whistling down, and I had also seen comrades killed.

Two minutes to go before the release of the bombs. I could hear Frank from the bomb aimers position giving Emmie occasional corrections as we neared the target and aiming point. I was watching dead astern, plenty of bombers following us... 'Fifty seconds to go.' We all kept quiet. No one talked unless it was really vital. 'Forty seconds.' I looked above and could see a Lanc. He was just far enough behind us for his bombs to miss. The bomb doors, like ours, were open and I could see his clusters of flares and markers, plus 1,000-pound high explosive bombs set in the middle of the bomb bay and one [4,000-lb.] Cookie.

'Thirty seconds to go.' I was wishing very hard now to drop the bombs and get the hell out of the danger zone. 'Six, 5, 4, 3, 2, 1 — NOW!' Willie lifted suddenly. 'BOMBS GONE!' came Frank's voice, buoyant![166]

Those few desperate minutes belonged to the bomb aimer, lying face down in the nose of the aircraft, guiding the skipper with his running commentary:
'Photoflash in place, pin out... Two degrees port.'
'Two degrees Port.'
'One degree Starboard.'
'One degree Starboard.'
'Left, left...Okay skip, hold it... hold it... steady... right a bit...
hold it... hold it...'
Against whatever barrage the enemy was throwing up, holding the plane steady was vital. Once relieved of its deadly burden, the air-craft had to fly straight and level for another thirty seconds so an accurate photograph could be obtained. Beneath the plane the flash would explode, dazzling everything in a burst of 1 million candlepower light and adding to the illumination of the searchlights and fires. Only after the picture had been taken could the crews turn on a course for home.

The Butt Report

Churchill's scientific adviser, Lord Cherwell — formerly Professor Frederick Lindemann — had been doubtful about Bomber Command's effectiveness for some time. Pictures taken by Spitfires of the Photographic Reconnaissance Unit suggested that not only were crews failing to hit their targets, they were failing to find them altogether. Under the orders of Lord Cherwell, D M Butt, a member of the War Cabinet Secretariat, undertook an independent analysis of 650 photographs taken by bomber crews on 100 raids over France and Germany throughout June and July. The results — even for one who harboured doubts as to Bomber Command's accuracy — were startling. On 18 August, the report landed on Churchill's desk.

What the Prime Minister read was grim:

i.   Of those aircraft recorded as attacking their target, only one in three got within five miles.

ii.   Over the French ports, the proportion was two in three; over Germany as a whole, the proportion was one in four; over the Ruhr, it was only one in ten.

iii.   In the full moon, the proportion was two in five; in the new moon it was only one in fifteen.

iv.   In the absence of haze, the proportion is over one half, whereas over thick haze it is only one in fifteen.

v.   An increase in the intensity of AA fire reduces the number of aircraft getting within five miles of their target in the ration of three to two.

vi.   All these figures relate to aircraft recorded as attacking the target; the proportion of the total sorties which reached within five miles is less by one third.[167]

For Churchill, who, in 1940, had placed so much faith in the bomber offensive, the Butt Report was abysmal reading. The figures and estimates, Cherwell conceded, might not be wholly accurate, but it was, he asserted, an urgent testament to the need to improve Bomber Command's methods of navigation. Churchill agreed. So did Portal, who was championing a plan to bring Bomber Command's strength up to 4,000 bombers. In the wake of Butts's findings, Portal outlined a scheme to launch a series of massive, devastating attacks against

Germany. These would be area attacks, the prime objective being the destruction of forty-three selected German towns, each with a population of more than 100,000.[168]

With his 4,000 bombers, Portal was confident Bomber Command could bring Germany to her knees within six months. Whitehall was intrigued but apprehensive. As early as June, the secretary of State for Air had warned Portal to expect opposition. Ministers, he wrote, were reluctant to devote vast quantities of resources to a solitary method of warfare.[169] Undaunted, Portal sent his proposal to the Prime Minister in late September. Churchill's reply, on 27 September, was short on enthusiasm, arguing that instead of an increase in strength, why not improve Bomber Command's accuracy?

It is very disputable whether bombing by itself will be a decisive factor in the present war. On the contrary, all that we have learnt since the war began shows that its effects, both physical and moral, are greatly exaggerated. There is no doubt the British people have been stimulated and strengthened by the attack made upon them so far. Secondly, it seems very likely that the ground defenses and night-fighters will overtake the air attack. Thirdly, in calculating the number of bombers necessary to achieve hypothetical and indefinite tasks, it should be noted that only a quarter of our bombs hit the targets. Consequently, an increase in the accuracy of bombing to 100 per cent would in fact raise our bombing force to four times its strength. The most we can say is that it will be a heavy and I trust a seriously increasing annoyance.[170]

Since the first day of war, Bomber Command had provided Britain with a means of waging an offensive campaign. Now Churchill had deemed its impact upon the Nazi regime as nothing more than an 'annoyance.' Putting pen to paper, Portal struck back on 2 October. 'I see no reason to regard the bomber as a weapon of declining importance,' wrote Portal, who reminded Churchill the prolonged bombing of Germany had been a 'fundamental principle' in Britain's war strategy since the fall of France. Putting Churchill to the test, Portal wrote that if the Prime Minister had truly lost faith in the bomber offensive, the worst thing he could do would be to permit the RAF to continue to the campaign.[171] Portal, notes historian John Terraine in his study of the RAF's war years, understood that to give up any large offensive campaign was akin to handing the enemy a major victory. It was a lesson learned in the carnage of the First World War.[172]

Churchill responded that same day, taking a softer stance but still pointing out the need to look beyond bombing as a sole offensive strategy:

We all hope that the air offensive against Germany will realize the expectations of the Air Staff. Everything is being done to create the bombing force desired on the largest possible scale, and there is no intention of changing this policy. I deprecate, however, placing unbounded confidence in this means of attack, and still more expressing that confidence in terms of arithmetic. It is the most potent method of impairing the enemy's morale we can use at the present time. If the United States enters the war, it would have to be supplemented in 1943 by simultaneous attacks by armoured forces in many of the conquered countries which were ripe for revolt. Only in this way could a decision be certainly achieved. Even if all the towns in Germany were rendered largely uninhabitable, it does not follow that the military control would be weakened or even that war industry would not be carried on.

...It may well be that German morale will crack and that our bombing will play a very important part in bringing the result about. But all things are always on the move simultaneously, and it is quite possible that the Nazi war-making power in 1943 will be so widely spread throughout Europe as to be a large extent independent of the actual buildings in the homeland.

He concluded:

...One has to do the best one can, but he is an unwise man who thinks there is any certain method of winning this war, or indeed any other war between equal strengths. The only plan is to persevere.[173]

Thus, Churchill had no intention of laying to waste Bomber Command's strategic policy — he was, however, considering actions on a broader scale and holding out for an Anglo-American alliance. While these words reassured Portal, the findings of the Butt Report hung over Bomber Command like a black cloud. For Peirse, it was a particularly sour pill to swallow. He found it hard to correlate the findings with the damage he believed his force had done, and a slew of excuses soon followed. He argued the weather was bad during June and July and the cameras had only been given to crews whose skills were thought to be in need of improvement. 'I don't think at this rate,' he said, 'we could have hoped to produce the damage which is known to have been achieved.' Surprised by the findings as he was, Portal did realise that improving night bombing was 'perhaps the greatest of the operational problems confronting us at the present time.' Notes the Official Historians: 'Thus, for the first time in air force history the first and paramount problem of night operations was seen at the highest level to be not merely a question of bomb aiming, though that difficulty remained, but of navigation.'[174]

Perhaps as a direct result of the Butt Report — and Peirse's desire to prove its findings otherwise — Bomber Command would suffer its most gruelling loss yet.

Berlin Catastrophe

The meteorological map at Bomber Command HQ showed violent activity over Germany on 7 November. A storm was gathering strength over the Reich, threatening thunder, hail and severe icing. Spurred by strong winds blowing from the west, heavy black clouds — their tops reaching 20,000 feet — rolled across the Ruhr and Berlin. It was into these conditions that Peirse sent Bomber Command on its largest operation to date. On the night of 7 November, he dispatched 169 aircraft to Berlin. Another 223 were thrust against various objectives throughout north-western Europe.

The flight to Berlin was a violent excursion. The route was thick with cloud. The bombers were buffeted and thrashed in the stormy conditions. Thick layers of ice formed on wings and airscrews and crept menacingly across the windscreens and turrets. The smell of vomit permeated many aircraft as men succumbed to violent bouts of airsickness. Icicles formed inside the planes as temperatures dropped to nearly 70 below zero. Any skin left exposed quickly succumbed to frostbite. For some, the conditions were too much and they chose to attack alternative targets such as Lübeck, Kiel and Rostock. Only seventy-three aircraft reached the general area of Berlin. The resulting bombing was scattered and largely ineffective. One man who flew that night was Captain John P Dobson of No. 218 Squadron. He and his crew were taken POW after their Wellington was shot down. In 1945 he recorded that night's ordeal in his diary. Although Dobson was now a veteran, his crew was flying for the first time. Over Berlin, their Wellington, christened Kate, was ensnared in a searchlight. The situation rapidly deteriorated from there:

The intensity of the beam on one's face simply sapped all the strength from one, like blotting paper sucking up a blot. And the eyes burned like all the fires of hell...

Flak concentrated on us until it seemed as though the whole sky were a mass of flaming eye-scarring bursts. And the smell... cloying, fetid, lingering in the nostrils wide with fear. Burst after burst followed our steady evasive action; not steady, nerve racking, making one wish to dive to do anything to escape the screaming shrapnel all around.

A particularly heavy burst threw the nose violently backwards, jerking the stick back against my stomach like a living thing. The port wing went down and we commenced to dive down in ever decreasing spirals, which would end in a tight spin. Completely out of control isn't fun at any time, but in a welter of upcoming flak our predicament was terrible. The crew were in a frenzy, yelling and screaming over the inter-com like mad men. Remember, it was their first experience with a flak-happy skipper.

A terrific crack, like a whip going hard against naked flesh, and Perspex flew all over my knees whilst the gale roared through the hole the flak had created. Then a very nucleus of bursts held us in thrall, smashing into the fuselage at every point, tearing huge gaps from the geodetic construction and flinging their steel slithers like darts into the steel plating of my cabin. I hardly heard the second-dickey yell that half the port wing had gone, paying no attention to the oil, which smothered me from a rent glycol pipe. The main thing on my mind was to keep the kite steady.

For a full 45 minutes we fought against that barrage, tossed up, blasted down and each time thinking that the last burst would be our end. 2,000 feet showed on the clock now and still the flak came on. The controls were all held in the grip of ice, frozen to hell, and old Kate had had her time. She was now almost out of control and her time had come... 'BALE OUT!' Just those two words, the difference between life and death; the opportunity to begin, when the war would end, a new life unfraught [sic] with danger and strife.

One by one, the crew filed passed my seat and dropped through the opening at my feet. When the last one had vanished, I trimmed Kate, tail heavy, so that in a few moments her nose would come up and she would spin to her complete destruction. Then, still holding the stick, I slid from my seat and, as the aircraft swayed slowly backwards, I fell forward through the hole in the manner approved. The time was 0005 by the office clock. Height 1,500 feet. My chute opened with a savage jerk, which seemed to tear me about in half. And as I swayed this way and that on the silken cords I beheld Kate slowly turning and plunging downwards with a scream that sounded high above the noise of the elements.

Everything seemed so very peaceful after the hell of eardrum-shat-
tering noise and I felt drowsy as I hung suspended twixt heaven and
earth.[175]

For those who survived the outward trek and the time over the target, the
weather was equally vicious in its ferocity on the return journey, forcing
many aircraft down to 300 feet to escape the hellish conditions at higher
altitudes. At the various bomber bases throughout England, wireless
operators sat and listened on their station's allotted frequencies. Through
the static came the urgent voices of desperate men, preparing to ditch in
the sea as their stricken bombers consumed the last of their fuel. Over
the North Sea, Wellingtons, Hampdens, Whitleys, Stirlings and Halifaxes
of Nos 1, 3 and 4 Groups began splashing into the cold churning grey
— many sinking beneath the waves with their crews still on board. Other
crews made visual contact with England, only to slam into the English
coastline.[176]

Of the 392 aircraft dispatched on operations, thirty-seven failed to
return — a 9.4 per cent casualty rate, and more than double the previous
highest loss for night operations. Berlin had claimed twenty-one aircraft
and 120 men. Seven of the fifty-five raiders targeting Mannheim that night
were destroyed, as were nine of the forty-three bombers sent to the Ruhr.
In the wake of such carnage, Peirse was quick to shield himself behind a
battery of excuses, placing blame on the weather and on the meteorologists for failing to forecast such horrendous conditions. Then there were
the crews, who, Peirse claimed, were insufficiently trained for long-haul
flights in such adverse circumstances. The Vice Chief of the Air Staff,
deemed this a 'damning admission,' arguing if crews were not properly
trained then it was up to Peirse and his group commanders to see they
were. But, as it stood, Peirse's explanations initially placated a concerned
Portal and Air Staff. But Churchill took umbrage, writing to Portal and the
Chiefs of Staff on 11 November. He argued there was no profit in presently
attacking Berlin, as Bomber Command could not afford the heavy losses
invariably involved with such an endeavour. There was no point, he wrote,
fighting both the Germans and the weather.[177]

The Prime Minister insisted Bomber Command conserve its 'strength
for the spring.' Portal and the Chiefs of Staff accepted this, but, already,
Peirse had voiced his opposition to a curtailing of operations. He argued
doing such would hurt the already fragile morale of his men. On 10
November, he wrote to Portal:

I am always preaching to the Command that they have a man-sized
job to do; a job on which all eyes are turned; a job on which too much
care and preparation cannot be expended, and above all a job which
must be pushed right through to the conclusion if results are to be

obtained. If… the Powers-that-Be did not consider this to be the case, or that there is any hesitation in the handling of the Force, doubt must immediately arise in the minds of the air-crews, and doubt spells irresolution. In other words, it is damned hard to fight a force like Bomber Command at a subdued tempo.[178]

But concerns of a greater urgency would soon burden Peirse, as Portal — increasingly dissatisfied with Peirse's excuses — inquired further into the tragedy that was 7 November, a day remembered as Black Friday. Under the weight of Portal's investigation, it was soon revealed that meteorologists had warned Perise of the hellish weather conditions over Germany by 4 p.m. of the afternoon in question. Furthermore, one group commander, Air Vice Marshal Jack Slessor, AOC 5 Group, unhappy with the forecast, opted to send his Hampdens to Cologne instead of Berlin — all of which returned safely from operations. Slessor's decision to tackle the safer option followed a briefing with his senior meteorological officer who said, in 'no unmeasured terms,' that dispatching the group's Hampdens to Berlin would result in catastrophe.[179]

Portal's inquiry also uncovered one station commander who insisted on sending out only his most experienced crews that night. When they returned, there was little more than vapour fumes in their fuel tanks. Peirse had blundered in a major way. Despite these revelations, Portal and the Air Staff were apprehensive in the launching of a full-scale investigation lest they damage Bomber Command's increasingly fragile morale. There was further consternation in presenting these findings to the Prime Minister. It was at the insistence of Sir Archibald Sinclair, Secretary of State for Air, that Portal showed Churchill the relevant papers on 4 January while the two men were in Washington, meeting with their new ally in arms. Four days later, Sir Richard Peirse was relieved of his duties as C-in-C Bomber Command and dispatched to the Far East. Portal had already approached Air Vice Marshal Arthur Harris, then head of the permanent RAF delegation to the United States, asking him to assume control of Bomber Command. It was a choice backed by both Churchill and Sinclair — and a major turning point in the Allied bomber offensive.

VII

A New Dynamic

The Gloves Come Off

According to Josef Goebbels, Hitler's minister of propaganda, all one had to do was look into Arthur Harris's eyes to see an unquenchable thirst for blood and a passion for slaughter.[180] Amongst the German populace, Harris's name is 'indelibly associated' with the fiery destruction of Germany's cities. With his appointment as C-in-C Bomber Command, the RAF was ready to play rough.[181]

The Channel Dash

Until Harris arrived on the scene, Air Vice Marshal 'Jack' Baldwin — commander of No. 3 Group — served as Bomber Command's acting C-in-C. Following 7 November — per Churchill's orders — conservation became the keyword by which the force operated. Through January and February, British bombers continued their attacks on Germany — Bremen, Hannover, Munster, Emden and Cologne — though in smaller numbers. The cruisers at Brest remained a primary concern. Through the rising smoke screens and heavy flak, Bomber Command flew 627 sorties against the port in January. Two more raids followed in February. Then, in the late hours of 11 February, the *Scharnhorst* and *Gneisenau* — accompanied by the *Prinz Eugen* — slipped out of Brest in a daring bid for the Baltic port of Kiel. They left the harbour just short of midnight with a heavy air and destroyer escort. The Germans used the cover of darkness to outmanoeuvre the British patrols in the Channel, preferring to brave the Dover batteries by day.[182]

February 12 was damp and grey. Clouds hung low over the water, providing the cruisers maximum concealment as they pressed through the Channel and hugged the occupied coast. Not until 1125 hours — after a Spitfire of Fighter Command spotted the cruisers off Le Toquet — did the Royal Navy learn of the German scheme. By now the warships were closing rapidly upon the Straits of Dover. Frantic orders were issued to all available RAF and Royal Navy units. The batteries along the Dover coast opened fire and unleashed a thunderous volley into the afternoon murk, as the first contingent of five British motor torpedo boats put to sea. The first aircraft of Bomber Command were airborne at 1335 hours. For the British, it was a military and intelligence nightmare.

Because of the inclement weather, most of Bomber Command had been stood down for the day and only 5 Group remained on four-hours notice. Now everything Bomber Command could muster was sent to hunt and destroy the ships. The battle was joined by RAF Fighter and Coastal commands and the Fleet Air Arm. Despite the hardware mobilised — including a flotilla of World War 1 destroyers — mist, rain and heavy cloud worked against the British. In three successive waves, 242 bombers were dispatched to attack. Thirty-nine bombers found their targets, but the shield of fire provided by the accompanying destroyers and the Luftwaffe escort kept the bombers at bay. One man who was supposed to go up that day was airgunner Johnson Biggs:

> It was a cold, grey morning. I had only just completed my six weeks of airgunner's training and had yet to fly my first real operation. When news came through that the German warships were on the move, there was a great commotion and we were all ordered to our aircraft. My commanding officer, Squadron Leader Stevens, said to me, 'Right, this is it. You're going up with me.' But as the store was locked, I couldn't get a parachute, so I was stood down.
>
> Conditions that day were terrible. The cloud was down to the sea, making it very hard to see what was going on and where things were. Squadron Leader Stevens took off, but never returned. The bodies of him and his crew were never recovered from the sea. I still think about it often. I think how that could have been me, and how sorry I am for those who lost their lives that day.[183]

The fighting continued until six that evening. Beaufort torpedo bombers were unable to penetrate the German convoy's heavy defences and fighter screen. British efforts failing, the ships slipped out of the Channel.

That night, as they closed in on their home objective, both the *Scharnhorst* and the *Gneisenau* ran into mines laid by Bomber Command the previous nights off the Frisian Islands. The *Scharnhorst* was in dock for six months. The *Gneisenau* beached herself at Wilhelmshaven.

Not since the 17th century, opined *The Times*, had the Royal Navy been so humiliated in its home waters. Bomber Command's efforts were derided as a fiasco. Flying against fast-moving targets — heavily defended by sea and air — fifteen bombers had failed to return and not one explosive had found its mark. In the wake of such tumult, Bomber Command's policy of conservation came to an end. On 14 February, 1942, one week before Harris's arrival at High Wycombe, Churchill wrote to Portal: 'The Brest question has settled itself by the escape of the enemy. I am entirely in favour of the resumption of the bombing of Germany, subject always, of course, to our not incurring heavy losses owing to bad weather and enemy opposition combined.'[184] That same day, a new directive from the Air Ministry — Directive 22 — reached Baldwin at Bomber Command HQ:

You are authorized to employ your effort without restriction, until further notice, in accordance with the following directions.

It has been decided that the primary object of your operations should now be focused on the morale of the enemy civil population and in particular, the industrial workers. With this aim in view, a list of selected area targets is attached... You will note that Berlin has been included amongst the targets. In this case, your operations should be of a harassing nature, the object being to maintain fear of attack over the city and to impose A.R.P. measures... Essen is the most important of the selected primary targets. I am to suggest that this should be selected as your initial target... Finally, I am to say that, although every effort will be made to confine your operations to your primary offensive, you should recognise that it will on occasions be necessary to call upon you for diversionary attacks on objectives, the destruction of which is of immediate importance in the light of the current strategic situation. In particular, important naval units and the submarine building yards and bases may have to be attacked periodically, especially when this can be done without missing good opportunities of bombing your primary targets.[185]

So here it was: the order to commence large-scale area attacks. Great swaths of Germany were now rendered prime targets for fire, thermite and high explosives. 'Primary Industrial Areas,' in addition to Essen, included Duisburg, Dusselforf and Cologne, while 'Alternative Industrial

Areas' included Bremen, Frankfurt, Hanover, Kiel, Mannheim, Stuttgart and Schweinfurt. Furthermore, the Directive referred to Gee (Ground Electronic Engineering), Bomber Command's new navigation aid with which 10 squadrons had been equipped by February 1942:

> TR 1335 (Gee) will confer upon your forces the ability to concentrate their effort to an extent which has not hitherto been possible under the operational conditions with which you are faced. It is accordingly considered that the introduction of this equipment on operations should be regarded a revolutionary advance in bombing technique which, during the period of its effective life as a target-finding device, will enable results to be obtained of a much more effective nature.[186]

Under development at the Telecommunications Research Establishment (TRE) since the summer of 1940, Gee was Bomber Command's first navigational aid ready for operations. Using a Gee box, a cathode-ray tube inside the aircraft, a bomber's navigator could pinpoint the plane's location with a high degree of accuracy. The Gee box received radio signals from interspersed stations in England. The navigator plotted the point at which signals were received on a grid chart, enabling him to accurately track the aircraft's route. It was estimated, however, that Gee would only be effective over Germany for six months before the enemy discovered a way to jam the signal. Bomber Command was therefore ordered to operate at maximum strength during this period to ravage Germany's war-making abilities and 'support the Russians.'[187]

The switch from precision bombing to the attacking of broad-based industrial areas was made prior to Harris's arrival at High Wycombe, though he is generally vilified as the architect of such policy. The fallacy of 'precision' bombing at night had been exposed. The idea of attacking urban areas had been a strategy sought by Portal since 1940, as a city was the easiest objective for crews to target regardless of conditions.[188] And lest there be any confusion as to what it was Directive 22 was instructing Bomber Command to do, Portal wrote on 15 February: 'Ref the new bombing directive: I suppose it is clear that the aiming points are to be the built-up areas, not, for instance, the dockyards or aircraft factories… This must be made quite clear if it is not already understood.[189]

Enter Harris

One week later, on 22 February, Air Vice Marshal Arthur Harris, two months shy of his 50th birthday, arrived at High Wycombe as Air Officer Commander-in-Chief Bomber Command headquarters. At the helm of Britain's bomber offensive, Harris would embrace the area bombing initiative not as a means of destroying German morale, but of destroying Germany itself. 'It was only after careful study of the blitz in England,' he wrote, 'that it was observed how immediate and serious was the effect on war production itself [with]... the destruction of large town areas.'[190] Over Germany he would wage a bloody war of attrition, pitting bomber and crew against metropolis. On the day Harris arrived at High Wycombe, he tells us he had: '378 aircraft serviceable with crews, and only 69 of these were heavy bombers. About 50 aircraft in the force were not even medium bombers but the light bombers of No. 2 Group... In effect, this meant that we had an average force of 250 medium and fifty heavy bombers until such time as the Command really began to expand.'[191] Harris faced an uphill struggle as such expansion was at the continual mercy of the war in the Middle East and the Admiralty's need for resources in the Battle of the Atlantic.

To those who worked alongside him, he was known as 'Bert.' To his crews he was affectionately known as 'Butcher.' To everyone else he would come to bear the name of the machine he wielded with such deadly consequence: 'Bomber.' By the time he was finished, more than 300,000 Germans would lie dead amongst the ruins of the Reich's once-proud cities. By the time Harris arrived at High Wycombe, Bomber Command had already lost more than 7,000 men. At the end of the war, total Bomber Command casualties would hit 73,741, meaning 'that more than one in every two Bomber Command operational aircrew suffered wounds, imprisonment or death.'[192] Under Harris, Britain's bomber offensive would emerge as one of the bloodiest and most controversial campaigns of the war.

His belief in the bomber was absolute. 'There are a lot of people who say that bombing cannot win the war,' he said. 'My reply to that is that it has never been tried yet. We shall see.' But his ardent faith in airpower was equalled by his contempt for the army and navy. Bombing, as far as Harris was concerned, was the only means of Allied victory and he was quick to share that sentiment with anyone. In a 1943 meeting with General Sir Alan Brooke, Chief of the Imperial General Staff, Harris credited Russian victories in the east with Bomber Command's nightly efforts over Germany. If it was left to him, the airman said, the war would soon be over.[193]

Harris's introduction to military life was via the army, having fought in the 1st Rhodesia Regiment in South-West Africa against the Germans in 1914-15. He had arrived in Rhodesia at the age of 18 in 1910 and worked at a number of jobs — including tobacco farming and mining — in the years leading up to the Great War. Following his African adventure he returned to England with thoughts of joining the British cavalry. A lack of vacancies, however, forced his attentions to the Royal Artillery. When that proved impossible to join, he looked to the Royal Flying Corps. He spent the remainder of the war as an anti-Zeppelin night pilot over London and flying operations over the entrenched Western Front. A major when the war ended, Harris was awarded a permanent commission as squadron leader in 1919 with the world's first independent air branch — the Royal Air Force — formed on 1 April 1918, with the amalgamation of the Royal Flying Corps and the Royal Naval Air Service.

The post-war years saw him command squadrons in Iraq and India, as well as England. He served the Air Ministry in various capacities and attended Army Staff College. In 1937 he was given command of 4 Group, but was then promoted to air vice-marshal after a year and sent to command the RAF in Palestine. Two years later he was back in England, commanding No. 5 Group for the first year of the war. He was sent to America in November 1940 as head of the RAF purchasing delegation in Washington. But less than two years later he would return to Britain and set about his newly-appointed task of reducing Germany to a pile of scrap.

Harris's arrival at High Wycombe coincided with Bomber Command's darkest period yet. The scars of Black Friday were still fresh and questions concerning the bombing offensive's efficiency were being asked. As Harris set about tackling the realities of the task at hand, Sir Stafford Cripps, Lord Privy Seal and Leader of the House of Commons, blasted the bombing campaign in a speech before the House on 25 February 25, concluding a two-day debate on the British war effort:

Another question which has been raised by a great number of Members, is the question of the policy as to the continued use of heavy bombers and the bombing of Germany. A number of Hounourable Members have questioned whether in the existing circumstances, the continued devotion of a considerable part of our efforts to building up this Bomber Force is the best use we can make of our resources... I would remind the House that this policy was initiated at a time when we were fighting alone against the combined forces of Germany and Italy and it seemed that it was the most effective way in which we could take the initiative against the enemy. Since that time we have had enormous support from the Russian Armies... and also from the great potential strength of the United States. Naturally, in such circumstances the original policy has come under review. I can assure the House that the Government are fully aware of other uses to which our resources could be put and the moment they arrive at a decision that the circumstances warrant a change, a change in policy will be made.[194]

In the United States, the speech was published in the *New York Times*, fuelling the arguments of those in America who disagreed with the Grand Alliance strategy of 'Germany first.' One such critic was Admiral Ernest King of the US Navy, Commander-in-Chief of the Fleet and the Chief of Naval Operations. He cared little for the European theatre and was only intent on avenging the destruction of the US Pacific Fleet. The Cripps statement was a matter of grave consternation for the RAF Delegation still in Washington DC. The day following the speech, the head of the delegation penned a letter to Portal: 'Unless authoritative reaffirmation of our belief in the Bomber Offensive is supplied immediately, effect both on strategic and production planning here may well be irremediable.'[195] But in the end, Cripps pulled little weight in government circles and his words would soon be lost in the wake of greater events.

Directive 22 was implicit in its instructions. It asserted the primary function of Gee was to bring about, over one target, a large enough concentration of aircraft to destroy the city. Per the Directive, the best means to such an end were heavily concentrated incendiary attacks.[196] Bomber Command would thus destroy Hitler's Reich by fire. To blast buildings and alter the contour of roads, raids would commence with the dropping of high explosives. As air raid sirens wailed and anti-aircraft guns thundered away, massive craters would be opened in the ground and thoroughfares would be choked by falling debris, preventing emergency services from reaching the devastated areas. The main attack would follow, unleashing a heavy concentration of 4,000-lb. blast bombs and reducing buildings to mere skeletal remains. Thousands of incendiaries would then be dumped through the pulverised roofs and shattered windows. Fires would ignite and grow to raging proportions, fuelled by air sucked through the devastated spaces.[197]

Harris would succeed where the Germans failed. Writing after the war, he noted 'If a rain of incendiaries is mixed with high explosive bombs there is an irresistible temptation for the fireman to keep his head down. The Germans again and again missed their chance, as they did in the London blitz that I watched from the roof of the Air Ministry, of setting our cities ablaze by a concentrated attack.'[198]

Nurturing the Offensive

To counter Parliamentary opposition and neutralise demands from certain quarters to split Bomber Command up among the army and navy, Harris knew he had to succeed where his predecessor had failed. Among the attached list of alternative targets sent to High Wycombe on 14 February was the Renault factory at Boulogne-Billancourt, west of Paris, where motorised vehicles were being produced for the German military. This would be Harris's first major target.

Already, a tactical plan had been devised to utilise Gee as a blind-marking aid. This method, code-named Shaker, called for attacking bombers to raid the target in three separate waves. The leading wave, the Illuminators, would consist of Gee-equipped bombers flown by the most experienced crews. They would arrive over the target at zero hour and drop triple flares. At zero + 2, the Target Markers would fly in and drop the maximum load of incendiaries on the flares. The majority of the force, the Followers, would bomb at zero + 15, dumping full loads of incendiaries and high explosives on the now writhing conflagration. The raid on the Renault factory would employ a derivative of Shaker. The bombers were to attack in three waves, but without the use of Gee as it was not yet ready for operations. So it was that on the night of 3 March, Harris commenced Bomber Command's new offensive not with an area attack, but a pinpoint precision raid.

A force of heavy bombers — Stirlings, Manchesters and Halifaxes — made up the advanced echelon. Unleashing a fiery cascade of green and yellow, they commenced their attack, dropping flares in the light of a full moon and bombing through visual means. A violent spectrum of colour erupted below as the bombers turned and dropped rows of flares upwind to guide in the proceeding waves. Additional flares and 1,000-lb. explosives were dropped on target as the second wave attacked in prelude to the Followers. The final wave stoked the inferno with 4,000-lb. blast bombs. Of the 235 aircraft dispatched, 223 reached their objective and released more than 400 tons of incendiaries and high explosives. Approximately forty per cent of the factory was destroyed, halting production for one month and costing the German military 2,100 vehicles. One aircraft was lost. On the ground, French casualties exceeded 300 — the heaviest number of casualties inflicted by British bombers yet. But the French Resistance drew inspiration from the raid. Georges Gorse, future mayor of Billancourt and serving with the Free French Forces in London, urged his countrymen after the attack to 'clench their teeth' and persevere under the harsh conditions. The British bombardment, he said, brought with it the promise of eventual liberation.[199]

Although the factory lacked flak defences and was not typical of what lay in the heart of Germany, the raid was a resounding success for Bomber Command and a vital public relations victory. The raid was typical of the early operations Harris ordered. While their overall strategic importance was questionable, they gave his crews a taste of something they were not yet accustomed to: success. Furthermore, they proved that Bomber Command was capable of hitting a target and hitting it hard. Elsewhere that night, Bomber Command's newest aircraft flew its first combat operation, when four Avro Lancasters of 44 Squadron laid mines off the German coast. Sleek and powerful, the Lancaster carried the payload of two Flying Fortresses. His arsenal expanding, Harris turned his attention elsewhere.

Essen was a target of vast strategic importance. At its very centre lay the massive Krupps armaments factory. On the morning of 8 March, Harris ordered the first of what would be eight major raids against Essen throughout March and April. Pursuant to Directive 22, this was to be the primary target in Bomber Command's campaign against Germany's industrial abilities. That night a force of 211 aircraft was dispatched on what would be the first operation utilising Bomber Command's new navigational aid. Again, the attack would be defined by the Shaker method. Each of the twenty Illuminating bombers — all equipped with Gee — carried twelve bundles of three flares to be dropped at ten-second intervals over the target. The flares were dropped up wind with the goal of illuminating 'the target at zero hour with lanes of flares approximately six miles long which would drift over the target and keep it so illuminated for twelve minutes.'[200]

While the flares were still falling, the Target Markers — sixty-two Gee-equipped bombers — appeared over the city and dropped the maximum load of incendiaries to create a heavily concentrated area of fire. The conflagration would guide the main attack force — the Followers, who were not equipped with Gee — when they made their run ten minutes after the two initial waves. The Followers disgorged maximum loads of high explosives and 'Cookies' into the flames below. Essen, with its vast belt of groping searchlights and devastating anti-aircraft fire, was an exceptionally fierce objective. A storm of flak and tracer destroyed eight bombers and, although weather conditions were clear, the city was veiled beneath a thick industrial haze typical of targets throughout the Ruhr. In their primary objective — the destruction of the Krupps factory — the bomber crews failed. Of the twenty Illuminators, only eleven dropped flares based on their Gee reading. The others tried to establish visual contact with Essen, but were thwarted in their attempts by the haze. Fewer than 200 aircraft reported actually attacking the target.

Over the next two nights, Bomber Command floundered through the Ruhr's industrial fogs. Heavy haze and bad weather resulted in the scattered bombing of more than twenty towns. British bombers targeted Essen five times that month. On the night of 26 March, intense night fighter activity en route to the target and heavy flak over the city claimed eleven bombers — an eleven per cent casualty rate among the 104 aircraft dispatched. Not all Gee raids that month proved to be failures. One such raid on Cologne two weeks ealier resulted in serious damage to two rubber factories and a railway repair workshop. But Harris knew the failures over Essen needed to be counterbalanced by an overwhelmingly-astounding success. In the destruction of Lübeck, he got one.

Epitaph for a City

Lübeck was an old Hanseatic town situated on the Trave River, fourteen miles in from the Baltic Coast. The town was a jumble of ancient wooden buildings and narrow, cobbled streets lightly defended and easy to locate because of its position on the river. 'It was,' wrote Harris, 'a city of moderate size, of some importance as a port, and with some submarine building yards of moderate size not far from it. It was not a vital target, but it seemed to me better to destroy an industrial town of moderate importance than to fail to destroy a large industrial city.' Because of its wooden construction, the town was deemed an ideal guinea pig on which to test the effects of a heavy incendiary attack. The 'main object of the attack,' explained Harris, 'was to learn to what extent a first wave of aircraft could guide a second wave to the aiming point by starting a conflagration.'[201]

Though it was a target of minimal strategic importance, Lübeck was listed among the targets included in Directive 22. Note the Official Historians: 'The inclusion of such a relatively unimportant place as Lübeck, which happened to be especially flammable... showed the extent... to which a town might become a target mainly because it was operationally vulnerable.'[202] Crews were briefed to fly in low that night, for the city's weak defences would enable the raiding aircraft to drop as low as 2,000 feet. Taking part were 234 Wellingtons, Manchesters and Stirlings, guided, as with the raid on Billancourt, by a full moon and clear weather. The town lay beyond Gee's 350-mile range, but the device was used to assist outward navigation. However, the aiming point was the town centre — the *Altstadt* — inhabited by 30,000 people. The force was split into two waves, with Harris ordering a half-hour interval between the first and second attack. This would allow time, Harris explained, for the initial fires to 'get a good hold before the second wave arrived.'[203]

The end result was destruction on a scale never before achieved as the city was pounded mercilessly. Of the 234 crews dispatched, 191 reported bombing the town, dropping more than 400 tons of bombs — two-thirds of which were incendiaries — on the target, destroying and damaging sixty-two per cent of the city's buildings, including a factory manufacturing oxygen apparatus for U-boats. More than 1,200 people were either killed or wounded. After the bombers left, fires raged for thirty-two hours and consumed 200 acres of city. Throughout Britain, the news of Lübeck's destruction — a vengeful blow for the slaughter bestowed upon London, Coventry, Birmingham, Liverpool, Plymouth and other cities — was received with euphoria. In Germany, it was a portent of things to come as Harris made his presence felt. It left the German populace deeply disturbed and, more importantly, shocked the Nazi hierarchy. On March 30, Goebbels received a report from the shattered city's propaganda minister. Sitting in his office, he flipped through its pages and balked at the descriptions of mass devastation. Parts of the city had descended into chaos, the report stated. Entire neighbourhoods had been demolished in a sea of flame. Goebbels at first accepted the report as a major exaggeration. Only when further dispatches from the city began crossing his desk did he realize the severity of the situation. It quickly became obvious that no German city had ever sustained such a beating.[204]

Five days later, Goebbels was shown a newsreel of the devastation. He sat and watched in shocked silence as flickering images of enormous damage played out on a wall-mounted projection screen in his office. The destruction surpassed what he had envisioned in his mind's eye. Corpses lined the streets as the news camera panned slowly across a smoking wasteland. Goebbels could only be thankful the attack befell people in northern Germany, which, he claimed, were tougher than those who lived in the southern part of the country. Such a thought, however, was small consolation. It was apparent the British raids were increasing in strength and severity. A bombardment along similar lines carried out continuously over the next several weeks could, Goebbels feared, push the German people to capitulate.[205]

At this point, Goebbels need not have worried. British casualties on the Lübeck operation were twelve aircraft lost — 5.5 per cent of the attack force — shot down by night fighters on the return journey. It was a rate which could not be sustained for any period of time, lest Harris risk crippling Bomber Command's already struggling expansion. Nevertheless, the die was cast. Harris had begun his systematic destruction of Germany. 'On the night of March 28-29,' he later wrote, 'the first German city went up in flames.'[206]

An Unfeasible Action: The Augsburg Raid

After Lübeck, Harris continued his attacks against the Ruhr. These included repeat visits to Essen. Again, adverse weather and the industrial haze under which the target dwelled hampered bombing efforts. On 10 April, Essen's defences devoured fourteen bombers. Two nights later, the last in a gruelling series of disappointing raids was carried out against the city. Although the Krupps factory was hit, it was not destroyed. In the eight raids Bomber Command had prosecuted against Essen, 1,555 aircraft had dropped thousands of tons of incendiaries and high explosives to little effect. These raids, experimental grounds for Gee, were followed by another experimental operation. This was the Ausburg raid, a low-level, daylight action prosecuted by a force of the new Avro Lancaster. The target: The MAN Diesel Engine Works in Bavaria, where U-boat engines were being cranked from the assembly line.

Twelve Lancasters from Nos 44 and 97 Squadrons were tasked with the operation. The raid — led by Squadron Leader J D Nettleton of No. 44 Squadron — was preceded by a week of low-level flying training. The plan, states the Operation Records Book of No. 44 Squadron, entailed 'Six aircraft from each Squadron loaded with four 1000 G.P. bombs to take-off at 15.15. hours… Each Squadron flying in formations of two sections of three would proceed to the target without fighter escort.' In lieu of accompanying fighters, diversionary raids were to be staged in the Pas de Calais, Cherbourg and Rouen areas by 'fighters and bombers commencing fifty minutes before our aircraft were due to cross the French Coast so that enemy fighters, in addition to being fully employed, would probably require to re-fuel and re-arm before being able to intercept.'[207]

At twelve minutes past the prescribed hour on 17 April, the first section of three Lancasters from 44 Squadron, led by Nettleton, took off from RAF Waddington. They were followed two minutes later by the second section of three, led by Flight Lieutenant Sandford. All crews airborne, a course was set for the cross-over point on the English Coast at Selsey Bill. Twenty minutes earlier, Lancasters from No. 97 Squadron, led by Squadron Leader J G Sherwood, had left the runways of Woodhall Spa and also set course for Selsey Bill. For the six Lancasters of 97 Squadron, the outward journey progressed smoothly. They thundered across France — soaring over the landscape at a mere fifty feet — and roared into Germany. They feigned a track toward Munich before turning sharply north for Augsburg. 'All six aircraft flew over France and low over Germany and successfully reached their target,' reads the entry in 97 Squadron's records book. 'All dropped their bombs. S/L SHERWOOD AND W/O MYCOCK were seen to be hit by flak over the target, caught fire and crashed near the target area. F/LT HALLOWS aircraft was badly damaged and all the other aircraft received a certain amount of damage, but they all managed to reach base safely without any casualties.'[208] The same could not be said for Nettleton and his crews.

Nettleton reached the target first, but suffered heavily on the outward track. The six aircraft of 44 Squadron crossed the French Coast at 1645 hours. Ten minutes later, 'both formations were intercepted by between twenty-five and thirty fighters and a running fight ensued as a result of which Sgt. Rhodes (Aircraft No. L.7536.H.) was firstly shot down...' The Lancasters were flying at 100 feet when the attack by Bf 109s of II/JG 2, operating from the Beaumont-le-Roger airfield, commenced south of Paris. The fighters came in at 'Port Quarter to Astern, aiming at the engines' and opened fire with their cannons before breaking away at 400 yards. The 'rear and mid-upper gunners of formation leader opened fire at 500 yards and gave bursts until breakaway. Approximately twenty attacks were made. The rear and mid-upper gunners gave mutual fire support to the other aircraft.' The engagement lasted approximately fifteen minutes during which time the aircraft flying off Nettleton's starboard side 'was hit and seen to dive into the ground on fire.' Although suffering a badly-damaged wing, one aircraft —piloted by Flying Officer Gerwell — managed to make it to the target area. The second wave of three were not so lucky. The entire formation was wiped out.[209]

Twenty-one of the 43 men who left RAF Waddington that afternoon were dead by 1515 hours. Another seven had been shot down. The diversionary raids by thirty Bostons and 800 aircraft of Fighter Command had failed in their intent as they took place 'a little too soon to have their desired effect.' The two remaining aircraft continued on their course, approaching the target from Lake Ammer and skimming the trees in a bid to avoid further detection. At Mering they crossed the Munich-Augsburg railway line and 'although the intention was to fly direct to the target, it was decided otherwise, owing to the number of chimney stacks which would necessitate an unnecessary increase of height.' Instead, Nettleton and Gerwell followed the Loch River and approached the target from an easterly direction.[210]

The ground defences opened up as the bombs fell and forced the Lancasters to take 'violent evasive action.' Nettleton threw his plane in a desperate turn. His front gunner, Sergeant Huntley, fired on the anti-aircraft guns and their crews and 'silenced one of the main defensive gun posts.' Meanwhile, the bombs — set for an eleven-second delay — detonated, blasting whole sections of the factory buildings into the sky. Clouds of light and heavy flak continued to explode everywhere, mortally wounding Gerwell's Lancaster. The plane burst into flames and came down in a field several miles west of the town. 'The tail section was seen to break away from the centre turret.'[211]

Of the twelve Lancasters originally dispatched to Augsburg, eight made it to the target. Of those, only five would return home. The four aircraft of 97 Squadron that made it back to Woodhall Spa were all badly damaged. Nettleton's Lancaster, number R. 5508, B-Beer, was the sole aircraft from 44 Squadron to make it back to England — but severe damage forced it to land away from base. 'Heartiest congratulations to all concerned on a magnificent raid yesterday,' wrote the station commander the following day. 'Deepest sympathy over those who failed to return.'[212]

The Augsburg raid was a spectacular undertaking. Despite the heavy loss of life, it proved Bomber Command was capable of low-level precision attacks. It also underlined the risks — one again — of daylight operations over enemy territory without fighter protection. For the Lancaster in 1942, such operations were too deadly a proposition to repeat.[213]

Back to the Baltic

Less than one week later, Harris again turned to the Baltic. This time he aimed further north and brought his sights to bear on the ancient town of Rostock. Like Lübeck, Rostock was a weakly-defended jumble of Hanseatic architecture and narrow streets. Of some importance was its port from which supplies to the Russian front were shipped and goods from Sweden received. Targets of strategic military value included the Heinkel factory in the southern suburb of Marienehe and the shipyards — the Neptune Works — north-west of the town. Bomber Command's actions against Rostock would be a violent blend of precision blast-bombing and incendiary area attack. Components of 5 Group would attack the Heinkel factory, the remainder of the force would ravage the city.

Lying more than a 1,000 miles away, Rostock lay beyond the range of Gee, but the device would be used to aid navigation. Ahead of them, crews faced a seven-hour round trip to be repeated over four consecutive nights on 23-27 April. The first two nights of bombing yielded poor results. Incendiaries and high explosives fell over a widely-scattered area and the Heinkel factory was left unscathed. On the third night, Rostock fired back, catapulting skyward a storm of flak and tracer. Despite the strengthened opposition, Manchesters from 106 Squadron, led by Guy Gibson, successfully attacked the Heinkel complex. Recalled Gibson in his memoirs:

By now all our aircraft were equipped with cameras, but these would not take good pictures below 4,000 feet. I couldn't understand at the time why they wanted photographs which would mean bombing from above 4,000 feet, and so not being as accurate, when they could have given the order for all aircraft to bomb lower and hit the hangar, even though the photographic results would be negligible. Anyway, I told my boys to go in at 2,000 feet, hit the hangar and damn the photographs! A dawn reconnaissance showed that the factory was hit. But the next night they went again to finish the job.[214]

The final night wreaked more devastation and inspired in the German vernacular a new word: *Terrorangriff* (terror raid). Aircraft numbering 107 thundered over Rostock that fourth night. From Nos 1 and 4 Groups, fifty-two bombers descended upon the town, while fifty-five bombers from Group Nos 3 and 5 targeted the Heinkel works. The factory was hit hard in a series of low-level attacks as bombers swooped in from 6,000 and 2,000 feet. Both town and factory were savagely mauled. Over that four-night period, Bomber Command dispatched 521 sorties against Rostock and dropped 721 tons of bombs. Only twelve aircraft failed to return.

In his diary, Goebbels vented his hatred for the British, claiming they were a race of people one could only talk to after kicking the teeth out of their heads. On 29 April, he wrote that seven-tenths of the city had been obliterated, forcing more than 100,000 people to flee. Rostock, he wrote, was in panic.[215] Although a victory for Harris and his crews, British bombers had yet to achieve such success against a major German target. Harris himself noted:

There remained the problem of the first-class target, the major industrial town round which the enemy was bound to concentrate effective and heavy defences. So far all that the Lübeck and Rostock attacks had proved was that we could saturate the passive defences of a town by concentration of attack; it remained to be seen whether the active and passive defences of a vital industrial area could be similarly overcome.[216]

Between the Augsburg and Rostock operations, raids against Hamburg and Cologne provided little to boast about, though Hamburg did lose 60,000 bottles of alcohol when a bomb landed on a bottling complex on the night of April 17. Severe icing and haze resulted in bombing across a forty-mile stretch of the Ruhr on the nights of 14 and 15 April as crews flew through the murk trying to locate Dortmund. The night after the final Rostock operation — 27 April — ninety-seven aircraft succeeded in bombing out nearly 1,700 people in Cologne and destroying a telegraph office. That same night, thirty-one Halifaxes and twelve Lancasters were dispatched to the Trondheim Fjord in Norway to attack the *Tirpitz* and other German warships.

RAF reconnaissance had shown the *Tirpitz* was anchored close to shore. The British Admiralty believed spherical mines could be dropped by Bomber Command in such a way that they would roll down the embankment of the Aalsfiord, hit the water and sink beneath the ship's waterline where they would detonate and blow in the hull. Flying that night was Wing Commander D C T Bennett of No. 10 Squadron. His Halifax was loaded with five mines, each weighing 1,000lbs.

Anti-aircraft fire strafed the bomber as it passed over the enemy coast and tore into the rear gunner. Bennett, however, held the aircraft on its course and crossed the assigned datum point at 2,000 feet. Sitting at his small table — surrounded by maps and charts — the navigator began his stop watch, as did Bennett who began to lower the plane, staying on course as he adjusted the speed. Through the Perspex windshield, the world outside glared white and cold as the frozen landscape rocketed beneath the aircraft. The mountains loomed grey and white and dropped off into the murky meanderings of the fjord, where the smudged grey forms of German warships could be seen through a hovering mist. The mist, Bennett noted, was not the work of nature, but a manmade smoke-screen.[217] The haze grew denser as Bennett continued the aircraft's descent. Looming at an ever-decreasing distance was the shape of the *Tirpitz*. She was well protected, covered as she was by a fleet of gun ships. Bennett's Halifax had already taken a beating. The flak that ripped through its structure as it crossed the coast had set the starboard wing alight. By the time the primary target was visible from the cockpit, the bomber's damaged wing was ablaze. Flames — fanned by the harsh force of the wind — were slowly devouring the wing's length. The red and orange glow of burning aircraft stood out in stark contrast against the hazy milk shade of the smokescreen. On the frigid decks of the ships below, gunners took notice, their radios coming alive as their compatriots raised the alarm.

At the controls, Bennett saw the flashes of the gun barrels below. They were off to the left of the aircraft's path. Where only moments earlier beyond the windshield there had been just the man-made mist, there were now dirty patches of black. The sound of shrapnel battering the bomber's exterior echoed through the length of the plane, which rocked back and forth. During all of this, Bennett had continued bringing the Halifax down to the height required for its bomb run. Now at 200 feet, the aircraft was fast approaching the point of bomb release. In his ear, Bennett should have heard the voice of the bomb-aimer relaying the subtle changes needed at the cockpit controls to align the Halifax with the target. What he heard instead was the bomb-aimer saying that visibility was zero. The *Tirpitz* had vanished. Having descended to 200 feet, the Halifax was now hurtling through the thick of the smokescreen — its density being much greater when flying through it. All the while, the gunships continued to throw up their relentless barrage. Bennett wondered how much longer the aircraft could sustain such a pounding. Already, the controls were growing sluggish in his hand. Suddenly, the massive form of the *Tirpitz* passed under the aircraft. The target vanished back into the haze as quickly as it had appeared, denying the bomb-aimer an opportunity to release the plane's deadly cargo.[218]

As the aircraft shook violently around him, Bennett hoped he could keep it airborne long enough to make a second run at the target.[219] The Halifax was in critical shape — and its condition was only worsening. Much of the starboard wing was now ensconced in flame. The starboard undercarriage had collapsed under the constant burden of assault and the starboard flap was malfunctioning. The aircraft was becoming increasingly resistant to Bennett's command at the controls. He weighed the options before him and decided there was little doubt as to what he had to do. He told his crew to prepare for a second run and turned the bomber back into the maelstrom. Now flying on sheer instinct, Bennett turned the craft in the direction of the *Tirpitz* and hoped for the best. At the moment he believed the ship would again pass under the bomber, he ordered his bomb-aimer to drop the mines they were carrying. Upon the release of the mines, the Halifax — no longer burdened by the excess 5,000-lb.s — bounced upwards in a minor fit of vitality. By now, the plane's — and therefore the crew's — predicament had become all the more dire. Flames continued to gnaw away at the aircraft's construction, and what benefit there had been from releasing the mines seemed only temporary. Bennett decided not to hang around and see where the mines went. The impulse to stay alive and common sense suggested he wing his way out of the enemy's line of fire. By this point, it seemed unlikely the bomber would be landing back in England.[220]

Not wanting to bring the aircraft down over open water, Bennett turned the stricken machine east towards neutral Sweden. It was a desperate flight for the crew as the plane fell apart around them. At the controls, Bennett now harnessed little power over the plane's actions. He tried to increase the bomber's altitude, but the Halifax failed to respond. The frozen landscape below was not a welcoming scene, yet Bennett had no other options. Temporary survival, at least, meant bailing out. He spoke into his helmet's mic and ordered his crew to get ready to bail out. The flight engineer had to work his way back through the aircraft's narrow crawl spaces and help the injured rear gunner out of his turret. In the claustrophobic confines of the tail, the flight engineer helped the gunner get his parachute on before both men made their way back to the front of the craft.[221]

One of the crew, ready to jump, opened the emergency hatch in the cockpit's floor. There was an arctic blast of air and a violent cacophony of noise that deafened the crew to everything but the wind. By now, the starboard wing had collapsed, forcing Bennett to hold the aircraft's wheel to port so the plane would fly on an even keel. One by one, the crew dropped through the hatch into the open space below while Bennett maintained his position at the controls. When the last man was through, he lowered himself to the floor, all the while keeping a hand on the wheel. He sat himself at the edge of the opening and dropped his legs through, immediately feeling the relentless pull of the wind. With one last look around the cockpit, he let go of the wheel and plummeted through the hatch. [222]

His parachute deployed without a problem and he descended to the frozen earth without injury. Although still in occupied Norway, Bennett was able — through the help of the local populace — to make his way to Sweden. From there, he promptly returned to England and rejoined the war effort. Not everyone in his crew, however, was so lucky. Out of the seven men, four evaded capture. Three — including the badly wounded tail gunner — spent the remainder of the war in a POW camp. [223] Four Halifaxes and one Lancaster were lost on the operation. For all the effort involved, the *Tirpitz* was not hit. Not until 12 November 1944 — following a succession of deadly attempts — would Bomber Command succeed in destroying the German warship, inflicting 1,000 casualties upon her 2,000 sailors.

VIII

The Gathering Storm

The Singleton Report

'We must first destroy the foundations upon which the German war machine runs — the economy which feeds it, the morale which sustains it, the supplies which nourish it and the hopes of victory which inspire it. Only then shall we be able to return to the continent and occupy and control portions of his territory and impose our will upon the enemy... It is in bombing, on a scale undreamt of in the last war, that we find the new weapon on which we must principally depend for the destruction of German economic life and morale.' So wrote the British Chiefs of Staff in July 1941 as the Germans cut a destructive swath towards the heart of Soviet Russia.[224]

While the Red Army was torn through with unheralded brutality, British aircrews — entangled in the widening searchlight belts and savaged by the ever-increasing night-fighter menace — continued winging their way through the flak-tortured skies over Germany. Bomber Command struggled with its ultimate goal; struggled to reach a scale of bombing 'undreamt of in the last war.' But Sir Stafford Cripps's speech before the House of Commons had made public the question of necessity. With the Soviet Union and the United States now aligned with Great Britain in its once lonely struggle, was such a bomber force even needed? Bomber Command's intended objective was clear: the destruction of Germany's industrial capabilities and the morale of its people. Lord Cherwell believed what the bomber offensive needed was a means by which the gradual devastation of the Reich could be measured. This, he argued, would strengthen support for Bomber Command. Bearing out this assumption, he put pen to paper and on 30 March 1942 delivered the following report to the Prime Minister.

The following seems a simple method of estimating what we could do by bombing Germany:

Careful analysis of the effects of raids on Birmingham, Hull and elsewhere have shown that, on the average, one ton of bombs dropped on a built-up area demolishes 20-40 dwellings and turns 100-200 people out of house and home.

We know from our experience that we can count on nearly 14 operational sorties per bomber produced. The average lift of the bombers we are going to produce over the next fifteen months will be about three tons. It follows that each of these bombers will in its lifetime drop about forty tons of bombs. If these are dropped on built-up areas they will make 4,000-8,000 people homeless.

In 1938 over 22 million Germans lived in fifty-eight towns of over 100,000 inhabitants, which, with modern equipment, should be easy to find and hit. Our forecast output of heavy bombers (including Wellingtons) between now and the middle of 1943 is about 10,000. If even half the total load of 10,000 bombers were dropped on the built-up areas of these fifty-eight German towns the great majority of their inhabitants (about one-third of the German population) would be turned out of house and home.

Investigation seems to show that having one's house demolished is most damaging to morale. People seem to mind it more than having friends or even relatives killed. At Hull signs of strain were evident, though only one-tenth of the houses were demolished. On the above figures we should be able to do ten times as much harm to each of the fifty-eight principal German towns. There seems little doubt that this would break the spirit of the people.

Our calculation assumes, of course, that we really get one-half of our bombers into built-up areas. On the other hand, no account is taken of the large promised American production (6,000 heavy bombers in the period in question). Nor has regard been paid to the inevitable damage to factories, communications, etc., in these towns and the damage by fire, probably accentuated by breakdown of public services.[225]

The problem with such a theory was the foundation upon which it was built, namely, that Bomber Command would reach the staggering size of

10,000 bombers. With the United States now at war, Bomber Command could not rely on American production to boost its numbers. Expansion aside, problems with navigation and bombing accuracy still abounded. Cherwell's paper was based on conditions which had yet to be met — some of which never would be. Portal and Sinclair knew this, but kept quiet. For Cherwell had provided a foundation upon which the bomber offensive could be built.

But there was a dissenting voice: Sir Henry Tizard, Scientific Member on the Air Council. Tizard argued that exerting so much energy into the bombing offensive would leave Britain deficient on its other fighting fronts. The War Cabinet found itself caught in the crossfire of Cherwell's and Tizard's dissenting opinions. It sought to quell the matter with an outside analysis and approached Mr Justice Singleton, a High Court judge who had already conducted a government study on the strength of the Luftwaffe. The question Downing Street posed to Singleton was: 'What results are we likely to achieve from continuing air attacks on Germany at the greatest possible strength during the next six, 12 and 18 months respectively?'[226]

To answer this question, Singleton examined all RAF records pertaining to bombing operations over Germany from August 1940 to June 1941. While Singleton and his committee exmained the evidence at hand, Bomber Command, under its new leader, was busy obliterating the MAN diesel works factory at Augsburg and incinerating Lübeck and Rostock. It seems unlikely that Singleton's conclusions were not prejudiced by the publicity garnered by these operations. Singleton presented his findings to the War Cabinet on 20 May. Although the report disputed Harris's firm belief that bombing alone could win the war, it did assert the benefits of the campaign — one of which was its assistance to the Russians:

I think there is every reason to hope for good results from a sustained bombing policy. I do not think it ought to be regarded as of itself sufficient to win the war or to produce decisive results; the area is too vast for the effort we can put forth; on the other hand, if Germany does not achieve great success on land before the winter it may well turn out to have a decisive effect, and in the meantime, if carried out on the lines suggested, it must impede Germany and help Russia... If Russia can hold Germany on land I doubt whether Germany will stand twelve or eighteen months' continuous, intensified and increasing bombing, affecting, as it must, her war production, her power of resistance, her industries and her will to resist (by which I mean morale).[227]

The report continued, hitting upon what had long been the bane of Bomber Command: 'The important matter is to reach a greater degree of accuracy.'

With the exception of the incendiary raids on Lübeck and Rostock and the attack on the Billancourt Renault Factory on 3 March, recent bombing results, Singleton wrote, had been less than encouraging. Only when flying in ideal weather did Bomber Command drive home an efficient attack, 'and there are few nights in the month on which such conditions can be expected, and few targets on which a night bombing attack can be really successful. At the same time, reports appear to show that the effect of our bombing is being more seriously felt in Germany than it was a little time ago.'

Problems of navigation were being tackled. In the meantime, crews had Gee to assist them — a device Singleton believed had yet to prove itself. Instead, he thought a trained 'target-finding force' would better hone Bomber Command's efficiency. He concluded his report on a cautionary note:

> To sum up, I do not think that great results can be hoped for within six months. I cannot help feeling that the six-months period ought to be looked upon as leading up to, and forming part of, a longer and more sustained effort than as one expected to produce results within a limited time. Much depends on what happens in Russia. The effects of a reverse for Germany, or a lack of success, would be greatly increased by an intensified bombing programme in the autumn and winter. And if this was coupled with knowledge in Germany that the bombing would be on an increasing scale until the end, and with the realisation of the fact that the German Air Force could not again achieve equality, I think it might well prove the turning point — provided always that greater accuracy can be achieved.[228]

The analysis was a refreshing counterbalance to the morbid revelations of the Butt Report, though it illustrated the apparent lack of a 'really successful' operation. It also resolved nothing. There was ample material for those on both sides of the fence to draw from and fuel their arguments. As the merits of Singleton's findings were debated, Harris was well into planning a devastating display of Bomber Command's full potential. It was code-named Millennium and would prove more than any bureaucratic report ever could.

Millennium

Languishing in prison after the war, Albert Speer, Hitler's armaments minister, had plenty of time to reminisce. Pondering the destruction that ultimately engulfed his country, Speer pinpointed 30 May 1942 as the night Britain offered Germany a bitter 'foretaste' of what lay in store. On that night, Cologne fell under the onslaught of more than 1,000 bombers.[229] The 'Thousand Raid' was audacious in concept and symbolism. Germany would bear painful witness to British resolve in the unheralded destruction of a major metropolis. It would also play upon the collective imaginations of the Americans and Russians — a fact not lost on the military and political minds in Britain. Portal enthusiastically endorsed the scheme. Churchill, too, in a late-night meeting with Harris at the Prime Minister's official retreat at Chequers, voiced his support, saying he was prepared to lose 100 bombers for such an operation.

Now Harris faced the challenge of amassing 1,000 bombers for the greatest air assault in history. It was Harris's intent to provide 700 aircraft from Bomber Command's own resources. This already exceeded the Command's current frontline strength of 600 bombers. Scouring every resource at his disposal, Harris approached Army Cooperation, Coastal, Fighter and Training commands to make up the missing numbers. In a letter to the various commanders, Harris bluntly stated his ambition 'to annihilate one of Germany's main industrial centres by fire.'[230] Responding to the call, Air Chief Marshal Sir Philip Joubert, C-in-C Coastal Command, pledged 250 aircraft to Millennium. But the Admiralty — which exercised operational control over Coastal Command — denied Harris Joubert's generosity. With the battle against the U-boat raging in the Atlantic, the First Sea Lord was loath to divert his precious resources to another venture. In the end, Harris was forced to bleed Bomber Command dry. Into Millennium he thrust his entire frontline strength and that of his reserves. 'Such a bold action might produce a great triumph,' note the Official Historians, 'but if anything went wrong, the disaster might well be irremediable. The whole programme of training and expansion might conceivably be wrecked.'[231] Scraping together every machine available, Harris and his Senior Air Staff Officer, Sir Richard Saundby, assembled a force of 1,047 aircraft. It broke down like this:[232]

No. 1 Group: 156 Wellingtons

No. 2 Group: 134 Wellingtons, 88 Stirlings

No. 4 Group: 131 Halifaxes, 9 Wellingtons, 7 Whitleys

No. 5 Group: 73 Lancasters, 46 Manchesters, 34 Hampdens

No 91 Group: 236 Wellingtons, 21 Whitleys (Operational Training Unit)

No. 92 Group: 63 Wellingtons, 45 Hampdens (Operational Training Unit)

Flying Training Command: 4 Wellingtons

Except for the four Wellingtons provided by Flying Training Command, every aircraft came from within Bomber Command. Now for the target. There were two options: Hamburg and Cologne. Both cities were easy to identify and lay on the western fringes of the Reich, thus minimising the amount of time over enemy territory. Hamburg was Harris's initial choice. Hamburg was a centre of U-boat manufacturing. From its factories and docks silent killers slipped beneath the waves. Destroying Hamburg would go some way to placating the Admiralty, but Cologne lay within the operational range of Gee. Vital to Millennium's success was the light of a full moon. The operation was set for the night of 27 May, or any night from then until 31 May — the full moon period — when ideal weather conditions prevailed.

'The weather in those days,' wrote Harris, 'had absolute power to make or mar an operation. In this instance, as I saw it, the weather had the power to make or mar the future of the bomber offensive.'[233] From 27 to 29 May, black clouds hung over the Continent and threatened Harris's grand scheme. The weather over England was clear on the morning of 30 May, but stormy conditions lingered over north-west Germany. The 'Thousand Bomber' force had been on stand by since final orders were issued on 26 May. Harris faced a dilemma. 'If I waited, I might have to keep this very large force standing idle for some time, and I might lose the good weather over England; to land such a force in difficult weather would at that time have been to court disaster and for so many aircraft it was necessary to have a large number of bases free from cloud. But if I sent the force that night, the target might be cloud-covered, and the whole operation reduced to naught and our plan disclosed.'[234] At five o'clock that evening, Harris was presented with the final met. forecast. It read:

Cologne: Broken cloud with some large breaks. Route: Much cloud and occasional thunderstorms going out, improving somewhat for return. Homebases: Conditions at takeoff generally good, very good, but local interference owing to thunderstorms possible. On return, local visibility troubles possible, particularly 1 and 5 groups, but even then no more than 25% of bases will be affected.[235]

The conditions were far from ideal for an operation of such magnitude — but further postponement meant jeopardising the entire endeavour. Too much planning and political maneuvering had been done to throw such an opportunity away. Harris was not going to risk this prime chance to finally prove Bomber Command's lethal effectiveness. This was his opportunity to silence — in Britain — the critics of the air offensive and to unleash — in Germany — a wave of destruction, the likes of which had never been witnessed. In short, it was now or never. Harris, sitting at his desk in the underground operations room at Bomber Command HQ, knew his decision — if wrong — would have dire consequences on the whole course of the air war. He turned and cast a glance at Wing Commander Dudley Saward, his Chief Radar Officer and future biographer, then returned his attention to the maps and charts in front of him. The atmosphere in the room seemed to suddenly weigh on the shoulders of those who were present. If Harris made the decision that was expected of him, it would elevate the war's destruction to an unforeseen level. Long before Harris arrived on the scene, the war-makers had cast any sense of chivalry aside. Hitler, in his stunning conquests of 1939 and 1940, had exercised sheer brutality with an enthusiastic abandon in the bombing of Warsaw and Rotterdam. And now, Britain, still fighting for its life against a regime that knew only violence and slaughter, could not take the tender-hearted route. This was something Harris knew all too well. Six decades on, it's easy to look back and shake one's head at the war's destruction and point fingers at those responsible for such devastation. But in 1942 — with much of London and other British cities in ruins — it was not the time to be weak or cater to what might be deemed today as political correctness.

Harris had stood on the roof of the Air Ministry building and watched German incendiaries and high explosive rain down on London. It was now Britain's time to return the favour. Harris — his face, emotionless and carved of stone — studied the charts on his desk. His jaw was set tight, and between his teeth was clamped a cigarette holder with an American Lucky Strike protruding from the end. Stretched out in front of him was all of Germany and its numerous metropolitan and industrial centres waiting to go up in flames. Harris surveyed the drawn landscape, a wisp of smoke rising from the growing ash at the end of his cigarette. He ran his finger over the map, tracing imaginary routes and pondering the risks those journeys would entail once his men climbed aboard their planes. He was not ignorant of the risks involved or the suffering they endured. The men of Bomber Command — Harris strongly believed — had a right to be proud of the work they were doing. They were the only ones landing blows against the enemy.[236] But the affection he harboured for his men and the esteem in which he held them did not mean those under his command were in for an easy ride. On the contrary, he expected a third of all airmen to perish on their nightly forays over Germany.[237] It was because his crews were willing to brave such daunting odds that he held them in such high esteem. Now, on this fateful day, he was all too cognisant of what his decision might mean.

He continued to run his finger over the map of Germany, passing it over cities and towns like a roving crosshair searching for its final target. Earlier in the year he had expressed his intention towards Germany in no uncertain terms when he told the press if he had the resources to do so, he would send 1,000 bombers over Germany every night. The devastation wreaked would surely end the war by autumn, he said. He asserted that the Germans would soon be begging for mercy as their country crumbled in flames around them. He hoped the screaming would begin on this night. There was silence in the underground room as staff watched Harris ponder the map. Finally, his wandering finger came to rest. The target of his choice was hidden beneath the tip of his finger. He drew heavily on the cigarette and sent a cloud of smoke drifting up towards the ceiling. Pulling his finger away, he revealed what city would bear the brunt of everything Bomber Command could throw at it. The target was Cologne.[238] What silence there had been now disappeared in a burst of feverish activity.

With all the risks entailed in his decision to go ahead, Harris displayed the true grit of a real commander.[239] The raid would be spearheaded by the Gee-equipped aircraft of Nos 1 and 3 Group attacking west to east, commencing the ninety-minute assault with a fifteen-minute downpouring of incendiaries and high explosives over the city centre. The main brunt of the attack would follow, with maximum loads of incendiaries falling on aiming points a mile north and south of the city centre. The Halifaxes, Lancasters and Manchesters of Nos 4 and 5 Groups would raid the city in the assault's final fifteen minutes. RAF Fighter Command — along with Blenheims of No. 2 Group — would fly intruder operations against German night-fighter bases along the bombers' route.

That evening — as crews all over England were briefed — the full scale of the operation was revealed for the first time. The plan called for 600 aircraft per hour to pass over the city, dropping eleven tons of bombs per minute.[240] It was payback for the likes of Coventry and London, Portsmouth and Liverpool. It was vengeance by fire for the many thousands lying dead amongst the ruins of Britain's shattered cities. Bombers took off from fifty-two airfields that evening and streamed across the English landscape, towards the North Sea. Over the sea clouds were dense and icing was severe. Guns froze, rudders jammed and elevators stuck, forcing 100 of the older aircraft to turn back. Conditions cleared as the remainder of the force reached the Dutch coast. They flew over Holland and thundered into Germany, through searchlights and flak and on to Cologne.

At 0047 hours — as the first aircraft passed over the city — the first bombs fell. Within minutes, the city centre was a mass of flame expanding in all directions. The sky glowed crimson: a vision seen from more than 100 miles away. The onslaught of British bombers overwhelmed the German nightfighters. No longer did British bombers penetrate German air space one-by-one. They swarmed over enemy territory in a thundering horde, for it was against Cologne that the British debuted the Bomber Stream.[241] Piloting a Manchester of No. 50 Squadron and flying in the final wave that night was 20-year-old Flying Officer Leslie Manser. Everything was cast in vibrant colour — the glow of the flames, the blue and white glare of the searchlights and the flash of guns and bombs — as Manser lined his aircraft up for the bombing run. Rocked by all that was erupting around it, the Manchester shook and rattled as Manser held it steady at 8,000 feet on the final approach to the target. Then, as a searchlight locked onto the aircraft, all was lost to a near-blinding whiteness. Three satellite beams swept in from three opposite directions and fixed the Manchester in a brilliant cone of light. It was now an easy target for the overwhelmed defences. Flak tore into the starboard engine and set it ablaze. In the nose of the aircraft, Manser's bomb aimer maintained his running commentary as the pilot held the aircraft steady on its bomb run.

Not until the bombs had been dropped on target did Manser turn from the city and try to evade the searchlights' grip. In this he succeeded, but not before the bomber was again battered by the ground defences. Manser struggled to maintain altitude as the aircraft — flying on one engine — limped away from the blazing city. The crew threw out everything they could to lighten the load, but still the altimeter needle ticked away the feet as the plane continued its slow and steady descent. By the time they crossed the German-Belgian border, the Manchester was flying at only 2,000 feet. Manser ordered the others to bail out, knowing the aircraft would not be landing safely in England. The young pilot refused a parachute, opting instead to hold the bomber steady as the others dropped through the emergency hatch. As they descended through the darkness at the end of their parachutes, the Manchester finally fell. It smashed into a field and disintegrated in a fiery blast with Manser still at the controls. For his sacrifice, Manser posthumously received the Victoria Cross.[242]

Manchester L7301 was one of forty-one bombers lost raiding Cologne, thirty-six of which were shot down by night fighters. At 0225 hours that morning, the last bombs fell. The twin towers of Cologne's ancient cathedral now stood morbid over a burning landscape. More than 2,000 fires raged. Some 3,330 buildings were obliterated. In total, 12,840 buildings were either destroyed or damaged, of which 2,560 were industrial complexes. The city was left without water and electricity. The docks and railways took a beating and the main telephone exchange was destroyed. More than 5,000 people were injured and 469 killed. The number of those bombed out of their homes totalled 45,132. In the immediate wake of the raid, 150,000 people fled the city. It was Bomber Command's first major victory. The façade of German invincibility had finally cracked. It was an operation wrote 'Hap' Arnold, Commanding General of the US Army Air Forces, 'bold in conception and superlative in execution.'[243]

For the Germans, it was a different story entirely. Albert Speer and Field Marshal Erhard Milch, State Secretary in the Air Ministry, were, by chance, summoned to meet with Goering the morning after. They found him in poor spirits and doubting the veracity of reports coming out of Cologne. He was screaming into a telephone, berating a Cologne city official for telling him blatant lies. How could the British, the Reich Marshal demanded to know, muster such numbers? It simply wasn't possible. Speer and Milch stood idly by and watched Goering work himself into an ever-increasing frenzy. He ranted, raved and stormed about the room. Sending him further over the edge was the thought of reporting the news to Hitler.[244]

In one audacious stroke, Harris had revitalised the bomber offensive. 'My own opinion,' he wrote, 'is we should never have had a real bomber offensive if it had not been for the 1,000 bomber attack on Cologne, an irrefutable demonstration of the power of what was to all intents and purposes a new and untried weapon.'[245] But the Germans had proved themselves to be a resilient people. From the ruins of Lübeck they emerged, restoring the city to near normal capacity within days. In Rostock, the Heinkel factory was operating again within weeks. This would apply to Cologne. Those who fled returned within two weeks as the city made great strides in its struggle for normality. But the effects of Operation Millennium had already ingrained themselves in the Allied consciousness. The war, in substantial measure, had been brought to the Germans. It was the first big step in Harris's grand scheme: destroying Germany by bomber. 'We are going to scourge the Third Reich from end to end,' Harris declared. 'We are bombing Germany city by city and ever more terribly in order to make it impossible for her to go on with the war. That is our objective; we shall pursue it relentlessly.'

Flight of the Mosquito

As rescue workers shifted through the rubble the following day and the skeletal remains of Cologne's buildings crumbled amidst smoke and flame, five aircraft from 105 Squadron took to the English skies. The first took flight at 0400 hours. The last didn't take off until 1710. Their objective was to photograph damage done to Cologne and drop a few high explosives to shake things up. The city's anti-aircraft guns hit one raider. Its two-man crew was killed when it plunged into the North Sea. The remaining four returned safely. Three reported bombing the target though no photographs were taken because of poor weather and the heavy pall of smoke languishing over the ruins. It was an inauspicious debut for an aircraft that would emerge alongside the Lancaster and Spitfire as one of the outstanding machines of the Second World War: The DeHaviland Mosquito.

It was a light, twin-engined bomber of plywood construction relying on speed and altitude for survival, though a night fighter variant was later introduced and proved a deadly nemesis for those who flew against it. Ideal for low-level, high-speed attacks, it would serve with the Pathfinders and form the core of the Light Night Striking Force later in the war. The men who flew it could boast flying up to 350 mph and soaring to 35,000 feet over a range of 3,500 miles. By 1944 it was blasting Berlin with the 4,000-lb. Cookie. Not only was this four times the bomb load of its original design, but it was equal to the standard carrying capacity of the U S Eighth's B-17. In his war memoirs, Air Vice-Marshal Donald Bennett recounts a visit to a Mosquito airfield made by Mrs Ogden Reid (Helen Rogers Reid), of the *New York Herald Tribune*. During the course of their evening together, he and the reporter watched a number of Mosquitoes roar into the darkening sky.

'I suppose the destination is Berlin?' Reid asked, notebook and pencil in hand. 'Can you tell me their bomb load?'

Bennett made no comment regarding the planes' final destination, but told his inquisitive visitor that the Mosquito was capable of carrying a 4,000-lb. bomb to the German capital.

'What do the B-17s carry to Berlin?' Reid asked after a moment of brief contemplation.

'With the routing which they use and the larger load of ammunition necessary for daylight operations, they are carrying 3,500 lbs.,' Bennett said. 'In any case, they cannot carry a blockbuster, as it is too large for their bomb bays.'

A grave look passed over Reid's face. 'I only hope,' she said, 'the American public never hears those facts.'[246]

Bennett was quick to note, however, that more direct routing and the carrying of less ammunition allowed B-17s to exceed the 4,000-lb. bomb load on operations against Berlin.[247] Regardless, the comparison stands as testament to the Mosquito's exceptional power and performance.

After Millennium

Harris now hoped to transpose the Cologne experience upon Essen. He sent 956 bombers to the city on the night of 1 June. Thick cloud topped out at 8,000 feet and the city lay veiled beneath its industrial fog. Marker flares dropped by an advanced echelon of Wellingtons from No. 3 Group were distorted by cloud, resulting in the scattered bombing of eleven cities. The failure came at a heavy cost. Thirty-one bombers were destroyed, and 212 airmen were lost. Harris was undaunted. Bomber Command flew 1,607 sorties against Essen and its Krupps Armaments factory over the next fortnight. It cost Harris eighty-four bombers. Damage to Essen remained minimal. The Thousand Bomber Force was then reassembled for a raid on Bremen. For this operation, Harris mustered 1,067 aircraft.

Like the raids on Rostock, the Bremen operation — on the night of 25 June — was to be a fiery amalgamation of precision attack and area bombing. The Focke-Wulf factory was to be pinpointed by 142 aircraft of No. 5 Group. Twenty Blenheims were to target the A G Wesser Shipyard, while Coastal Command would bomb the Deschimag shipyard. A contingent of Blenheims, Bostons and Mosquitoes would fly Intruder operations against German night-fighter bases along the bombers' route. Because it was situated on the Wester River, Bremen should have been an easy target to identify. Instead, crews found themselves flying through heavy cloud, which effectively covered everything. Bombing through the haze, they still managed to inflict some considerable damage, flattening an assembly shop at the Focke-Wulf factory and battering the Vulkan shipyard and Atlas Werke. Some 6,600 houses were destroyed or damaged, rendering 2,378 people homeless. Deaths totalled eighty-five. In its primary objectives, however, the Bremen operation was a failure.

Bomber Command suffered heavier casualties against Bremen than it did against Cologne or Essen in a single raid. Forty-eight aircraft were lost. It was the greatest single-night loss suffered by Bomber Command thus far. Flying through everything the Reich could throw at them that night were 198 aircraft of Operational Training Unit 91 Group. Over the extended distance to Bremen, they suffered grievously as night fighters, flak and searchlights picked off twenty-three training aircraft and crews. The reason for such losses was attributed to the use of older aircraft — such as the Whitley, now retired from front-line service — and the greater distances involved. Training units would continue to reinforce Bomber Command's frontline strength until mid-September. They would fly in operations against Düsseldorf on the nights of 31 July and 10 September. Both operations wreaked widespread damage, but bomber casualties amongst both the front-line squadrons and the training units were heavy. On the night of 31 July, twenty-nine of 630 bombers were lost — eleven of those destroyed were from 92 (O.T.U.) Group, which put up 105 aircraft. Against the same target on 10 September, thirty-three of 479 raiders failed to return. Five of thirteen Wellingtons dispatched by training units were destroyed. Training units shed blood again over Bremen on the night of 13 September and then Essen three nights later.

On 1 March 1942 an article written by Gustav Krupps appeared in the German media. Wrote the German armaments magnate: 'If Germany should ever be re-born and shake off the chains of Versailles one day, the

1. Arthur 'Bomber' Harris sitting at his desk examining documents. (IWM HU4382)

2. Berlin, December 1943: victims of a bombing raid are laid out for identification and burial in a gymnasium decorated with Christmas trees. During the war as a whole between 300,000 and 600,000 Germans died as a result of Allied strategic bombing. (IWM HU12143)

3. A devastated Hamburg following the July 1943 raids. (IWM C4131)

4. *Opposite above:* A day shot of Lancasters flying in formation.

5. *Opposite below:* Avro Lancasters of No. 1 Group, lined up in the dusk at RAF Scampton, Lincolnshire, England before an operation. (IWM CH8785)

6. A night attack on Lorient showing a U-boat factory being blasted. (IWM 3387)

7. *Opposite above:* Squadron Leader Peter Hill, briefs crews of No. 51 Squadron RAF on the forthcoming raid to Nuremberg in the Operations Room at Snaith, Yorkshire. No. 51 Squadron lost six Handley Page Halifaxes that night, 30/31 March 1944, and 35 men were killed, including Squadron Leader Hill. Seven men were captured and made prisoners of war. (IWM CH12598)

8. *Opposite below:* Winston Churchill standing on an airfield watching a Stirling take off for an operation over enemy territory. (IWM H10314)

9. An impressive shot of the incredible flak barrage RAF bombers encountered on operations over Brest. (IWM C1856)

10. A Stirling crew is debriefed following a major operation against Berlin. (IWM CH11640)

11. A Wellington that returned from an operation with its entire rear turret shot away. (IWM CH9866)

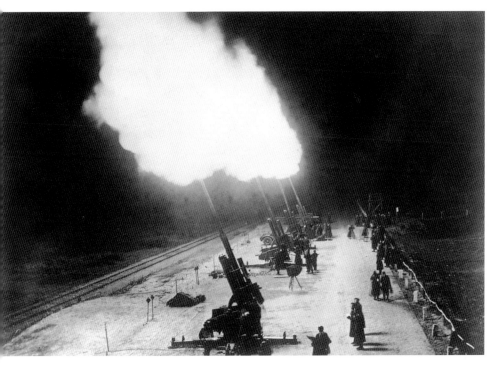

12. A German 88mm anti-aircraft battery striking back during an RAF bombing attack. (IWM MH13407)

13. A Handley Page Halifax of No. 6 Group, Bomber Command, flying over Wanne-Eickel oil refinery in the Rhur, October 1944. (IWM C4713)

14. A Lancaster dropping bundles of incendiaries and a 4,000lb blast bomb over Duisburg on 14 October 1944. (IWM CL1404)

15. A Halifax continuing on its bombing raid despite having half its tail shot off. (IWM CE154)

16. *Right:* A close-up shot of a 4,000-pounder being dropped over a Luftwaffe equipment depot. (IWM C4525)

17. *Below:* One of the massive flak towers that formed part of Hamburg's defence. (IWM CL2503)

18. Two aircraft of the Royal Air Force Bomber Command during a raid on the industrial transport centre of Pforzheim, south-east of Karlsruhe. The white 'cascade' is caused by the glowing target indicators. This image is a still from a film made by the RAF Film Production Unit. (IWM C5007)

19. RAF armourers loading a Stirling from No. 7 Squadron. (IWM CH5285)

20. Armourers show off bombs for a comparison in size at the bomb dump at Woodhall Spa, Lincolnshire. (IWM CH12450)

21. *Above:* A Lancaster of No. 467 Squadron Royal Australian Air Force, May 1944, showing emblems denoting 98 operations flown. (IWM HU2668)

22. *Left:* A bomb-aimer in position inside a Lancaster. (IWM CH11540)

23. *Left:* Sentries standing outside the underground Operations Block of Bomber Command HQ, High Wycombe, Buckinghamshire. (IWM CH3275)

24. *Below:* The RAF pound Hamburg with 22,000lb bombs. (IWM C5197)

Krupps concern had to be prepared again. I wanted and had to maintain Krupps in spite of all opposition, as an armament plan for the future. After the rise to power of Adolf Hitler, I had the satisfaction of being able to report to the Fuhrer that Krupps stood ready. We are all proud of having thus contributed to the successes of our army.'[248] The Krupps armaments works was an imposing symbol of German military superiority, consuming more than two square miles of Essen's city centre. On the night of 16 September — as Essen's guns blazed away — a stricken bomber, loaded with incendiaries, fell from the sky and slammed into the factory. Further havoc was caused by the impact of fifteen high explosive bombs. It was Bomber Command's most successful operation against Essen yet, though thirty-nine of 369 bombers were lost. Airgunner Sid Brans, flying with No. 97 Squadron, survived the ordeal and wrote about it in a letter home:

> Essen was our next effort, and although it was announced that 39 planes were lost that night, strangely enough it proved to be one of the quietest trips so far. Essen, of course, is smack in the centre of the Ruhr district and very heavily defended, in fact I was reading in the *Daily Telegraph* that one squadron leader estimates that there are something like two to three thousand guns in the area. But it wasn't the guns that impressed me as much as the searchlights. There were literally hundreds of them in just one great solid belt and it seemed impossible that anything could penetrate them. Having learnt our lesson at Frankfurt we didn't hang about, but dropped our bombs and got out...[249]

Frontline squadrons operated alone for the rest of the year. The night skies were becoming an ever bloodier arena as the number of men and machines destroyed ominously increased. It eventually reached the point, where, 'in the later months of 1942, the enemy appeared to have gained a serious degree of tactical superiority.'[250] In the face of mounting casualties and strengthening German defences, Bomber Command continued its offensive, lashing out against Mainz, Osnabrück, Hamburg, Saarbrücken, Duisburg, Wilhelmshaven and repeated visits to Bremen — but in decreased numbers. During this period, Harris — who had thus far experimented with mass formations, precision daylight raids and training units — ordered another experimental raid.

The Polish port city of Danzig — now Gdansk — lies on the Vistula river, four miles inland from the Baltic Sea. Following the German conquest of Poland in 1939, Hitler united the city with Germany. On 11 July forty-four Lancasters were tasked with the destruction of the Danzig U-boat yards. The operation entailed a 1,500-mile round trip journey. The outward 750 miles were to be flown in daylight. The Lancasters' task was to bomb the target at dusk and return to England under the cover of night. To thwart German fighters, routing was carefully planned. The aircraft were to fly in a low-level formation over the North Sea. The formation would split up and — using cloud for cover — fly over Denmark and the Baltic and approach the target separately. It would be Bomber Command's heaviest daylight attack against a German target thus far.

The outward trek to Danzig remained free of Luftwaffe intervention. Twenty-four of the forty-four Lancasters succeeded in bombing the yards, but some crews had trouble locating the target and bombed after dark. The flak was heavy and the searchlight activity intense. Despite the heavy defences, only two Lancasters were lost. The remaining forty-two returned safely to England, though eight landed with a significant number of holes in them. The force had bombed from 15,000 feet, inflicting some damage but not enough to put the yards out of action. Prior to this operation, six Mosquitoes of 139 Squadron were sent to Flensburg on 2 July in a daring low-level, daylight raid against U-boat construction yards.

Nevertheless, Harris was proving himself to be a flexible commander. He was hurling his forces against major objectives and experimenting beyond the normal scope of night operations. He had, in the five months since arriving at High Wycombe, revived faith in Bomber Command and its offensive. It was something not lost on the Prime Minister. 'Proof of the growing power of the British bomber force,' Churchill declared, 'is also the herald of what Germany will receive city by city from now on.'

IX

The Pathfinders

A Trial over Frankfurt

The first real effort of this Squadron in its new role as Pathfinders. An Incendiary raid on FRANKFURT. Of the eleven sorties detailed, two had to be abandoned owing to engine trouble, two did not return...[251]

Marker flares were dropped across the bombing point in prelude to the main attack and, through the haze, could be seen a brilliant technicolour display of luminescence. The defences were heavy and there was a rumble and the smell of cordite as flak exploded against the Stirling and ruptured a starboard petrol tank. There were tracer streams and searchlights and the lurid glow of burning planes. The sky mirrored the shattered and burning nightmare below as flames were carried high in the thickening pall of smoke rising above the city. That evening, the briefing had been tense. The lines of red tape stretching across the map of north-west Europe converged on Frankfurt. Over this formidable objective, they would be acting in a new capacity — that of Pathfinders.

Now, flares dropped, the Stirling crew — flying with a hole in a starboard petrol tank — made a bid for the coast. But the German anti-aircraft batteries had found their range and were unleashing their barrage with uncanny accuracy. The next hit severed the oil pipes on the port side and — with a grinding shriek of metal — sheared off that side's inner propeller and gear. There were mad yells over the intercom as the plane dipped violently and the captain struggled to maintain control. As the flight engineer shut off feed to all useless pipe lines, the plane was hit again. The port engine was ripped from the wing and fell off into the night. Now the pilot yelled for help at the controls. Leaving his station, the wireless operator joined the pilot in the cockpit and helped apply pressure to the rudder bar and control column to keep the plane on an even keel.

Against what seemed to be amazing odds, they made the Dutch coast but were losing height. The sky still throbbed with searchlights and tracer. Beneath the plane there came a heavy thudding as enemy fire ripped the length of the Stirling's bomb doors. Out of desperation, all moveable objects were jettisoned to lighten the load. The plane floundered through the coastal defences and out over the water, towards the sanctuary of England. As they passed over the English coast — after a desperate North Sea crossing — the starboard inner engine began to cough, then, with an unimpressive sputter, it cut out. The Stirling slammed into the ground, tearing up a field near King's Crossing. The impact tore the bomber apart and killed all on board.

Going for the Kill

Stirling BF-355. Clouds held the light of the moon as the bomber dropped through a layer of cumulous. Frankfurt lay black beneath the weaving searchlights. As the first flare dropped, Flight Sergeant Michael Elelman, in the rear turret, watched tracer arc skyward. Within minutes the main force had arrived and the first white flashes of bombs finding their mark were clearly visible. The scene was one of exuberant colour and illumination. In moments a river of flame seemed to wind its way through the tortured geography below and, with each white flash of exploding bomb, that river grew. Flares continued to fall. Elelman was amazed at what he saw. Below him, he could see the awesome silhouettes of other bombers against the growing clouds of dense smoke and the dazzling display of a city burning.

One bomb that fell resulted in a massive upthrust of flame: a blazing column that shot nearly a thousand feet into the sky. A fiery torrent was now devouring the blackness that had shrouded the city prior to the RAF's arrival. Reflected light, wild and erratic, played upon Elelman's turret. The Perspex was bathed in a reddish glow and doused in the white of a passing searchlight. The plane weaved gently, though never straying from its course. Deadly starbursts erupted never far off and the concussion of the blasts shook the plane. Twelve bundles of flares had been dropped and the plane banked in a turn to set them on a course for home. Even as the city fell back farther in the distance, the raging fires could still be seen, tattooed upon the sky and rising smoke.

They were twenty-six miles south-east of Cambrai when Elelman saw the JU 88 following them 1,500 feet below on the starboard quarter. For five minutes it shadowed the Stirling, as if the German pilot was unaware of the heavy bomber's presence. When the Junkers commenced the attack, it did so in a rapid climb, ascending to within 600 yards of the Stirling. 'Enemy aircraft approaching from below starboard quarter,' Elelman said, and opened fire with a short burst. He knew the plane was too far away for the Stirling's Brownings to be effective, but he hoped the fire would serve to send the Junkers on its way. The enemy craft continued its rapid ascent. 'Dive to port!' Elelman yelled, and the pilot dropped the plane according to his rear gunner's instructions. As the Stirling peeled away, the Junkers shot up over them and out of sight, though the direction in which it broke away was not observed.

All was relatively quiet. The sky was devoid of flak and there was no searchlight activity emanating from below. The Stirling dropped 500 feet before returning to its proper course at 11,000 feet and a 180 knots. 'Keep an eye out.' The pilot's voice crackled in Elelman's ear piece. There was a three-minute lapse between the initial encounter and the second attack. 'Enemy aircraft!' Elelman said, 'Port quarter! 600 yards!' The Junkers did not carry any lights, but was well illuminated by the full moon. The fighter closed in quickly to 400 yards and fired its cannons. Elelman opened up with his guns again. There was an exchange of tracer — red and green — violent streaks of light that fell away into space as the Junkers broke away and the Stirling dropped in another dive to port.

'We've got two of them!'

As the Stirling dived away and the JU 88 broke off its attack, a Foke-Wulf 190 emerged from the night and attacked on the bomber's port quarter. There was the sound of metal being punctured as cannon fire and tracer tore into the Stirling's port side from the wing to the rear turret. Elelman returned fire, but the barrage went wide as the FW 190 broke away to starboard. Again, Elelman fired on the aircraft as it fell in an evasive manoeuvre. All the while, the Stirling continued in its twisting dive. Plunging and turning. Again came a burst of enemy fire and a heavy thudding from underneath on the starboard side. The Stirling's elevation had dropped to 9,000 feet. When the rear guns had ceased firing, the pilot pulled out of the dive, but kept tilting the plane heavily from starboard to port before executing a violent 180-degree turn. 'Enemy aircraft, starboard quarter about 500 yards!' came the voice from the mid-upper gunner. In his turret, Elelman was unable to get a clear shot. He pirouetted the turret round to starboard as, again, the Stirling was plunged in a desperate evasive action. As this happened, the FW 190 opened fire at about 350 yards and continued to fire as it closed to 150 yards. By now, there was no sign of the JU 88, but the Stirling was hit again as the enemy aircraft tore away to port.

'Port outer hit!'

The rear turret shuddered with the force of its guns as Elelman fired at the FW 190 in the midst of its evasive action. Tracer could be seen striking the enemy aircraft. There was a multitude of sparks and smoke belched from somewhere. In Elelman's ear there came an ecstatic cry of jubilation. The pilot pulled the Stirling out of its dive and the FW 190 passed underneath trailing smoke as it went. 'The bastard's been hit!' From his post, the wireless operator watched the Focke-Wulf break away in a vertical plunge. In its wake it left a trail of smoke and sparks, interspersed by brief outbursts of flame. It disappeared beyond a subtle bank of clouds. Moments later there was lavish flash of red that filtered through the cloud below and lit everything briefly like a crimson dawn. Then all was quiet. The Stirling had taken a considerable beating. The flight engineer made a list of the damage done. During the first attack, hydraulics to the mid-upper gun turret had been severed. All vacuum instruments were damaged. Additionally, pipe lines to number four and number two port petrol tanks had been punctured, and a piece had been shot out of the port elevator. Also, the starboard undercarriage was damaged. There were no casualties among the crew. The pilot brought the Stirling back up to height as the flight engineer limited flow to the damaged pipes. They passed over the Dutch coast without major incident, threading an erratic path through the defences out to the North Sea.

The crew of Stirling 'T-Tommy' were doing the same thing when they found themselves intercepted by a JU 88. Cannon fire exploded from below the port quarter. It struck the aircraft, tearing into the starboard wing and fuselage. An explosion of sparks erupted within the cabin. The wireless operator screamed and slumped forward. Not until the Junkers broke away on the starboard beam — travelling on a parallel course at about 400 yards — was visual contact made by the mid-upper gunner. He fired his guns and tracer was seen on all sides of the enemy aircraft, but there was no hit. It turned sharply, crossing ahead to port bow at a right angle. The pilot threw the Stirling in a sharp forty-five degree turn to port to bring the front guns to bear. But again the Junkers turned, then plunged in a deep dive to port beam below and disappeared — moving too quickly for the front gunner to get a clear shot.

The Stirling was flying on three engines, the starboard outer having been put out of action. The wireless equipment had also been destroyed in the attack, the wireless operator shot in the chest, shoulder and knee. The navigator laid him flat on the floor of the cabin where a puddle of blood formed in moments. And then the second attack began. A Focke-Wulf 190, 500 yards up on the starboard beam and 900 yards out. It made a diving attack, its machine guns and cannon firing red tracer as it sped towards them. The Stirling's mid fuselage and tail plane were punctured in several places as the pilot turned the heavy into the attack. The fighter continued to fire as it dived past the bomber, disappearing beneath it before the Stirling was in a position for its gunners to respond.

'Enemy aircraft dead astern! 1,200 feet!'

An ME 109. Its nose dropped in a sharp angle as it fell towards them — slightly to starboard — and opened fire at 300 yards. Several shots pierced the rear turret from above, missing the gunner by mere inches and slamming into the bulkhead behind him. The air was scorched. The rear gunner opened with a prolonged burst as the Stirling dived in a violent evasive manoeuvre, dropping to port and turning wide in a complete circle, losing 1,500 feet in the process. Visual contact with the Messerschmitt was lost, but there was a further burst of enemy fire from the starboard quarter. The wing on that side burst into flames as red tracer tore along it and ripped into the inner engine. The FW 190 had rejoined the fray.

Both enemy aircraft executed simultaneous attacks from the beam and quarter. Shells exploded along the length of the fuselage and the starboard flap disintegrated in a hail of cannon and machine gun fire. Another bevy blew in the bauble of the mid-upper turret, killing the gunner immediately. The front and rear turrets were both immobilised. In the cockpit, the pilot held the bomber hard over to port and trimmed the throttle on the outer port engine to compensate for full port rudder in a vain attempt to keep the plane on an even keel.

When the bomber hit the sea, it did so with its nose pointing slightly upward. The tail made contact first and the fuselage promptly split in two. A wave boiled over the broken halves. When it rolled away, the tail could just be seen protruding from the water. The front half rolled on its side. Within seconds, both halves were sucked beneath the surface, taking all on board with it. Such violent and traumatic ends were commonplace. For others, death was more instantaneous. Airgunner Jack Catford remembered the sight of a Pathfinder plane taking a direct hit on a raid over Stuttgart:

Very gradually it was becoming darker, although all the aircraft were still visible for several miles. We had climbed after dropping our bombs and were now at 22,000 feet. It was at that moment that I saw the Mother of all explosions! A bomber had been hit with a full bomb load on board. The cause was not apparent as it was quite a ways behind us and there was no flak at the time. A fighter could have crept in and scored a lucky hit. Anyway, there it was, a small red and orange blast which multiplied at an amazing speed until it resembled the mouth of a blast furnace. Green, red and yellow flames mingled with the orange so it must have been a Pathfinder aircraft. The debris spread over a large area of the sky, and gradually flaming and glowing embers fell, glittering as they did, into a slow curve to the ground far below. All that was left in the sky was a patch of black oily smoke, drifting, where moments before there had been an aircraft and seven men. Because of the nature of the calamity, no parachutes were seen.

Final Approach

'Wireless operator here,' said a voice over the intercom. 'Switching off jamming switch and turning IFF on.' IFF — Indicator Friend or Foe — transmitted a recognisable signal to British radar. Scientific Intelligence disputed its merits and argued the Germans could hone in on the transmission, but High Wycombe insisted there was no harm in letting crews believe it served a purpose to their benefit.[252] At 5,000 feet, the Stirling crossed the coast and a course was set for the airfield at RAF Oakington in Cambridgeshire. An ETA for base was set and the navigator gave the pilot a slight change of course. The aircraft banked gently on its new heading. Looking up from his charts, the navigator said, 'Fifteen minutes to base.'

Closing in on the airfield, the pilot put himself through to ground control to receive instructions for landing. The navigation lights of other aircraft could be seen all around, as weary crews circled the airfield's perimeter and waited for their chance to land. Below, another bomber touched down. 'Hello Q Queen, this is Foxtrot three. Your turn to land is three. Repeat: Your turn to land is three.' The flying control operator provided each aircraft circling above with the barometric pressure at ground level. This allowed the pilots to adjust their altimeters accordingly. When the aircraft made contact with the ground, the altimeter would read zero. And now it was Q Queen's turn to land. The front gunner had made his way up from his turret to the cockpit where he served as second pilot on takeoffs and landings.

'2,500 revs,' called the pilot.

'2,500 revs,' the second-pilot confirmed, making the adjustment.

The propeller pitch was set to fine and the flaps adjusted to one-third.

'Wheels going down,' said the pilot. The second pilot repeated this as he pulled the necessary lever. In the back, the flight engineer moved along the fuselage to the rear of the aircraft to check the tail wheel had lowered into place. 'Tail wheel is Okay.' Three red lights flashed on the instrument panel, signalling the wheels were down and locked in position. The Stirling banked in a graceful turn as the pilot steered it into the funnel lights. 'Full flap going out.' The airspeed began to taper off. Levelling the plane out, the pilot called for the engines to be cut. Immediately, the second pilot pulled back on all four engine throttles. The plane touched down with a heavy jolt. Not until the Stirling was nearly halfway down the flarepath did the tail wheel make contact with the ground. As the runway unravelled behind the aircraft, the bomber's speed continued to drop rapidly, until it was moving along the end of the runway at a mere 10mph. The bomber was then guided along the perimeter track — the pilot informing the tower his craft was clear of the flarepath — and into its parking bay. There, the engines were shut down. After listening to their constant thrumming for up to ten hours on some nights, the sudden silence was deafening. Airgunner Jack Catford recalls his post-landing ritual.

> I loosened the straps and hauled myself out of the turret then crawled on my hands and knees to the exit hatch. I was first out, with my arms full of parachute and sundry other gear. The ground crew were waiting by the exit and Robbie gave me a hand down. I dropped everything and fumbled in my pockets for cigarettes and lighter, at the same time trying to answer all Robbie's questions about the trip. The first puff on the cigarette was marvellous, after which I hurriedly moved away and attended to the very urgent needs of nature.

The action against Frankfurt on the night of 24 August — the second raid spearheaded by the Pathfinders — was not a complete success. Many aircraft bombed through heavy cloud, sending their incendiaries and explosives cascading into the open country around Frankfurt. Casualties that night were also heavy. Sixteen bombers out of a force of 226 were destroyed — a casualty rate of seven per cent. Five of those sixteen were Pathfinder aircraft. Among the dead was the commanding officer of No. 7 Squadron.

Prelude to Pathfinding

Bombing by night was an exceptional challenge. Visibility was often limited and the glare of searchlights made the task of accurately identifying targets a formidable one. The night — often coupled with clouds, haze or bad weather — was among an objective's best defences. To render Bomber Command impervious to such conditions, a special force was created: the Pathfinders. Its duty was to fly ahead of the main attack force — sometimes flying in low beneath cloud and haze — to search for the correct aiming point by use of flares. The Pathfinders would drop coloured markers to indicate points where the bombers should turn onto the target. Once the correct aiming point was located, it would be marked in such a way that the main force would have a definitive point of reference onto which they could drop their bombs.

By the summer of 1942, the idea of a Target Finding Force was a well-bandied concept. In November 1941 Group Captain Sydney Bufton, the recently-appointed Deputy Director of Bomber Operations at the Air Ministry, suggested creating such a force comprising six squadrons and their specially-selected crews. Bufton was a man not without experience, having flown ops and commanded Nos 10 and 76 Squadrons. It was while flying with the former that he pioneered the concept of using flares to identify the target and guide bombers on the correct course through the use of coloured verey lights. In the fading twilight of Peirse's reign at High Wycombe, Bufton put his proposal forward. But under Peirse, it came to nothing. When Harris took over Bomber Command, Bufton presented his idea again. Harris, too, rejected it.[253]

The new C-in-C and his Group Commanders did not like the idea of a *corps d'élite*. The formation of such a group, Harris argued, would foster jealousy and resentment among crews not deemed worthy enough for selection. Squadrons would also suffer from having their best crews taken from them. They were, said Harris,

> the very men who were needed most to raise the general level by their example and precept and who were required as Squadron and Flight Commanders in their own units; the formation of a *corps d'élite* seemed likely to lead to a good deal of trouble and might be thoroughly bad for morale.[254]

The Singleton Report had addressed the concept of a Target Finding Force. Singleton interviewed two airmen in the course of his investigation, later writing:

> They are both completely satisfied with the accuracy of TR 1335 (Gee) provided that it be used by specially trained crew... The crews are not by any means all of the same calibre, and the officers to whom I refer are firmly convinced of the desirability of a specially trained Target Finding Force, which, they believe, would lead to greatly increased efficiency and bombing.[255]

Harris wanted to keep such a force at the group level. Instead of forming a separate Target Finding Group under its own senior commander, he suggested each Bomber Group be led by the squadron within that respective group that netted the previous month's best bombing results. On 12 June, he wrote a letter to Portal and put forward his thoughts on the subject. Portal responded two days later, stating he understood Harris's objections to forming a *'corps d'élite.'* He continued, however, arguing that bringing the best crews from each bomber group together into one unit would guarantee the 'continuity of technique' and the continual improvement of methods employed by the new Target Finding Group.[256]

Essentially, Portal was laying down the law and ordering Harris to abandon his protestations. Harris had no choice but to reluctantly agree. He was not, however, burdened by total defeat and did manage to secure several official concessions. Men assigned to the Target Finding Force were to fly sixty operations, including those already flown with their old squadrons. As such, Harris requested that each man be promoted by one rank once he proved himself efficient in his new role as a Target Finder. After several weeks, this was agreed upon by the Treasury. Furthermore, Harris christened the new force himself, abandoning 'The Target Finder Force' in favour of 'The Pathfinder Force' (P.F.F.). Finally, he 'proposed... that the men wear some sort of distinguishing badge; as we were compelled to have *corps d'élite* it seemed to me necessary to carry the principle through to its logical conclusion.'[257]

On 11 August 1942, Harris received the official order from the Air Ministry calling the new force into existence. The Pathfinder Force was not immediately deemed an independent Bomber Group. Its orders would be issued by High Wycombe via 3 Group Headquarters. Six days after the official order was issued, the Pathfinders were allocated airfields throughout Cambridgeshire and Huntingdonshire.

Its initial composition — a squadron from each bomber group — resulted in a nearly all-inclusive range of aircraft: the Stirlings of 7 Squadron, the Halifaxes and Lancasters of 35 Squadron, 83 Squadron with its Lancasters, the Wellingtons of 156 Squadron and the Mosquitoes of 109 Squadron.

The Man from Down Under

In discussing who would assume command of this new elite, several names were mentioned. One was that of Basil Embry, a pilot of notorious reputation whose escapades during the Battle of France had secured for him a certain cult of celebrity within the RAF. In a two-week period, he 'brought home a damaged aeroplane on fifteen occasions' before his Blenheim was finally shot down.

> His ensuing adventures included escaping, though wounded, from a prisoner-of-war column, knocking his [guards] when recaptured, hiding in a manure heap, pretending to be an Irish Republican refugee terrorist and speaking Urdu when told to speak Gaelic, and eventually reaching the south of France on a bicycle.[258]

But whether Harris thought Embry too much of a wild card can only be guessed. In the end, he opted for Air Vice-Marshal Donald C T Bennett. Bennett recalled his conversation with Harris as blunt and to the point. The idea of a separate Pathfinder Force rankled Harris, for he believed it would weaken the overall strength of Bomber Command by taking its most accomplished crews and forming a *corps d'élite*. His resistance, however, had buckled under orders from the Prime Minister, which were delivered by the Chief of the Air Staff.[259]

Donald Clifford Tyndal Bennett was born in Queensland, Australia, on 14 September 1910. He joined the Royal Australian Air Force when he was 30 and soon transferred to the RAF to complete his pilot's training in England. By the time he was appointed commander of the Pathfinders, he was already a man of vast flying experience and held several long-distance flying records. Prior to the war, he served briefly as a fighter pilot before going on to become a flying boat pilot with 210 Squadron — commanded by Arthur Harris. Aside from his piloting abilities, he soon earned a reputation as a highly-skilled navigator and began lecturing at the RAF School of Navigation.

He left the RAF in 1935 and went to work in civil aviation, joining Imperial Airways for whom he piloted flying boats around the Mediterranean. By the time Hitler's hordes were devouring great swaths of Europe, Bennett was flying between Southampton and New York for British Overseas Airways Corporation. But with Britain at war again, the RAF beckoned. In 1941 Bennett rejoined the service and was given command of No. 77 Squadron and its Whitleys. He was then appointed Commanding Officer of No. 10 Squadron in April 1942. It was while with this squadron he was shot down leading a raid against the battleship *Tirpitz* in Norway. For his efforts, he was awarded the Distinguished Service Order upon his return to England. Then, on the day he was set to leave with No. 10 Squadron to the Middle East, he was summoned to see Harris at High Wycombe. On 5 July 1942 Bennett was promoted to Group Captain and tasked with leading the Pathfinders into combat.[260]

Off to do Their Best

The new group captain faced a daunting task.

The training of his crews was Bennett's top priority, for the success of future operations depended on their performance. Equipping his men with the latest navigational technology was second on Bennett's list, followed by devising a way to illuminate targets in such a manner that crews would not be fooled by decoy methods employed by the Germans.[261] The formation of the Pathfinders coincided with the Germans' first successful jamming of Gee — on the night of 9 August — when 192 aircraft attacked Osnabrück. The new force was coming into play with few advantages. Flak and searchlights over German cities were pushing the bombers higher, and night fighters were inflicting increasing casualties. Summer was rapidly waning and the crews would soon be flying in winter conditions. At home, there was no time to train. The day the force was transferred to its new airfields, Harris ordered that crews be ready for operations that night.

Though bad weather kept the Pathfinders grounded that first night, they were leading their first raid the next evening, 18 August. The target was Flensburg, an inlet on the Baltic Coast north of Kiel and a centre of U-boat construction. The crews were neither properly trained nor equipped for the task. Arming his bombers with parachute flares and wishing his men success, Bennett dispatched his crews to do the best they could.[262] Thirty-one Pathfinder aircraft flew with a force of 118 bombers. And in their inaugural effort, they would fail. The winds encountered en route were not as forecast, and the bombers were blown of course. What the Pathfinder crews — operating visually without the benefit of any improved navigational devices — thought to be the target was actually an inlet on the Danish coast, north of the intended objective. Parachute flares were dropped and the main force bombed accordingly. No bombs landed on Flensburg.

Three nights after the Frankfurt raid of 24 August, the Pathfiners were over Kassel. Cloud cover was minimal and marker flares were accurately dropped over the target. All three factories of the Henschel aircraft company — located within the city — were heavily damaged. But the apparent success of the operation was blunted by the loss of thirty-one aircraft, most of which were shot down by night fighters. Then the next night it was Nuremberg. In the belly of the Pathfinder aircraft were Target Indicators, 250-lb. incendiary casings filled with a highly flammable mixture of benzol, rubber and phosphorous that burned for prolonged periods of time. Over the city it blazed a dazzling red and was referred to as 'Red Blob Fire.' Crews were ordered to bomb from as low an altitude as possible, but Nuremberg's defences were fierce and the bomber force was severely bled. There was some damage to the city centre, but bombing was too scattered to have any concentrated effect. Along the outward and return routes, night fighters hunted their lumbering prey and inflicted further losses. Twenty-three of 159 aircraft were shot down.

Upon assuming command, Bennett declared there would be no living VCs in the Pathfinders.[263] It appeared, from these bloodied beginnings, the declaration would stand.

Basic Operating Procedure

Over Bremen on the night of 4 September the Pathfinders commenced the raid with a multi-waved assault that would become their basic operating procedure. At zero + 5, the Finders would fly over the target and mark the aiming points with flares. The Illuminators would back these up, dropping lines of white flares across the designated points. The well-lit area would then be bombed with coloured Target Indicators by the Primary Markers. The final wave — in prelude to the attack force — were the Backers-Up, and would dump maximum loads of incendiaries and douse the area in flame.

Barometric fuses sealed inside and set to burst between 200 and 500 feet would ignite the Target Indicators. Aircraft in the main bomber stream would line up on the flares and approach them from the same compass heading and drop their bombs as they passed over the marker. Throughout the attack, Pathfinder aircraft would remain over the target, dropping flares to keep the target area well marked. It was a complex process — one that would be refined with devastating precision in the coming months. As it was, the new method of marking debuted over Bremen wreaked great damage upon the Atlas Shipyards and the Weser Aircraft factory. The city's docks were severely blasted and an oil storage facility was blown sky high. Bremen's post raid report claimed anti-aircraft guns shot down one bomber — a number that provided little comfort to the suffering population. Throughout the city, it was known the flak defences were inadequate.[264]

But the risks of implementing the Pathfinder Force were inherent. If the marking went wrong, so did the entire raid. On the night of 1 September, instead of marking the industrial town of Saarbrücken, the Pathfinders inadvertently illuminated the small town of Saarlouis and its surrounding villages. Local residents were forced to seek shelter against the maelstrom of high explosives and incendiaries in the bunkers of the nearby Siegfried Line. Harris expressed no displeasure over the mistake, Bennett recalled indifferently. In fact, the C-in-C expressed his satisfaction at the news the Pathfinders were able to keep bombers concentrated on a specific target.[265]

Bremen and Beyond

Bremen was bombed again on the night of 13 September. Flying on this raid was Airgunner Sid Brans. He penned a letter to his brother one week later and described the experience:

> Since last writing you I have been able to add three more trips to my quota: Bremen, Essen and a mining effort. The Bremen trip was especially interesting for me, as it was there I went on my first 'op' when at Cottesmore. It was a bit different going in a Lancaster this time.
>
> When we got there we found plenty of opposition from the ground defences and the atmosphere was not at all healthy, in fact it's the hottest spot I've struck so far. We were hit by flak on our bombing run-up and found nine holes in the plane on our return to base, including one through the engines. The flight engineer had all the fun and games this time and one piece of shrapnel nearly parted his hair for him. However, the pilot never lost control and we got away with it all right, though coming out we nearly knocked down a night-fighter, which fortunately made no attempt to interfere with us.
>
> We were bucked on our return to find that our photograph showed that we had scored a direct hit on the aiming point, and in view of this we were given one of those 8,000-lb. toys to take to Wilhelmshaven the next night, but circumstances beyond our control prevented us from taking off at the last moment.

The raid inflicted further damage on Bremen's already battered industry. The Focke-Wulf factory was put out of action for more than a week. Five aircraft near completion were destroyed along with nearly 850 houses. The night before, 479 bombers left 20,000 people in Düsseldorf without a home — but thirty-one aircraft and crew failed to return. Frankfurt, Duisburg, Wilhelmshaven and Essen also came under heavy fire that month as casualties on the ground and in the air mounted. Frankfurt was the target on the night of 8 September. The raid caused little damage, but Sid and his crewmates were nearly killed. In a letter dated 10 September 1942 Sid again described his experiences over Germany to his brother:

We went to Frankfurt again and believe me it's the nearest I've been to 'missing on ops' yet. Our journey out was more or less uneventful, apart from the usual flak barrage on the French coast, and we arrived at the target to find several good fires already burning. There was a very large number of searchlights, though not as many as the 200 or 300 I saw reported in the press, but in spite of these we stooged over quite happily looking for a place to drop our bombs. We then turned round to make a second run-up, and trouble caught us good and proper. A burst of 'flak' hit us right under the tail and threw the plane into what was more or less a slow roll. Everybody and everything in the kite were deposited hither and hither and as we started to hurtle downward I remember thinking this was 'it.'

Fortunately the pilot had other ideas and managed to pull us out, and by violent evasive action we steered clear of trouble. Once outside the danger area, and finding that nothing was seriously wrong, our skipper decided to go in again. This was sticking our necks out for trouble, and believe me, it wasn't long coming.

On the next run-up a searchlight caught us, and in next to no time we were nicely coned, as pretty a target as any A.A. gunner could wish for. Hell and corruption burst all around and one shot blew in the Perspex of my turret. Had I been sitting in the turret instead of the bomb-aimer [position] well, there is no doubt that I should now have been nothing more than a nasty mess and an obituary notice in the local paper. The pace was too hot for us and, dropping our bombs, we beat it, the skipper literally throwing us all over the sky to avoid trouble. By the time we got clear, I felt as sick as a dog, in fact our navigator literally was sick.

Throughout the month, Mosquitoes of 105 Squadron flew several brazen operations in the face of the enemy. On 19 September six 'wooden wonders' raided Berlin by day. 'Berlin appeared in brilliant sunshine on E.T.A.,' notes the squadron's Operation Records Book, 'the cloud having broken abruptly. Bombs were dropped at 1600 hours and one burst was observed approximately ½ mile to the south of centre. Heavy flak was encountered and evasive action taken. Two fighters were seen, but these were evaded. The rest of the trip to the Dutch coast was done at low level. Flak was again encountered over the Frisians.'[266] All but one aircraft returned. Six days later they were at it again with another daylight attack — this time blasting the Gestapo Headquarters in Oslo from 100 feet.

All the while the Pathfinders struggled in adapting to their new role. That first month saw the force suffer a nine per cent casualty rate — a loss that would have proved catastrophic had it continued into September and beyond. By October, however, as the selected crews grew more comfortable with their specialized task, casualties dropped to just below three per cent and would fluctuate thereon out between 1½ and 4½ per cent. It was a rate, noted Bennett, which could be sustained without wiping out the newly formed force.[267]

October and Onwards

As Bomber Command continued to evolve, remnants of its fledgling years were retired from the front line. The Hampden — following a raid on Wilhelmshaven on the night of 14 September — was removed from operations. It had served its purpose valiantly, but was rendered obsolete in the shadow of the new four-engined heavies. With the Manchesters out and the Hampdens gone, the Lancasters of Bomber Command were concentrated in No. 5 Group. This had been Harris's old command, and it is perhaps because of this he assigned it operations that transcended Bomber Command's normal parameters. One such task was the 17 October raid on the Schneider Armaments and Locomotive works at Le Creusot, more than 300 miles inside France, near the Swiss border.[268]

Le Creusot was a small town of 22,000 people, yet its factory was the largest steel works on the Continent. To minimize casualties among the local French populace, the raid was to be a daylight operation, carried out at low level without fighter escort. On 1 October, designated crews from nine squadrons began low-level flying exercises over England in preparation for Operation Robinson. Ninety-four Lancasters — led by Wing Command L C Slee of No. 49 Squadron — would take part. The primary target was to be attacked by eighty-eight bombers. The remaining six were to bomb a nearby transformer station supplying the factory's electricity.

The force crossed the Atlantic at 500 feet — flying below the German radar screen — and dropped to 100 feet as they rocketed into France. They skimmed the tops of trees, avoiding German fighters — but not the occasional flock of birds. Four bombers were damaged when they collided with startled fowl. The sun was setting as the Lancasters reached their objective, climbing to heights of 2,500 and 7,500 feet. The flak was light as the raiders dumped 160 tons of high explosives and incendiaries in a mere seven minutes. All aircraft escaped damage by enemy fire. Only one aircraft was lost when — attacking the transformer station at low level — it slammed into the building.[269]

The crews returned to base believing they had inflicted much damage upon the factory. But images captured by RAF Photographic Reconnaissance showed the majority of bombs had blown apart the housing for the factory's workers. Many bombs had fallen short. Operational Research at Bomber Command, states the Official History, believed

...this was partly attributable to the failing light and the smoke which soon began to drift across the target, but they also thought the tactics adopted had been inappropriate and that the bomb-sights had not been properly used. They suggested that the outcome was the penalty of employing night crews in complex daylight operations without giving them more than a few days' training.[270]

In the days prior to Le Creusot, the Pathfinders led assaults against Osnabrück and Kiel. In the case of the latter, high-capacity blast bombs blew away 250,000 square metres of roofing tile and 150,000 square metres of glass.[271] Harris refocused some of his attention on Italy in late October. The Anglo-American armies were preparing for Operation Torch — the Allied invasion of North Africa — and British General Bernard Montgomery and his Eighth Army were readying themselves for the offensive at El Alamein, scheduled to begin on 23 October. The night before the Eighth Army began its push, a force of 112 Pathfinder-led Lancasters pounded Genoa. The Italian defenses were weak and the city centre suffered for it as 180 tons of bombs came crashing down. Not one bomber was lost. The British returned in force the following night, but heavy cloud and thick palls of smoke from the previous night's effort spared Genoa another fierce battering.

The next afternoon, Bomber Command dropped 135 tons of bombs over the centre of Milan in less than twenty minutes. The bombers flew individual routes over France, rendezvousing at Lake Annecy before soaring over the Alps. They encountered little resistance in their approach, but one Lancaster was shot down over the city. A university, the offices of the local fascist party and the Caproni Aircraft factory were all ravaged. Two hospitals were also hit. One Lancaster, according to Italian witnesses, thundered over the city at roof level as the front and rear gunners blazed away, cutting people down in the streets. Then, the damage done, the bombers turned for home, losing two more over northern France. Another, damaged by flak, crashed on its return to England, killing all on board. A storm swept across the Alps that night and scattered a force of Stirlings, Wellingtons and Halifaxes en route to Milan, saving the city from further punishment.

Foul weather battered Britain and northern Europe for the next two weeks, restricting Bomber Command's activities until the night of 7 November. Three days had now passed since the British victory at El Alamein and on the eve of the Allied invasion of North Africa, Bomber Command returned to Italy. The target was Genoa. It was the beginning of a month-long campaign against Italian objectives in support of the Allied desert war. 'Against such weak defences and with the excellent visibility that was usual in the Italian climate it was easy to get a good concentration of attack without any navigational aids,' Harris later wrote.[272]

Flight Sergeant Rawdon H Middleton, an Australian pilot with No. 149 Squadron, flew against Turin on the night of 28 November. Dropping to 2,000 feet, Middleton swept his Stirling across the city three times, trying to locate the proper aiming point. At such an altitude, he was an easy target for the light flak guns, which riddled the Stirling with holes. One shell exploded in the cockpit and tore into Middleton's legs, chest and face — blowing away his right eye and knocking him unconscious. The second pilot, Flight Sergeant L A Hyder, and the wireless operator were also hit. Despite his wounds, Hyder managed to maintain control of the aircraft, allowing the bomb aimer to eventually drop their payload on target. Though he had lost a lot of blood, Middleton regained consciousness and relieved Hyder of the controls. Through the pain, he set a course for home.

The flying was difficult. The cockpit was a shattered mess: the windscreen had been blown away and many instruments destroyed. Only through tremendous effort did Middleton succeed in reaching the English coast. Both his and Hyder's wounds were flowing freely; so severe were they, Middleton knew the bomber could not be landed safely. The dying pilot turned the plane on a parallel course to the coastline and ordered his crew to bail out. As his comrades disappeared through the emergency hatch, Middleton struggled to keep the Stirling steady. Two members of the crew opted to stay with Middleton, for he was too weak to jump. Together, the three men went to their deaths. The plane crashed into the Channel and sank beneath the waves. Middleton was posthumously awarded the VC. Hyder received the Distinguished Flying Medal.[273]

That same night, Guy Gibson dropped the first 8,000-lb. bomb of the war. 'Turin received it with displeasure,' he wrote, 'and I took a movie picture to show it bursting, and also to show the boys what it was like when we got home.'[274] Although the industrial cities of northern Italy remained the primary target throughout November, Hamburg and Stuttgart were attacked later in the month. Because of bad weather, the results were inconsequential. But technological breakthroughs in the field of navigation were around the corner — breakthroughs that would firmly set Bomber Command on the road to a devastating offensive.

X

The Technological Edge

Preparing for the Full Offensive

'Our experiences during the Blitz left us in no doubt as to the suffering and hardships of the population through the ever increasing attacks,' remembered D R Field, a pilot with 90 Squadron, after the war. 'But as with us, they had the alternative of evacuating the cities, finding adequate shelter or of surrendering. They had no consideration or sympathy for their own innocent victims and expressed only euphoria at Hitler's earlier conquests. The total regret one felt was that the Germans made it necessary.'[275]

Britain's third full year of war was now drawing to a close. Throughout 1942, the British bombardment of Germany had increased in its ferocity and forced the Germans to station more guns and fighters on its Western Front.[276] In the year ahead, Bomber Command would launch the full might of a total offensive against Germany and the USAAF would begin flying its first missions against objectives deep within the Reich. Together, British and American bombers would commence a round-the-clock campaign to shatter the Nazi homeland. But before 1942 ebbed into 1943, the daylight squadrons of No. 2 Group would undertake Operation Oyster, an exceptional raid against the Philips radio and valve factories in the Dutch town of Eindhoven. The date was 6 December.

The operation was tasked to ninety-three bombers — forty-seven of which were the new American-built Lockheed Venturas, a twin-engined bomber of questionable quality. Bostons and Mosquitoes made up the remainder of the force. The raid would be flown minus fighter cover, as the target lay out of range some seventy miles inland. Bostons would lead the assault and bomb from low altitude. A second wave of Bostons and Mosquitoes would bomb from no higher than 1,500 feet. The Venturas would then follow. American B-17s — escorted by Spitfires of Fighter Command — would fly a diversionary raid over Lille.

The losses were heavy. Fourteen of the ninety-three aircraft dispatched were shot down — a casualty rate of fifteen per cent. But the carnage wrought upon the Philips facility was extensive. Sixty tons of bombs ripped through the complex. Not until six months later would it again achieve full production. The surrounding town did not escape the blasts, as some explosions tore through the streets and killed 148 Dutch and seven German soldiers. Fifty-three of the surviving bombers arrived back in England peppered with holes. The number of aircrew lost amounted to sixty-two. Despite the significant bloodshed, the Eindhoven raid was an exceptional undertaking in accuracy and results. In the operation's aftermath, Bomber Command would benefit from breakthroughs which would ultimately improve its bombing accuracy by night.

Equipping for the Job

Oboe was similar in concept to the system used by the Luftwaffe in the bombing of Britain two years prior. An aircraft, tracked by two ground stations in England, would fly along a beam emanating from one station. The aircraft would bomb the target when the beam it was travelling intersected a beam broadcast by the other station (code-named MOUSE. The system was nearly two years in the making, but suffered three major limitations. Its operational range was no more than 300 miles, meaning it could guide British bombers to the Ruhr, but not Berlin. Secondly, there were only two sets of Oboe ground stations in England. Each pair of stations could only control six aircraft per hour, meaning that only twelve aircraft per hour could be controlled over the target. Also, once over the objective, the bombers had to fly straight and level for several minutes, making them easy targets for anti-aircraft fire.

In 1941 it had been tested as a blind-bombing device by Stirling crews attacking the German fleet at Brest. But the first operational trial of Oboe was not carried out until the night of 20 December 1942. It had been decided, because the number of aircraft Oboe could guide per hour was so limited, the Pathfinders — rather than the main force — would be equipped with the device. If it enabled the Pathfinders to mark the target accurately, it stood to reason the main force would bomb with greater accuracy. The first Oboe-dropped bombs were against a power station at

Lutterade, attacked by six Mosquitoes of 109 Squadron. Although crews reported good results, in subsequent reconnaissance photographs it was hard to determine which bomb craters were new and which were the product of a previous action.

Against Düsseldorf, two Mosquitoes put Oboe through its paces on the last night of the year. According to a report, six out of nine 'bombing incidents' hit industrial centres, though no severe damage was done. Later that night, three Oboe-equipped Mosquitoes attacked a night fighter control centre near Florennes, Belgium. Two of the three aircraft successfully managed to drop their high explosives from 28,000 feet through heavy cloud and hit the target. Operatives of the Belgian Resistance relayed the results back to London. Over the ensuing months, Oboe would establish itself as a beneficial system. In ideal conditions, under the guidance of Oboe, a crew could, on average, drop their payload within 600 yards of a target.[277]

Pulse

In the immediate wake of Oboe came another major breakthrough: H2S. A system of unlimited range, H2S was a ground-mapping radar aid, relying on the transmission and receiving of radar pulses from surface objects to create images of the ground below and display them on a cathode-ray tube inside the aircraft. Driven by an electric motor, the system's scanner rotated at 50 rpm and was mounted beneath the mid-upper turret of H2S-equipped aircraft. Developed at the Telecommunications Research Establishment, H2S was a link in the chain of the radar evolutionary process, a successor to Airborne Interception (AI) radar used in British night fighters and Air to Surface Vessel (ASV) radar used by the Royal Navy. Unlike the previous radar systems mentioned, H2S was developed with Bomber Command solely in mind.[278]

By December, some Halifaxes and Stirlings had been equipped with this new technology mainly through test installations. When flying on operations, the H2S operator would see on the cathode-ray tube nothing more than a flickering, shadowy image. Thus, using and interpreting the H2S-relayed information — being able to properly distinguish coastline from rivers and urban areas from open country — required skill and much training. There was an additional drawback. Over areas of mass urban congestion, the radar-relayed image would sometimes be indecipherable. This would be countered the following year with the introduction of a new version operating on a shorter waveband. At the moment, however, there was a more pressing concern.

The Battle of the Atlantic still raged. U-boats continued to take a heavy toll on Allied shipping. To counter this threat, the Royal Navy was using the magnetron-valved Air to Surface Vessel radar to hunt and sink German submarines. The same magnetron valve in the H2S system had yet to be flown over Germany. If a crashed bomber were to deliver that technology into the hands of German scientists, argued the Admiralty, the results could prove disastrous. They therefore urged the Combined Chiefs of Staff to delay Bomber Command's usage of H2S until March the following year. Fortunately for Bennett, who was anxious to equip his Pathfinder Force with the system, Churchill intervened. The Prime Minister was a great fan of technology and, on 6 May, wrote to Portal to say that he hoped nothing would interfere with the implementation of the new apparatus.[279] This had been preceded the month before by a memorandum to the Secretary of State for Air. Churchill was placing great hopes on the bomber offensive for the coming winter. The Air Ministry's top priority, he wrote, was to ensure that German cities suffer an unyielding onslaught of British fire.[280]

Churchill knew that if vast national resources were to be continually invested in Bomber Command, the bombing offensive's success was of paramount importance. So it was that on 22 December, Churchill — twice Lord of the Admiralty — sided with the Air Ministry. On 8 January 1943 the Combined Chiefs of Staff authorised the use of H2S over Germany. Thirteen Pathfinder aircraft equipped with Oboe led a force of Lancasters against Hamburg on the night of 30 January. The weather, however, was poor and the H2S system failed to yield the devastating results it would on future operations. During the day, six Mosquitoes raided Berlin. The masses had gathered that morning in the German capital to hear members of the Nazi upper hierarchy speak. The attacks were coordinated to interrupt the public diatribes of Goering and Goebbels. The air raid sirens wailed just as Goering ascended the podium that morning and again in the afternoon as Goebbels began his address. The bombings resulted in both speeches being postponed. One Mosquito of No. 139 Squadron was shot down. Squadron Leader D F Darling and his navigator, Flying Officer W Wright, were killed.[281]

As for H2S, its first success would not come until nearly two weeks later when, on the night of 11 February, the Pathfinders relied on the technology in their sky marking above Wilhelmshaven. This entailed the use of parachute flares of various colours to mark turning and aiming points in the sky. The city was totally obscured by cloud, but the flares were dropped with astonishing accuracy. The resulting bombing by 177 aircraft caused massive destruction on the ground. A great explosion ripped through the clouds. Crews reported the afterglow lasted nearly ten minutes. Bombs had landed on the naval ammunition depot to the south of the city. The resulting blast consumed 120 acres of surrounding dockyard and metropolis.[282]

Countermeasures

The Pathfinder Force became its own separate group — No. 8 Group — in January 1943 and Bennett — now promoted to Air Commodore — its first Air Officer Commanding. By the beginning of 1943, Bennett later recalled, his force had the men, had the technology and some experience.[283] The Pathfinders were now equipped with purpose-built target-indicators. The distinct, bright burning of reds, yellows and greens in the night skies above Germany could not be easily replicated by enemy decoy fires. Further technological advances were also made in the thwarting of German ground and airborne radar.

The slaughter of 18 December 1939 was attributed to the German use of Freya radar. For the Luftwaffe, it was the first line of defence. November 1943 would see the creation of a special force within Bomber Command — 100 Group — whose primary task would be to fly interference on British bombing operations and jam Freya through the use of a radio counter-measure known as Mandrel. This system was actually available in December 1942 and was fitted in the nose of several aircraft from each squadron. It was supported by a ground-based Mandrel station in Kent and Mandrel-equipped aircraft of Fighter Command that flew along the enemy coast, throwing up a 'Mandrel screen.' With Mandrel also came the development of Tinsel, a microphone fitted to the exterior of a bomber that could be adjusted by the wireless operator to tune in to German night fighter radio transmissions.[284]

While these and the introduction of other devices initially helped to slightly reduce casualties in Bomber Command, it wasn't long before the Germans were developing their own technology to thwart Britain's counter-measures. One incident seemed to play to the Admiralty's fears after an H2S-equipped Stirling crashed in Holland. Within months, the Germans had developed Naxos, a means of homing in on H2S transmissions. Nevertheless, the point remains, that 'after years of operating with virtually no technical aids, Bomber Command received Oboe, H2S, the target-indicator bomb and its first radio-countermeasures devices all in less than two months.'[285] The air war was on the eve of entering its most violent phase.

Sidelined

The force that had struggled for so long against poor bombing results, home-based criticism and, in the skies, deadly opposition was now poised at the beginning of 1943 to strike its thundering blow. 'At long last we were ready and equipped,' Harris boasted.[286] Bomber Command — by early February — had nearly sixty operational squadrons of which more than half were equipped with the four-engined heavies. The Bomber Command of 1940 was dead. The Bomber Command of 1943 would besiege Germany with devastation on an unprecedented scale. A directive issued on 8 September 1942 set the pace for the future bombing offensive. The American VIII Bomber Command would fly daylight operations. RAF Bomber Command would continue its night offensive. But Harris's much-anticipated campaign was sidelined on 14 January 1943, with the issuing of a new directive instructing him to carpet bomb 'the U-boat operational bases on the west coast of France.' It read:

> A decision has accordingly been made to subject the following bases to a maximum scale of attack by your command at night with the object of effectively devastating the whole area in which are located the submarines, their maintenance facilities and the services, power, water, light communications, etc. and other resources upon which their operation depend.[287]

Reason for the order was the 'recent serious increase in the menace of the enemy U-boat operations.' Included with the directive was a list of bases to be targeted by Harris's force: Lorient, St-Nazaire, Brest and La Pallice. Added the directive, 'you will initially undertake such an operation on the heaviest scale against Lorient.' For Harris, the directive was a grave frustration, resulting in the delay of a great offensive so long in the preparation. Since Bomber Command's previous diversion to maritime targets in March 1941, the Germans had set about encasing their submarine pens and construction yards in concrete shelters five metres thick. Not until the following year would Bomber Command have in its arsenal the 12,000-lb. bomb needed to penetrate such a barrier.

Lorient was pummeled on the night of 14 January. It was the first of eight raids against the French coastal town. By the night of 16 February Bomber Command had flown 1,853 sorties against this one objective — the only clear-cut result of which was the town's destruction. St-Nazaire, in accordance with the directive, was targeted next. Between the night of 28 February and 2 April, 794 aircraft were dispatched against the town. Again, St-Nazaire was destroyed while the U-boat yards, shrouded in their thick concrete shelters, suffered little. Despite the 6,000 tons of bombs dropped by the British at night and the 460 tons dropped by the Americans during the day on the two French objectives, the U-boat pens suffered little damage. On 5 April Bomber Command was released from bombing these objectives when it became clear they were destroying nothing more than the surrounding towns. 'We did, in fact,' noted Harris, 'devastate two perfectly good French towns.'[288]

The Casablanca Directive

In January Churchill and Roosevelt presided over their Chiefs of Staff at Casablanca. On the American agenda was the launching of a second front in northern Europe in 1943, a strategy backed by the strong support of Roosevelt's Chief of Staff, General George Marshall. The American war machine was fuelled by massive industry and seemingly unlimited reserves of manpower. It was a vast weapon Marshall wanted to wield quickly. Britain, an island nation of limited resources and only 48 million people, favoured a peripheral approach — slugging away at the edges and working inward. In Churchill's mind, changing the course of American strategic thought and delaying such an action would allow more time for the Russians and the Germans to wipe each other out. It also meant Germany would be forced to suffer the fury of an unrelenting bomber offensive long before any British or American soldier put a foot down in France.

Prior to the conference, Portal — on 3 November 1942 — submitted a paper to the British Chiefs of Staff. In it, the CAS proposed that an Anglo-American bomber force of 4,000-6,000 aircraft could wield enough destructive power to cripple Germany to the point where she would be unable to defend herself against an Anglo-American invasion. Portal summarised his plan:

(i) The paper assumes an Anglo-American bomber force based in the United Kingdom and building up to a first-line strength of 4,000-6,000 by 1944.

(ii) Such a force could deliver a monthly scale of attack amounting to 50,000 tons of bombs by the end of 1943, and to a peak of 90,000 tons by December 1944.

(iii) Under this plan of 1¼ million tons of bombs would be dropped on Germany between January 1943 and December 1944.

(iv) Assuming that the results attained per ton of bombs equal those realised during the German attacks of 1940-41, the results would include—

(a) the destruction of 6 million German dwellings, with a propor tionate destruction of industrial buildings, sources of power, means of transportation and public utilities;

(b) 25 million Germans rendered homeless;

(c) an additional 60 million 'incidents' of bomb damage to houses;

(d) civilian casualties estimated at about 900,000 killed and 1,000,000 seriously injured.[289]

It was a plan championed by Allied airmen on both sides of the Atlantic. Harris enjoyed a close, personal friendship with both Brigadier General Ira Eaker, Commander of the American VIII Bomber Command, and Major General Carl 'Tooey' Spaatz, Commander of the US Eighth Army Air Force. This friendship flourished despite American scepticism about area bombardment and British doubts concerning daylight precision raids. All were airmen in seats of power and understood the inherent struggles that plagued such a role. Just as Harris combatted the Admiralty for resources and his own strategic agenda, so too did Eaker and Spaatz struggle with Admiral Ernest J King, Commander-in-Chief of the US Navy, who favoured throwing everything at the Japanese.

In a letter dated 24 October 1942 Harris sought to help his American counterparts in a letter to Churchill, stating they were worried that the U.S. military would forsake the resources of American bomber forces in favour of the navy and army.[290] Harris received no reply, but Portal's paper, presented only days later, was officially endorsed by the British Chiefs of Staff on 31 December 1942. It was presented the following month at the Casablanca Conference with the full backing of the heads of the British and American bomber commands. If the Allies could not agree on the location of a second front, they could agree on the need of a combined bomber offensive. Notes *The Luftwaffe War Diaries*: 'The future fate of Germany at the hands of bombers was decided.'[291] On 4 February the Casablanca Directive was issued to the Allied bomber commands operating in the United Kingdom:

Your primary objective will be the progressive destruction and dislocation of the German military, industrial and economic system, and the undermining of the morale of the German people to a point where their capacity for armed resistance is fatally weakened.[292]

The primary objectives of this offensive, depending on weather and 'tactical feasibility,' would be the U-boat yards, German aircraft industry, transportation, oil plants and 'other targets in enemy industry.' The directive continued:

You should take every opportunity to attack Germany by day, to destroy objectives that are not suitable for night attack, to sustain continuous pressure on German morale, to impose heavy losses on the German day fighter force and to contain German fighter strength away from the Russian and Mediterranean theatres of war.[293]

'Whenever Allied Armies re-enter the Continent,' the directive reminded, 'you will afford all possible support in the manner most effective.' Strongly approved by Churchill and Roosevelt, the directive finally meant clear-cut backing for Harris and the men of Bomber Command. General Eaker and the American VIII Bomber Command would pour fire upon German industry. Harris and RAF Bomber Command would reduce German cities to alien landscapes of smouldering rubble. He was now free to pursue what it was he most craved: the complete destruction of Germany. On the night of 5 March he set about the task, commencing the first of his three great campaigns: the Battle of the Ruhr.

XI

The Battle of the Ruhr

And so it begins

For Harris, all Bomber Command had suffered and endured was a prelude to one specific point. Tormented by flak and searchlights and ravaged by night fighters, everything was but preparation for the main offensive 'that began at a precise moment'[294] when Harris launched his sustained campaign against the cities of the Ruhr. The first target was one previously deemed most worthy of destruction: Essen, a city against which Bomber Command had failed in all past efforts. But things would now prove different for 'at long last we were equipped and ready.'[295] Two minutes before nine that evening, the first red Target Indicators exploded above the Krupps Armaments factory. Led by five Mosquitoes of 109 Squadron equipped with Oboe, 443 aircraft descended upon the city.

Halifaxes would attack from zero + 2 to zero + 20. Wellingtons and Stirlings would form section two and bomb from zero + 15 to zero + 25. The last twenty minutes belonged to the Lancasters. As usual, an industrial haze blanketed the city, but as the plan of battle called for the Mosquitoes to mark solely on their Oboe fixes, it mattered little. Ahead of the main force, the 'Mossies' came in low and dropped yellow flares along the inward route to the city, stopping fifteen miles short of the main aiming point. Stirlings and Halifaxes of the Pathfinder Force — equipped with H2S — reinforced the marked trail and bombed the aiming point with green flares and incendiaries. The attacking aircraft bombed with one third high explosive and two-thirds incendiary, dumping more than 1,000 tons of bombs in forty minutes. The Battle of the Ruhr had begun.[296]

Through the wafting smoke and raging fires, photos taken by RAF Photographic Reconnaissance revealed the near-total devastation of Essen's city centre. Approximately 160 acres of city had been flattened — that included more than fifty buildings of the Krupps Armaments factory. Three thousand houses were destroyed and 500 people were killed. The city's defences had claimed fourteen bombers. It was not a bad result for Bomber Command's 100,000th sortie of the war.[297] Goebbels made note of the raid in his diary the following day, declaring Krupps had taken a particularly brutal beating. The severity of the British bombardment, Goebbels wrote, was making life extremely difficult for the German people and risked pushing the population over the mental edge. The Reich's anti-aircraft guns and night-fighter force were not scoring enough kills to deter Bomber Command on their nightly raids.[298]

The Battle of the Ruhr would consist of forty-three major attacks, half of which were intentionally brought to bear on targets at some distance from Germany's industrial centre, among them: Berlin, Munich, Stuttgart and Nuremberg. Objectives in Italy and France were also targeted. Three nights after Essen, British bombers were over Nuremberg. The city could not be visually identified. Flares were dropped late and through thick cloud. Bombing was scattered and the damage inflicted was minimal. The next night it was Munich, where 264 aircraft destroyed the aero-engine shop at the BMW factory. During these early operations, Bomber Command's casualties hovered between an 'acceptable' two and four per cent. But as the German night-fighter force reached its zenith, things would become increasingly bloody. British bombers were little match for those that hunted them. States the Official History:

Bearing enormous loads of bombs and petrol, these heavy aircraft, both because of their weight and on account of the need to conserve fuel for the long hours of endurance, travelled, by comparison with the German night fighters, very slowly, making an airspeed of perhaps 180 knots on the way out and 210 knots on the way home. Though they could perform the famous 'corkscrew' manoeuvre by which they sought to evade or at least present a more difficult target to the fighters, their manoeuvrability was, nevertheless, far inferior to that of their smaller and more speedy opponents. Restricted to .303-calibre machine-guns, they were substantially outshot and completely outranged by their cannon-equipped enemies. Their armour-plating was progressively removed, until little remained, to increase their bomb-lifting capacity. Belching flame from their exhausts as well as radar transmissions from their navigational and fighter warning apparatus made them all too apparent to those who hunted them. Once engaged in combat, they had little chance of victory and not much of escape, while large quantities of petrol, incendiary bombs, high explosives, and oxygen with which they were filled often gave spectacular evidence of their destruction.[299]

German ingenuity, too, played its part. Arriving over Stuttgart on the night of 11 March, crews saw flares and fires burning below and dropped their bombs accordingly, not realising the conflagration was ignited by Germans in open country outside the city. This failure was counterbalanced the following night when the Krupps Armaments factory was again severely blasted. The remainder of March saw Harris twice dispatch his forces on successful raids against the ports of St Nazaire, while prosecuting minor operations over occupied France and minelaying sorties off the Frisian Islands and Biscay ports. Skymarking was employed against Duisburg on the night of 26 March as flares exploded in the thick clouds above the city — but bombing results were poor, as they were the following night against Berlin. Two nights later, on 29 March, 329 Lancasters, Halifaxes and Stirlings returned to 'The Big City.' They were blasted and strafed by night fighters and flak, held by searchlights and blown out of the sky. Twenty-one aircraft — more than six per cent of the force — were wiped out. Not until 3 April would major operations resume with a 348-bomber strike against Essen.[300]

It was the first raid in which more than 200 Lancasters took part, with the force consisting of 225 Lancasters, 113 Halifaxes and 10 Mosquitoes. The night was cloudless and the bombing was severe. More than 1,100 buildings were either damaged or destroyed, including more than 100,000 square feet of the Krupps factory. Again, Bomber Command suffered a heavy toll as night fighters and the city defences destroyed twenty-one bombers. But on the ground, the situation was more dire. One week after that attack, Goebbels paid a visit to the city. He and his entourage had to walk to their hotel as the savaged roads could sustain nothing but foot traffic. Essen, Goebbels wrote in his diary that evening, was a complete write-off. The city's engineers estimated it would take twelve years to completely repair the damage. The Krupps factory lay in ruins, prompting Goebbels to speculate the British would now 'pounce' on Bochum, Dortmund or Düsseldorf.[301]

The next city in fact was Kiel, outside the Ruhr, followed by two consecutive raids over Duisburg on the nights of 8 and 9 April. Throughout April, for every attack Harris ordered against the Ruhr, he ordered an additional two against other targets in Germany.[302] It was an intense undertaking as night after night crews were sent into the maelstrom of some of Germany's most heavily defended cities. As the severity of the British bombardment intensified, so too did Goebbels' outrage, Churchill later wrote. In his diaries, Goebbels blasted the Luftwaffe for failing to stop Bomber Command.[303] But it wasn't for lack of trying. Against Stuttgart on the night of 14 April, twenty-three bombers were destroyed — five per cent of the 462 dispatched. Two nights later the casualty rate jumped to eleven per cent when thirty-six of 327 raiders were obliterated while attacking the Skoda Armaments factory in Pilsen. That same night, eighteen aircraft — nearly seven per cent of the 271 Wellingtons, Stirlings and Halifaxes — bombing Munich were destroyed. With the total loss of fifty-four aircraft, it was the bloodiest night for Bomber Command so far.

The bloodshed continued both on the ground and in the air as Germany stood hardened against the increasing ferocity of the bomber assault. Stettin — more than 600 miles from any English airfield — burned on the night of 20 April in a major conflagration that devoured more than 100 acres of city and thirteen factories. Twenty-one bombers failed to return, while eight of eighty-six Stirlings sent to blast the Heinkel factory in Rostock were lost that same night. In Stettin, nearly 600 people were killed. When RAF Reconnaissance arrived over the city thirty-six hours later, they photographed two dozen fires still raging out of control. On the night of 26 April Duisburg was bombed for the fourth time since the Ruhr campaign commenced. Essen was hit again four nights later. Since 5 March Bomber Command had flown 3,069 sorties against these two cities alone. And, from there, the Battle of the Ruhr passed into its second month.[304]

By this time, according to Albert Speer, Bomber Command's raids were beginning to make a serious dent in Germany's war production. The relentless bombardment brought the frontline to the German people, but failed to weaken their resolve.[305] As streams of British bombers poured over Germany's interior night after night, the burden of protecting the Reich's cities and industry began to wear heavily on Germany's fighting fronts.

One of the Reich's heaviest wartime expenses was the funding of the tens of thousands of anti-aircraft guns that pointed skyward, protecting Germany and keeping its enemies at bay on the western battlefields. The guns, wrote Speer, were desperately needed on the Eastern Front in the war against Russia. Had there not been a need for Germany to defend itself against Bomber Command, the nation's anti-tank defense would have doubled in strength. The hundreds of thousands of German troops required to man the nation's anti-aircraft guns was a detrimental drain on the country's fighting resources. Furthermore, Germany's optical and electronic industries were working at a frantic pace to supply the necessary hardware for the Reich's radar and communication networks. As a consequence, said Speer, Germany remained far behind the American and British armies in its supplying of frontline troops with modern equipment.[306]

The assault continued throughout May, though the month opened with minor operations against railways in France and mining off the

Biscay ports. On the night of 4 May 12 Venturas of 487 (New Zealand) Squadron were tasked with bombing a power plant on the outskirts of Amsterdam. From this operation only one bomber managed to make it back to England after the formation was set upon by nearly seventy German fighters. Noted the squadron's Operation Book: 'A very black day in the squadron history… a better set of boys could not be met in 30 years, everybody is feeling dazed by the news.'[307] The following night's objective was Dortmund, one of the most savagely hit cities of the campaign. It was the largest air assault since the Thousand Bomber raids a year before, with 596 aircraft participating. More than 1,600 people were either killed or wounded, while some 1,200 buildings went up in flame.[308] But if Duisburg was severely hit, then so was the force attacking it. From within the seething cauldron of the city's defences, thirty-eight bombers never emerged again. Two major operations against Duisburg and Bochum followed. Then, on the night of 16 May Bomber Command struck the Ruhr dams.

Ordeal by Water

No. 5 Group Operation Order No. B 976:

> The inhabitants and industry of the Ruhr rely to a very large extent on the enormously costly water barrage dams in the Ruhr District. Destruction of Target X alone would bring about a serious shortage of water for drinking purposes and industrial supplies. This shortage might not be immediately apparent but would certainly take effect in the course of a few months. The additional destruction of one or more of the five major dams in the Ruhr Area would greatly increase the effect and hasten the resulting shortage. Target Z is next in importance.[309]

The attack on the dams by nineteen Lancasters of 617 Squadron was an effort by Bomber Command to paralyze Germany's war production with the destruction of a single target.[310] The breaching of the Mohne and Eder dams would fail to inflict a crippling blow on the Ruhr's vast industrial arsenal, but it would stand, in terms of precision bombing and low-level flying, a feat unsurpassed in the war's many remaining months. Since the days of the Western Air Plans, the industrial destruction of Germany through the breaching of the dams had been a concept considered by the British planning staff. The Ministry of Economic Warfare in London had already identified the Mohne and Sorpe dams as those most vital to the Ruhr's water supply. Both dams controlled the level of the Ruhr river — from which the Mohne and Sorpe rivers flowed — used to transport tanks, steel and other products of war to and from the factories as well as supplying water for industrial and domestic purposes throughout the region.[311]

617 Squadron was formed for this specific task on 1 March 1943 under the leadership of Wing Commander Guy Gibson. At just 24 years old, Gibson had already flown 173 operations and served one tour of duty as a night fighter pilot. Crews, specially selected from within 5 Group, were assigned to the squadron, though the operation for which they had been selected was kept from them until the night of the raid. Training began immediately. Over the next six weeks, in burrowed Lancasters, Gibson led his crews in night-time, low-level runs over lakes and reservoirs through-out Britain. The bombs used for the task would have to be released from no more than sixty feet above the water and no farther than 600 yards from the wall of the dam at a speed of 250 mph.[312]

The specially-designed 'bouncing bomb' was the creation of Dr Barnes Wallis, an inventor and aircraft designer with Vickers Armstrong. Rather than a conventional explosive, Wallis envisaged a bomb that would bounce across the top of the water and detonate against the dam at a predetermined depth, utilising the 'tamping effect' of water to deliver the full brunt of the blast and destroy the structure. The weapon, code-named 'UPKEEP,' was perfected on 29 April — two weeks before the raid.[313]

Outline Plan

The twenty special Lancasters of 617 Squadron are to fly from base to target area and return in moonlight at low level... The Squadron is to be divided into three main waves, viz:-

(a)   1st Wave. Is to consist of three sections, spaced at ten minute intervals, each section consisting of three aircraft. They are to take the Southern route to the target area and attack Target X. The attack is to be continued until the Dam has been clearly breached. It is estimated that this might require three effective attacks. When this has been achieved the leader is to divert the remainder of this wave to Target Y, where similar targets are to be followed. Should both X and Y be breached any remaining aircraft of this wave are to attack Z.

(b)   2nd Wave. Is to consist of five aircraft manned by the specially trained crews who are to take the Northern Route to the target, but are to cross the enemy coast at the same time as the leading section of the 1st wave. This 2nd wave are to attack Target Z.

(c)   3rd Wave. Is to consist of the remaining aircraft and is to form an airborne reserve under the control of Group H.Q. They are to take the Southern Route to the target but their time of take-off is to be such that they may be recalled before crossing the enemy coast if the 1st stand 2nd waves have breached all targets.[314]

At dusk on 16 May, the first section of nine Lancasters took off from RAF Scampton in Lincolnshire. Led by Gibson, they flew in open formations of three and kept below 1,500 feet as they thundered across the English countryside. As land gave way to the North Sea, the bombers dropped to 100 feet to avoid the German radar screen and detection by enemy fighters. The Lancasters hurtled across Germany at chimney level. Although avoiding fighters, they were prime targets for ground-based anti-aircraft fire. One bomber in Gibson's wave was hit by flak and plunged into the ground, detonating the mine as it did so in a violent explosion.[315]

Ten miles from the target, the surviving aircraft climbed to 1,000 feet and continued their approach. Upon reaching the Möhne Dam, the small force assembled for a reconnoitering of the target then dispersed, waiting their turn as Gibson commenced his attack. He brought his aircraft down low, skimming the tops of trees as he aimed for the stretch of water leading up to the dam. The defenders situated on top of the structure laid down a heavy field of fire. Holding steady against the barrage, Gibson brought the Lancaster down to 60 feet. When the bomb aimer gave the word, the mine was dropped, sending up a huge plume of water. It bounced along the surface and exploded, sending massive waves sloshing up on the shore and against the wall of the dam. But it didn't breach the structure. As one Lancaster after another flew in, cutting headlong across the water against a maelstrom of tracer, Gibson piloted his aircraft up and down the reservoir trying to divert enemy fire. Despite his efforts, and those of Australian pilot Flight Lieutenant Mick Martin, one aircraft was blown out of the sky on its attack run and another was riddled with gunfire. As the fifth Lancaster, piloted by Dave Shannon, a 20-year-old Australian pilot, commenced its attack run, the wall of the Möhne Dam suddenly crumbled. Wrote Gibson *in Enemy Coast Ahead*, '…there was no doubt about it; there was a great breach 100 yards across, and the water, looking like stirred porridge in the moonlight, was gushing out and rolling into the Ruhr Valley towards the industrial centres of Germany's Third Reich.'[316]

Gibson ordered his W/Op to signal back to No. 5 Group HQ the predetermined code-word signifying a successful breach. The signal was

'Nigger,' the name of Gibson's black Lab. The message sent, Gibson and four other Lancasters set course for the Eder Dam some fifty miles away. The approach to the Eder was hampered by fog, and it was hard to distinguish the target from the surrounding hills. The positioning of the dam amidst the hilly valley also made the bomb run a difficult task. Shannon was the first to attack, but the final approach proved too tricky and he overshot the target. He made several more passes before opting to circle overhead and get a feel for the area. The second aircraft dropped its bomb too close to the target. The explosive detonated and ensnared the Lancaster in the explosion. The crippled plane flew over the dam and disappeared — the machine and its crew never to be heard from again.[317]

Dave Shannon then took another swipe. His bouncing bomb smashed into the centre of the dam wall — but the structure stood firm. Pilot Officer Les Knight's Lancaster was the last aircraft in Gibson's section still carrying a mine. Knight brought his plane in just right. The bomb was released and bounced three times along the water's surface before smashing home. As Knight pulled the nose of his aircraft up, the Eder crumbled. A thirty-foot wall of water came gushing through, flooding the valley and raged towards the towns below. Water churning beneath them, the four surviving Lancasters and their crews turned for home. Two had headed straight back for England from the Möhne. Of the original nine aircraft, five returned. One was shot down on the return trip.[318]

The second wave, tasked with attacking the Sorpe Dam, had crossed the German coast at the same time as the first wave, flying low and in close concentration. They had flown a different route and were ordered to attack the Sorpe from the lowest possible height. Only one Lancaster, piloted by Flight Lieutenant J C McCarthy, an American who joined Bomber Command prior to America's entry into the war, made it to the objective. En route, the defences had been fierce. One Lancaster had to turn back after it was savaged by flak. Two more were blown out of the sky and one had its bomb ripped from its undercarriage when it flew too close to the surface of the sea. On his own, McCarthy bombed the Sorpe but the single bomb failed to breach the structure.

The third wave of five Lancasters was to serve as an airborne reserve, but, like the second wave, suffered heavy losses when two of the bombers were destroyed by enemy ground fire. One Lancaster bombed the Sorpe, but the dam still stood firm. One aircraft, badly damaged, returned to England without dropping its bomb and one attacked the Schwelme Dam without success. The entire effort that night cost 617 Squadron eleven of the nineteen Lancasters dispatched. The cost in human lives was extreme. Of the fifty-six airmen to go down, fifty-three were killed. The remainder were taken prisoner. On the ground, nearly 1,300 people drowned in the tidal waves that swept the Ruhr and Eder Valleys. Together, the two dams held back 350 million tons of water. The initial damage was extensive:

2,822 hectares of farmland were destroyed, more than 6,300 heads of livestock were swept away in the raging torrent. Eleven factories were destroyed and 114 swamped with mud and water, causing severe damage. Numerous roads, bridges and railway lines were either destroyed or damaged — all of which had an impact on the Ruhr's industrial output, though it was one far from catastrophic.[319]

Had the Sorpe Dam been breached as opposed to the Eder, which was of no relevance to the Ruhr, the devastation would have been near complete. This simple mistake, wrote Speer, prevented the British from striking a blow that not even a thousand bombers could have delivered.[320] Though not an overall strategic success, the 'Dambusters Raid' was a propaganda coup hailed on both sides of the Atlantic. And it set the standard for low-level precision bombing. Gibson was awarded the Victoria Cross. The participating crews were honoured with thirty-four different decorations. Barnes Wallis continued designing aircraft until after the war, but would be forever haunted by the Allied loss of life suffered against the dams.[321]

Major operations resumed on 23 May with an 826-bomber assault on Dortmund. Throughout May and June, Bomber Command struck hard and sure throughout Germany. More than 700 machines levelled 1,000 acres of Wuppertal on the night of 29 May. Five industrial complexes were reduced to blazing ruins and 118,000 people were left homeless. Düsseldorf was struck again on the night of 11 June by 783 bombers. It was the city's second ordeal by fire in as many weeks. More than 130 acres of metropolis were flattened, rendering 140,000 people homeless. A sea of fire — measuring 8 km by 5 km — swallowed forty-two war factories and the local government headquarters. British casualties, too, were increasing nightly. Thirty-three bombers fell over Wuppertal. Düsseldorf's guns claimed thirty-eight. Over Mulheim, thirty-five aircraft were destroyed and forty-four failed to return from a raid over Krefeld. Rare now was the occasion when fewer than 500 bombers descended upon a city, leaving ever-increasing areas writhing in flames. Rare, too, was the occasion when bomber casualties fell below five per cent.[322]

Pointblank

American blood and machinery littered Germany by day. Flying the gauntlet of Luftwaffe day fighters, bombers of the United States Army Air Force were being mauled on a savage scale. Not until 27 January 1943 did American aircrews first cross the German frontier. Their objective was a fringe target: the harbours of Wilhelmshaven. The mission cost the Americans three bombers — an acceptable loss, but one that proved to be the exception and not the rule. More than ten per cent of bombers dispatched on the first four American missions to Germany were knocked from the sky by enemy fighters.[323] The Americans had brushed aside the warnings of their British counterparts who had learned early the hazards of daylight operations over Germany. They would pay heavily.

Churchill and his Chiefs of Staff travelled to Washington for the Trident Conference in May. Since January, the Allied bombing offensive had been waged under the aegis of the Casablanca Directive. In the months between Casablanca and Washington, American military planners behind the air war produced the Eaker Plan — a battle outline based on estimates reached by General Eaker. The idea was to coalesce the efforts of the British and American bomber commands and wipe out the German fighter arm. By Eaker's calculations, some 2,700 bombers would be needed by mid-1944 to adequately complete the task. The plan was endorsed by both Portal and Harris in April and presented to the British and Americans the following month and incorporated into the Allied air war as the Pointblank Directive.[324]

Issued on 10 June to British and American bomber forces in England, it asserted that American precision bombing of specific targets by day could be further enhanced by Bomber Command blasting the surrounding area at night. But the key to success lay in the destruction of the Luftwaffe's night- and day-fighter forces. In part, it stated:

> The increasing scale of destruction being inflicted by our night bomber forces and the development of the day bomber offensive by the Eighth Air Force have forced the enemy to deploy day and night fighters in increasing numbers on the Western Front. Unless this increase in fighter strength is checked we may find our bomber forces unable to fulfill the tasks allotted to them by the Combined Chiefs of Staff.

> In these circumstances it has become essential to check the growth and reduce the strength of the day and night fighter forces which the enemy can concentrate against us in this theatre. To this end the Combined Chiefs of Staff have decided that first priority in the operation of British and American bombers based in the United Kingdom shall be accorded to the attack of German fighter forces and the industry upon which they depend...

> While the forces of the British Bomber Command will be employed in accordance of their main aim in the general disorganization of German industry, their action will be designed as far as practicable to be complementary to the actions of the Eighth Air Force.[325]

Pointblank did little in cementing a combined bomber effort between the British and Americans.

In its wording — 'British Bomber Command will be employed in accordance of their main aim in the general disorganization of German industry' — Harris saw freedom to pursue his long-stated aim of destroying all of Germany's cities. As he later wrote: 'It gave me a very wide range of choice and allowed me to attack pretty well any German industrial city of 100,000 inhabitants and above.'[326] His forces were heavily embroiled against the Ruhr, and against this grand objective they would not deviate. By May, German fighters had forced the Americans back to attacking fringe targets in France and the Low Countries. Not until the last week of July would they again venture deep into Germany. Throughout June and the second week of July, the RAF continued its blitz on the Ruhr. A battered and scarred landscape of smouldering ruins bore testament to Bomber Command's growing strength.

Cologne again went up in flames on the night of 3 July. The homes of more than 70,000 people were consumed in the conflagration, as were twenty industrial plants. 'In no instance, except Essen,' Harris wrote afterwards, 'were we aiming specifically at any one factory... The destruction of factories, which was nevertheless on an enormous scale, could be regarded as a bonus.'[327] Amidst the searchlights and flak that night, British bomber crews faced a new threat: the Wild Sau, or Wild Boars. They were single-engine fighters of unit Jagdgeschwader 300, devised by bomber pilot Major Hajo Herrmann, and tasked with patrolling the skies directly above the targeted city. Wild Boar pilots were not restricted by the orders of ground controllers. They had free reign throughout the skies, pinpointing bombers against the illumination of the flares and fires below, the searchlights and the burning glow of stricken aircraft. The Wild Boars — who paid no attention to anti-aircraft fire — shot down twelve of the thirty bombers lost that night out of a force of 653.

Cologne was a city shattered. Three nights earlier, the RAF had delivered upon the city the most devastating raid to emerge from the Ruhr campaign. It left 4,300 people dead, and another 10,000 injured. By the time the bombers left, some 230,000 people were homeless. More than 20,000 buildings were levelled, including forty-three industrial complexes. But for Cologne, the ordeal was not over. The British returned on the night of July 8. High explosives and incendiaries blasted and burned a further 2,300 dwellings and 19 factories. In one week, 350,000 people had been made homeless in Cologne. 'There was, I believe, some surprise when the general public learned that we were attacking Cologne again, after damaging the city so severely in the 1000 bomber attack,' wrote Harris in his memoirs. 'But, of course, the 600 acres previously damaged left a good deal of Cologne still standing...'[328]

In the course of four months, Bomber Command ravaged Germany with 58,000 tons of bombs — a tonnage exceeding that dropped by the Luftwaffe on Britain during the Blitz, and more than British bombers had dropped in all of 1942.[329] Harris concluded the Ruhr campaign at the end of July. British bombers had flown 24,355 sorties against the Reich's industrial heart at a cost of 1,038 aircraft. Germany was burning, but its defences were still strong and its people far from weak. Harris — determined to break the enemy's spine — moved onto his next great scheme: the destruction of Hamburg.

XII

Gomorrah

The Battle of Hamburg

Harris planned the annihilation of Germany's second city in May as his forces waged their bloody war of attrition against the Ruhr. On 27 May, he issued Bomber Command Order No. 173:

> The importance of HAMBURG, the second largest city in Germany with a population of one and a half millions, is well known and needs no further emphasis. The total destruction of this city would achieve immeasurable results in reducing the industrial capacity of the enemy's war machine. This, together with the effects on German morale, which would be felt throughout the country, would play a very important part in shortening and winning the war.
>
> The 'Battle of Hamburg' cannot be won in a single night. It is estimated that at least 10,000 tons of bombs will have to be dropped to complete the process of elimination. To achieve the maximum effect of air bombardment, this city should be subjected to sustained attack.
>
> #### Forces to be employed
>
> Bomber Command forces will consist of all available heavies in operational squadrons until sufficient hours of darkness enable the medium bombers to take part. It is hoped the night attacks will be preceded and/or followed by heavy daylight attacks of the United

States VIII Eighth Bomber Command.

Intention

To destroy Hamburg.[330]

The operation was sadistically named 'Gomorrah.' But Hamburg presented a formidable objective with its fifty-plus batteries of heavy flak guns and twenty-four searchlight batteries. Amidst the weaving tangle of lights, crews would face a maelstrom of shrapnel, rocketed skyward by 166 88-mm guns, ninety-six 105- and 128-mm guns. More than a third of the U-boats stalking the North Atlantic sea lanes were built in Hamburg. It was a city boasting numerous ports and harbours. From its Blohm and Voss shipyards had been born the mighty *Bismarck*. Aircraft production and oil refining were also key industries. A mere fifty miles inland from the German coast, it was a prime target. Already, British bombers had appeared over the city 137 times since the war began.[331]

What Harris called 'The Battle of Hamburg' comprised four massive raids over a ten-night period, commencing on 24 July. That first night, Harris ordered a maximum effort and dispatched 791 bombers to do their devastating worst by the Hamburg populace. The crews would fly under the protection of a new scientific device code-named Window. Exceedingly simple in its design, Window was merely pieces of aluminium foil measuring 27 cm long by 2 cm wide adhered to strips of black paper. These strips were to be pushed out of the bombers through a chute at specific intervals during the run over Germany. These thousands and thousands of metallic strips clouding the skies would distort German radar with false echoes. The trials had been done. The theory was sound. Window had been in existence since early the previous year. Its use over Germany had been delayed because of the fears of Lord Cherwell. The premise of his concern was simple: if the RAF could jam German radar through such a primitive method, surely the Luftwaffe could utilise it for its own purposes over Britain. But Cherwell need not have worried. German bombers over Britain were rare in 1943. The majority had been sucked into the disastrous quagmire that was the Russian front. It was not until July — more than a year after Window's creation — following the personal intervention of the Prime Minister that the Chiefs of Staff approved its use. The confusion it would cause amongst the German defenses would cost Hamburg dearly.[332]

The first bomber — a Stirling of No. 75 N2 Squadron — took flight at 2145 hours, ascending into the clear twilight. From forty-two airfields across the United Kingdom they rose, silhouetted against the soft summer evening. Not until shortly after 2300 hours had the final bomber left English soil. As they hurtled across the black seascape, the first images began to appear on

German radar. It was coming up to midnight. Messerschmitts were scrambled from airfields at Stade, Vechta, Wittmundhaven, Wunstorf, Luneburg and Kastrup. But as the RAF intruders crossed the enemy coast — keeping north of the Elbe Estuary — it became clear something was wrong. The German radar screens in operation rooms along the coast were flooded with static. A signal officer in the operation room at Stade 'switched into the direct lines at the radar stations and asked what was the matter. He received the same answer from all of them: '"Apparatus put out of action by jamming."'[333] The German night fighters had been rendered blind.

The Pathfinders dropped yellow flares over the sea — just short of the enemy coast — to mark the way. A cascade of burning colour over Dithmarschen marked the stream's turning point. Bombing blind on H2S, Pathfinder aircraft dropped yellow Target Indicators and illumination flares above and around Hamburg at 0058 hours — two minutes before zero hour. Great swaths of the city were laid flat. More than 700 aircraft dropped 2,284 tons of bombs in fifty minutes. Twelve bombers were lost. Notes *The Luftwaffe War Diaries:* 'A major attack seldom cost the RAF so little. But for Hamburg there began a week of horror, the worst in its 750 years of history.'[334] In a rare joint effort between the British and American bomber commands, American bombers hit Hamburg the following morning through wafting palls of black smoke. They did so again the next day — flying a total of 626 sorties against the city — but were hampered once more by the thick blackness that drifted up from the ruins. Night brought the wail of air raid sirens on 25 July. Six Mosquitoes ventured to the scarred city and stoked the flames with more high explosives as the main brunt of Bomber Command's fury befell Essen.[335]

Firestorm

July had been an unseasonably hot month. Less than two inches of rain had fallen on Hamburg and the buildings were tinder dry. On the night of the second raid — July 27 — temperatures still hovered around 30° C by 1800 hours and humidity remained at a low thirty per cent. When the bombers arrived at 0057 hours, fires still burned. The sky glowed red and flames danced in the reflections carried by the clouds and smoke. Harris this time had dispatched 787 bombers, again setting zero hour for 0100 hours. At three minutes to, the incandescent yellow of the Pathfinders' Target Indicators flared above the city's shattered skyline. The Main Force was overhead within three minutes, unburdening themselves of their devastating cargo. The north-east section of the city bore the shock and — within a quarter of an hour — was a seething sea of flame. New columns of smoke ascended thousands of feet into the sky as maximum loads of incendiaries and high explosives were dumped amidst the conflagration. The big guns on the ground fired wildly, but accomplished little as the surrounding geography was swallowed by fire.

The city's cramped working districts went up like tinderboxes. In the district of Hammerbrook, the fires began to coalesce into one massive torrent of flame halfway through the raid. The city's emergency services were swamped. With water supplies dwindling, they were still struggling with the fires ignited during Bomber Command's previous visit. The unseasonably warm weather of what had been a pleasant July, the low humidity and little rainfall now played upon the Hammerbrook inferno. At 0120 hours the firestorm began. As the fire grew in its size and ferocity, so too did its rapid intake of air from surrounding areas. The more air the conflagration devoured, the greater it grew until it worked itself up into a fiery tornado that swept through the city with 150 mph winds. Streets turned to tar and terrified people exploded into flames as temperatures skyrocketed to 1,000° C. The convection currents sucked people into the fire and ripped trees and signposts from the ground. In the bomb shelters, thousands roasted alive and were reduced to ashes as the firestorm enveloped nine square miles of city. Some sought refuge in the city's canals, only to suffer burns on their faces and heads. Overcome by the heat, many simply drowned.[336]

In the raging hell that devoured Hamburg that night, 40,000 Germans died and nearly 320,000 buildings were destroyed — including sixty-one per cent of the city's housing and 580 factories. An additional 40,000 people were injured. Wrote Hamburg's Chief of Police in a report dated 1 December 1943:

> People who… attempted to leave their shelters to see what the situation was or to fight the fires were met by a sea of flames. Everything round them was on fire. There was no water, and with the huge number and size of the fires all attempts to distinguish them were hopeless from the start.

> …The fires spread with incredible speed because owing to the concentration of HE bombs and land mines, roofs were torn off, walls blown in, windows and doors torn from their frames or smashed, and the fires were therefore fed unhindered…

> [People in shelters] were already dead or unconscious from C.O. poisoning. The house had collapsed, or all the exits had been blocked. The fire had become a hurricane and made it impossible in most cases to reach the open.

Many of these refugees then lost their lives through the heat. They fell suffocated, burned or ran deeper into the fire. Relatives lost one another. One was able to save himself, the others disappeared. Many wrapped themselves in wet blankets, or soaked their clothes and thus reached safety. In a short time clothes and blankets became hot and dry. Anyone going any distance through this hell found that his clothes were in flames or the blanket caught fire and was blown away in the storm...

A population ready and prepared for the alarm were literally over-whelmed by fire, which reached its height in under an hour.[337]

By comparison, British losses seemed inconsequential. Seventeen of the 729 aircraft that successfully attacked the target were lost. The RAF had dropped 2,326 tons of bombs in a mere forty-three minutes. More than 550 bombloads devastated an area measuring only two miles by one mile.[338] It was destruction on an unheralded scale. The Nazi hierarchy was shaken to its core. It was the very fate Hitler had envisaged for London in 1940, as he explained that year at a dinner party attended by Speer. Maps of London, Hitler said, showed the city to be a cramped metropolis that — as history had once proved — could easily be consumed by a major conflagration. Goering, Hitler continued, had a plan to dump countless incendiaries on the British capital and create a massive fire storm that would overwhelm the city's emergency services.[339] Hitler and Goering, however, never put the plan into action.

The RAF, putting it to good use over Hamburg, 'put the fear of God' into Speer. Worried about the ultimate consequence, he warned Hitler that Germany's wartime production was dying a slow, painful death. If the British blasted six more major cities with the same ferocity as they had Hamburg, armament production would come to a complete halt.[340] But unlike other cities such as Berlin, Munich, Nuremberg, Frankfurt or numerous others, Hamburg was a relatively easy target. It did not require a deep or prolonged penetration into enemy airspace. Repeated attacks on near-successive nights on a city deep within the German interior threatened the risk of bleeding Bomber Command dry. And over Berlin and Nuremberg, the blood of British bomber crews would flow freely in the coming months.

In the immediate wake of the firestorm, 1,200,000 people fled Hamburg. Another 900,000 were left homeless. Like a spreading virus, a sense of dread emanated from the ruined city and infected the German popu-lace, according to Adolf Galland, Inspector of Fighters in the German Air Ministry. In military and political circles, there were slight murmurings that the war was all but lost.[341] But, as so many times before, the German people showed their resilience in the face of brutal adversity. The war was not over, and neither was Harris's obsession with Hamburg's destruction.

Two nights later, another 777 bombers returned. The city was exhausted and shattered, and the civil defences were helpless against the onslaught of another 2,300 tons of bombs. But the anti-aircraft fire — despite the British uses of Window — was more accurate and the German night fighters more determined. Twenty-eight bombers succumbed to enemy fire. It was the heaviest loss suffered by the British during the Hamburg campaign. A severe thunderstorm over Germany three nights later thwarted Harris's final strike. Four bombers were lost in the maelstrom of lightning and rain. The Battle of Hamburg was over.[342]

Nine thousand tons of bombs had changed the city forever. Bomber Command had flown 3,095 sorties against Hamburg over those four nights and lost only eighty-six aircraft. The use of Window, it is estimated, saved up to 300 bombers. 'No air raid ever known before had been so terrible,' Harris wrote afterwards. 'The second largest city in Germany, with a population of nearly two million, had been wiped out in three nights.'[343]

The Road to Berlin

The tide had turned. The war in North Africa was won. The cream of the German Army had been consumed amidst the wintry ruins of Stalingrad. German cities were burning on an unprecedented scale. From August until November, Bomber Command flew deep into Germany, hitting Nuremberg, Munich, Hannover, Mannheim, Bochum, Stuttgart, Frankfurt, Kassel, Bremen, Leipzig, Düsseldorf and Cologne on what became known as the Road to Berlin. On nights the British appeared over the German capital, the price paid in blood was heavy. More than twenty bombers were lost one night; nearly fifty on another. Such was the ferocity of the most heavily defended place on earth, even on nights with a waning moon and weather conditions ideal for the British. And while the British Eighth Army under Montgomery and the American Seventh Army under Patton were fighting their way across the island terrain of Sicily — en route to the Italian mainland — Milan and Turin were blasted from above.

On the night of 12 August, over Turin, a Stirling of 218 Squadron, piloted by 21-year-old Flight Sergeant Arthur Louis Aaron, was severely damaged by enemy fire. Shells tore through the fuselage, killing the navigator and wounding other members of the crew. Aaron was hit in the head. The shell smashed his jaw and ripped away part of his face. Another burst severed his right arm and one shell went through his chest and into his lung. The cockpit's windshield was blown out and the Stirling's hydraulic system was destroyed, along with one engine. Working through immense pain, Aaron levelled the aircraft out at 3,000 feet. The bombs jettisoned, the bomb aimer and flight engineer took control of the stricken Stirling and set a course for North Africa. They flew for four hours, as Aaron, unable to speak, relayed instructions on how to fly through a series of written messages he penned with his left hand. Eventually they crossed into North Africa and landed — after five attempts — under Aaron's guidance at Bone airfield. Nine hours later, Aaron died. He was posthumously awarded the Victoria Cross. The bomb aimer and flight engineer both received the Distinguished Flying Medal. Tragically, it was later established that the 'enemy' fire that wreaked so much devastation actually came from a nervous tail gunner in another bomber.

A target of supreme consequence, the German Research and Experimental Station at Peenemunde on the Baltic Coast — where the Reich's scientists laboured in their development of long-range rockets — was the target of 596 aircraft on the night of 17 August. The facility was scattered about a wide area and shrouded by smoke screens. To penetrate the veil, Group Captain John Searby of 83 Squadron would act as Master Bomber. He would pilot his Lancaster between the target below and the attacking aircraft above and relay to the Main Force the best Target Indicators to bomb. It was a daring role, putting him and his crew at risk from not only the ground defences, but the downpour of incendiaries and explosives. To throw off the night fighters, eight Mosquitoes flew a diversionary raid to Berlin and dropped flares above the city in a wild display of colour. By the time a contingent of Wild Sau fighters had descended upon the capital, the Mosquitoes had already left, leaving the German fighters to face the full brunt of Berlin's defences.

At Peenemunde there were three aiming points: the scientists' living quarters, the rocket factory and the experimental station. Not until the first bombs were dropped did the Luftwaffe realise what the real target was. The bombers attacked in three waves. As the final wave commenced its assault, German fighters arrived in force. Some were armed with the new *Schräge Musik* (known as Night Music, but more accurately translated as Jazz Music) weaponry — an upward-swinging cannon fitted in the cockpit of the twin-engined Messerschmitts. About 1,800 tons of bombs were dropped, the majority being high explosives that caused widespread damage and set the rocket programme back by about two months. Forty bombers were shot down: a casualty rate of nearly seven per cent and one deemed acceptable in light of the targets' importance.

But the bloodiest portent of things to come was two nights later on 23 August when 727 aircraft raided Berlin. Searchlights lit the sky like day and the murderous barrage of its anti-aircraft guns devoured bombers and their crews at an alarming rate. Fighter activity was extremely fierce and the sky swarmed with enemy aircraft. One bomber after another was annihilated, some detonating in mid-flight, others falling in flames in a long, spiralling descent. Fifty-six bombers were lost — 7.9 per cent of the force dispatched. Damage to Berlin was mildly significant with the destruction of more than 2,000 buildings and the loss of nearly 1,000 people. Thirty-three bombers were destroyed the following night over Nuremberg. On the last night of August, forty-seven bombers failed to return from another Berlin operation. Less than one week later — on 3 September — Berlin's defenders wiped out another twenty-two aircraft. Travelling the route to the German capital, Bomber Command lost its 5,000th aircraft on operations — a Lancaster, shot down over Hannover. By the morning of 19 October British bombers had flown 144,550 sorties over enemy territory for a loss of 5,004 aircraft.[344]

But there still remained a month of flights into the very heart of Germany before Harris launched what he hoped would be his masterstroke: The Battle of Berlin.

XIII

The Hardest Target

The Battle of Berlin

The raids on Berlin were a dazzling spectacle. Parachute flares threw a rainbow of color across the night sky and bathed the streets in shades of green and red and yellow. Grasping tentacles of blue and white light groped in the darkness, accompanied by the thunderous percussion of anti-aircraft guns and the seismic blast of high explosives. Thick columns of black and white smoke rose from the city as fires soaked the night in coats of red. On the ground, there would be much excitement at the bursts of blue and orange that signified the destruction of yet another bomber. To Albert Speer, the raids were visions of apocalyptic beauty, and he constantly had to remind himself of Berlin's harsh reality.[345]

Berlin. It was the hardest target and Harris's prime objective. On 3 November he penned a letter to Churchill. Behind the wording was Harris's unabashed faith in the destructive power of the bomber and his failure to grasp the basic truth that bombing alone could not win the war. 'We can wreck Berlin from end to end if the USAAF will come in on it,' he wrote. 'It will cost us between 400-500 aircraft. It will cost Germany the war.'[346] In recent weeks he had sent his forces to the German capital, but ignored the bloody portent inherent in the results. Between 23 August and 4 September, Bomber Command had flown 1,669 sorties against the 'The Big City.' The number of aircraft lost totalled 125. Another 114 returned suffering varying degrees of damage. The Berlin raiders had sustained a bloody fourteen per cent casualty rate. Any illusions the Allies harboured about the weakness of the German defences had just been violently shattered.[347]

Flying the on night of 23 August was Stirling R9288 of No. 214 Squadron. On board was Flight Officer Gordon Hart, the navigator. Their outward track was to take them over the Dutch coast and then south of Bremen to avoid the city's flak defences. 'We crossed the Dutch coast at Ijmuiden for Berlin,' Hart said. 'We were due to pass north of Amsterdam, but we were coned by searchlights as soon as we crossed the coast at 11,000 feet.'[348] Caught in the glaring brilliance, the pilot, Flight Sergeant H Triplow, threw the plane to starboard.

> I asked him to get back on track [said Hart] but he said it was impossible as there were too many searchlights. We were south of our intended track when we crossed Amsterdam and took a hit in the starboard inner engine. Immediately, the plane banked 90 degrees to port so that it was on its side and dropped like a stone because, at this point, it had no lift.

Casting an eye on the altimeter above his chart table, Hart watched the needle spin wildly as the plane plummeted towards earth. It slashed through the numbers —10,000, 9,000, 8,000 — all the while the searchlights maintained their hold. 'At 8,000 feet I realized I needed my parachute, but in circumstances such as this it was impossible to move. The pilot, needless to say, was doing everything he could to straighten the aircraft.' The plane dropped 4,000 feet before Triplow managed to level her out and escape the searchlights. But the plane was down one engine and still losing altitude. Hart concludes the story:

> Stirlings with a full bomb load and virtually full fuel tank cannot maintain height, so the bombs had to be dumped. Over friendly territory we always did our best to dump them in the sea, if possible, or open country. The call from the pilot was 'What shall we do, navigator?' We had to get back to base because we couldn't maintain height. We were equal distance from the Zuider Zee and the North Sea and I thought the North Sea route was the best as at least we were going in the right way back. I reckoned by the time we reached the coast we would be at 1,000 feet, but the pilot managed to stretch it so we arrived at 1,500 feet. I gave it a couple more miles and then told the bomb aimer to drop the bombs in the sea. This trip took two hours and 50 minutes. We were carrying 2 x 1,000lb. and 2 x 500lb. bombs. This trip counted as only half an operational trip.

The bombers that did make it to Berlin were savaged. A searchlight belt sixty miles in width surrounded the city and was reinforced by a flak area extending forty miles across. A maelstrom of light and shrapnel was thrown into the sky. German ground stations had monitored the British approach and established early on that Berlin was the target. Night fight-ers were dispatched accordingly. As the city's defences consumed the approaching bomber stream, the Luftwaffe swarmed in from all sides. Fifty-six bombers fell over the city. Three hundred airmen were lost. It was Bomber Command's greatest single-night loss yet.[349] But that number would be surpassed. Harris's belief that no more than 500 bombers would be lost in a prolonged campaign against the centre of Nazi Germany was a gross miscalculation. He also overestimated the American willingness to participate in such a venture.

Over Germany, the American VIII Bomber Command was not prosper-ing. Its losses were appalling and its casualty rates hovered near cata-strophic with each passing month. July had witnessed the loss of 109 American bombers. Another 107 followed in August. Bloodied and bat-tered, American airmen continued to press home their near-suicidal offen-sive despite the awful price paid in lives. 'The Americans gave us the best they had…' wrote Harris after the war. 'As for the American bomber crews, they were the bravest of the brave, and I know that I am speaking for my own bomber crews when I pay this tribute.'[350] Bravery wasn't enough. The American bomber offensive was on the fast track to a gory end. In September they flew fewer sorties and still lost eighty-three bombers in the process. But the worst came the following month with the US Eighth's second raid on Schweinfurt. The date was 14 October. Sixty of the 291 Fortresses dispatched were lost. Another seventeen were damaged beyond repair. The total casualty rate was a numbing twenty-six per cent.[351]

It was a stunning defeat for Allied air power and a startling victory for the Luftwaffe. Following this bloodletting, the Americans could not be expected to tackle a target of such ferocity as Berlin. Not until the advent of the long-range fighter would American bombers appear over the German capital — their first visit to which would be in March the fol-lowing year. In his venture to wage what he believed would be the 'the greatest air battle of all time,' Harris would have to fight alone. In his faith that it would end the war, he was resolute. He had not heeded the lessons of the Blitz. Far from pushing the British to the precipice of surrender, the destruction of their cities only strengthened their resolve. The Germans had not yet yielded under the massive onslaught of British bombs. This was not a matter of German character, Harris asserted afterwards, but a by-product of Hitler's dominance over his people. There was little the German populace could do, Harris believed, with the Gestapo breathing down their necks and the constant threat of deportation to the nearest concentration camp. The destruction of Berlin, however, would change that. So great would the death and carnage be, the enemy would have no choice but to lay down their arms. Bombs would indeed leave Berlin in shattered ruins, but its destruction would be wreaked by the Red Tide that eventually came crashing down from the east.

Harris purposely resisted orders throughout 1942 to send his men and machines to Berlin. He knew what it entailed and realised his force was not prepared to handle such a formidable opponent. The legacy of Black Friday had cast a long shadow over any intention to attack the German capital. By 1943 circumstances had changed and the time for an assault on the heart of the Nazi Empire seemed right — especially in the wake of Stalingrad. It was Portal's opinion that the British should pour a liberal amount of salt in Germany's wounds with further attacks on Berlin.[352] Three raids of little consequence followed in March. Then there were the bloody excursions in August and September before Harris commenced his full-throttle assault on Berlin on the night of 18 November.[353]

It would be the last of Harris's three great campaigns. British and American strategists were planning the conquest of Fortress Europe. While their bomber commands would continue to play a vital role in the deconstruction of German military might, it would be secondary to the contribution of the Anglo-American armies. Ironically, it was Harris's intention to render the invasion of Europe unnecessary. He was mindful of the apocalyptic bloodshed suffered by the Allies in the first war to end all wars. Contemplating the fiery holocaust that was Hamburg, Harris believed bombing 'to be a comparatively humane method. For one thing, it saved the flower of the youth of this country and of our allies from being mown down by the military in the field, as it was in Flanders in the war of 1914-1918.'[354]

Across the barbed-wire scarred landscape of France and the sun-baked regions of the Middle East, more than 900,000 Britons fell in the First World War. Aligned a second time against Germany, Britain would send 303,240 men to their deaths. They shed blood on the shores of Dunkirk and the sands of North Africa. They fell in the jungles of Burma against Japan and on the beaches of Normandy. The 'flower' of British youth might have been spared the catastrophic fate that befell the generation before them, but it had little to do with bombing and much to do with the amount of time that lapsed between the British Army's expulsion from France in 1940 and its part in the retaking of Europe four years later.[355]

By August — with the cities of the Ruhr burning and Hamburg virtually destroyed — Harris was confident that Germany was hurtling towards the brink. That month he wrote to Portal, expressing his firm belief that 'we are on the verge of a final showdown in the bombing war...' Like the Battle of the Ruhr before it, the air battle that bore Berlin's name would not be a set campaign against a single objective, but a series of raids against several targets. Berlin would bear the brunt of the assaults and throw at Bomber Command everything it had. It would be, for British bomber crews, the bloodiest season.

A Bitter Winter

Albert Speer was sitting in his private office at the Armaments Ministry in Berlin when the air raid sirens began to shriek. It had just gone 1930 hours on 22 November. The British had ventured to the city four nights earlier, but had caused only minor damage — a fact attributed to the heavy cloud cover that night. It was also perhaps the reason why the British themselves had suffered so lightly for their efforts. Few German fighters had succeeded in engaging the bombers. Only nine British aircraft were shot down. Now the bombers were back and would have to again contend with the shoddy weather conditions. Speer left his office, got in his car and drove quickly to a nearby flak tower to take shelter. Huddling masses were already there with blankets and food, waiting for the cannonade of bombs to begin. As he often did, Speer climbed a winding staircase along the tower's inner wall up to an observation deck at the top of the structure. Here he planned to watch the city burn yet again. But no sooner had he stepped out into the chilled night, than a massive explosion ripped the air from his lungs and rattled the tower's thick concrete walls. Speer hurriedly retreated inside, where the gathered crowd was attempting to make room for a number of injured anti-aircraft gunners. Another high-explosive detonated nearby and unleashed thick clouds of cement dust from the tower's walls and ceilings. Explosion followed explosion for nearly thirty minutes. The percussion of the blasts frayed nerves and jarred teeth. The air inside the tower grew thick with dust that stung the eyes and irritated the throat. When the bombers finally left, Speer climbed to the observation deck and took in the damage. His Ministry building was ablaze. He ran downstairs and leapt in his car, manoeuvring through the ravaged streets as fast as he could. When he reached his destination, in the place of his private office all he found was a massive crater.[356]

Berlin's three flak towers were formidable structures of concrete and steel. On top of each were eight 128-mm guns theoretically capable of destroying a bomber at 45,000 feet. Though the city lay shrouded beneath a heavy layer of cumulus, the bombers cut a destructive swath through the centre of Berlin. The damage radiated westward to the suburbs. Fires were rampant and thick columns of smoke ascended to 19,000 feet. The Ministry of Weapons and Munitions, the Waffen SS Administrative College and the Alkett tank works were among the numerous buildings either heavily damaged or totally destroyed. To the city, Harris had dispatched 764 bombers. They attacked in five waves as the guns atop the flak tower hurled their projectiles skyward. Twenty-six bombers were torn through and never returned. It was an acceptable 3.4 per cent casualty rate. On the ground, an estimated 2,000 people died under the bombs. Another 175,000 were left without homes. Nearly three whole army divisions — some 50,000 troops — had to be called in to help with the clean-up effort. For Berlin, it would prove to be the most devastating raid of the war.[357]

The battle for the German capital was underway, and would rage until March. It was destined to be a bitter winter for those on both sides. For the men in the bombers, it would be a vicious test of endurance. Beyond the range of Gee and Oboe, the city lay 650 miles from the nearest English airfield. The cover of darkness was vital to British survival over Germany, thus the distance would be flown amidst the coldest winter conditions and the longest nights. 'The whole battle was fought in appalling weather,' wrote Harris after the war, 'and in conditions resembling those of no other campaign in the history of warfare. Scarcely a single crew caught a single glimpse of the objective they were attacking and for long periods we were wholly ignorant, except from such admissions the enemy made from to time to time, of how the battle was going.'[358]

The wintry conditions also made it hard for the opposition. Thick layers of cloud prevented German searchlights from pinpointing specific targets for the defenders on the ground. But the glare of the searchlights emanated brightly from beneath the cloud and — coupled with the glow of the burning city — silhouetted the bombers against the haze making them clearly visible to the night fighters ranging above them.[359] This season marked the confrontational highpoint between the Luftwaffe and Bomber Command. Men and machinery faced off not only against one another, but wind, rain, snow and icing. Mannheim, Stuttgart, Frankfurt, Leipzig, Brunswick, Schweinfurt, Augsburg and Magdeburg were all subjected to massive area attacks. Explosives and incendiaries decimated entire neighborhoods.[360] Hearts were ripped from city centres, and structures that had stood since medieval times were swallowed by flame. Numbers ranging near the hundred of thousands — sometimes more — were left homeless in a single night. Germany, once proud and strong, was dissolving into a nation of shattered ruins. And still the bombers returned again and again to Berlin. A Royal Artillery major flying as an observer in a Mosquito over the German capital on the night of 26 November wrote the following after returning to base:

We approached Berlin from the West and observed the defences of Brunswick and Magdeburg in action — vast numbers of searchlights could be seen exposed in a dense wide belt all around Berlin. We flew at 31,000 feet… In about 20 seconds, we were illuminated by three to four search lights which exposed straight on to us. In a matter of seconds, these were joined by many other beams. I was able to count 31 beams dead on us and it was light as day in the aircraft.[361]

In the skies they dived and weaved, the gunners shrieking orders to the pilot as fighters throttled full bore towards them. Aircraft returned riddled with gunfire. Sometimes the remains of a gunner had to be hosed from a shattered turret. Sometimes the entire turret was shot away — occupant and all. The crews of the low-flying Stirlings suffered terribly. They were decimated by light and heavy flak and crippled by roaming night fighters. Since the vicious loss suffered over Berlin on the night of 23 August, 280 Stirlings had taken part in three major operations against the city. Being easy prey for all that was against them, thirty-seven failed to return. It was a casualty rate of more than thirteen per cent — one even Harris couldn't stomach. 'It's murder,' Harris was quoted as saying, 'plain murder to send my young men out to die in an aircraft like that!' The Stirling was withdrawn from bombing operations after the Berlin raid of 22 November. The task of battering Germany now fell to the Lancasters, Halifaxes and Mosquitos.[362]

By the end of November, more than 400,000 Berliners had been bombed onto the streets. Eighty-three bombers — the vast majority Lancasters — had been lost in three raids over the German capital since the night of 18 November. Total losses for the month numbered 170. They fell all over Germany. Leverkusen, Ludwigshaven, Cologne and numerous other cities were strewn with the ruins of shattered bombers. 'By November,' Harris wrote afterwards, 'the [German] fighter defence had been reorganised and strongly reinforced…'[363]

The first major operation of December was a raid over Berlin by 458 Lancasters, Mosquitoes and Halifaxes. Fighters were waiting. German ground stations had identified Berlin as the target nearly twenty minutes before the assault began. By the time the bombers arrived, they had already lost cohesion, scattered by winds incorrectly forecast and thick icing. The fighters swarmed in and out of the fractured bomber stream, annihilating one aircraft after the other to the accompaniment of flak from below. Bombing was widely scattered. Some explosives fell in the open countryside on the outskirts of the city. Damage was light, but British casualties were extreme. Forty bombers — nearly nine per cent of the attack force — were wiped out.[364]

Aside from its defences, Berlin's size and the layout of its streets worked against the British effort. The city covered 900 square miles, making it harder to inflict severe damage in heavily concentrated areas. The city's geographical layout did not provide any clear physical features on which H2S — relied upon by the Pathfinders — could easily home. It was a metropolis of large parks and wide streets — areas where incendiaries could fall and burn to little effect. During the four-month campaign, Berlin would be hit sixteen times. 'Thousands upon thousands of tons of bombs were aimed at the Pathfinders' pyrotechnic skymarkers and fell through unbroken cloud which concealed everything below it except the confused glare of fires,' wrote Harris.[365] The city — and its people — would remain defiant.

Ten thousand people were bombed out of their Berlin homes on the night of 29 December. The city could be seen burning from 200 miles away. It was the heaviest raid to befall the capital that month, and cost the British twenty of the 712 aircraft dispatched. The total number of bombers lost that month was 174. 'In consequence British Bomber Command,' states *The Luftwaffe War Diaries*, 'which in November, 1943, was confident that it had air sovereignty over Germany, was by December again suffering heavy losses. In January and February the casualty rate continued to ascend, and finally reached an all-time high in March 1944.'[366] But Harris, in early December, remained confident. On the second anniversary of Pearl Harbor, he penned a letter to the Air Ministry. He foresaw, within the next three months, having forty Lancaster squadrons at his disposal. He wrote: 'From this it appears that the Lancaster force alone should be sufficient but only just sufficient to produce in Germany by April 1st, 1944, a state of devastation in which surrender is inevitable.'[367] The words are deemed more ironic in hindsight as Bomber Command was on the verge of suffering its greatest loss of the entire war.

Victory Denied

British and American airmen bled and suffered by day and night in the vast expanse of the harshest of combat environs. Against the most determined foe they were outgunned and outmanoeuvred. But the tide turned in favour of the Allied air forces in December with the arrival of the North American P-51 Mustang. It was a hybrid of British and American ingenuity: an American body and armaments, powered by a British Merlin engine by Rolls Royce. Equipped with its disposable drop tanks, it boasted a top speed of 455 mph at 30,000 feet. Top priority was given to equipping the beleaguered US Eighth Air Force with the new machine. Over the next three months, the number of Mustangs taking to the skies would increase at an extraordinary rate. They would become the scourge of the Luftwaffe, reigning supreme over the German fighter force and inflicting devastating losses. But before that happened, Bomber Command would be severely bled.

Raids over Berlin on the first two nights of January proved ineffective. Fighters heavily engaged the bombers on both nights. Casualties were extreme. In two nights, Bomber Command lost fifty-five out of 804 aircraft. The bloodletting continued two weeks later on 14 January with the destruction of thirty-eight raiders over Brunswick. Another thirty-five were wiped out over Berlin one week later. On the night of 21 January fifty-seven bombers from a force of 648 were destroyed flying against Magdeburg. The German night fighter force were now relying on a new method of attack — Tame Boar tactics — to counter the British use of Window. Window, which had caused the German defenders so much grief, was being thwarted by a new German radar dubbed SN-2, operating on a frequency unaffected by the British proliferation of metallic strips in the sky. The new system was fitted into the twin-engine night fighters that had been rendered ineffective by Window. Now they could track the bomber stream to and from the target, flying amidst the enemy and shooting them down at will.[368] Such tactics had been used to great effect on the night Magdeburg was attacked.

Bombers were being churned out at a steady rate, as were the crews to fly them. This was just as well; Bomber Command was losing men and machinery at a terrifying rate. In spite of this, it still managed to inflict grievous wounds upon the Reich. Twenty-thousand Berliners were bombed out on the night of 27 January. It cost Harris thirty-three bombers. The following night, his forces returned and bombed out another 180,000 people. This time, forty-six aircraft failed to return. A Berlin report for the night of 28 January states: 'The casualties are still not known but they are bound to be considerable. It is reported that a vast amount of wreckage must still be cleared; rescue workers are among the mountains of it.'[369] The British raided Berlin six times in January. Bomber losses for the month reached a staggering 321.

Amidst the mass slaughter, 617 Squadron of Dambusters fame executed a daring low-level attack on the Gnome and Rhone aero-engine factory in Limoges, France. The raid was led by the squadron's new commanding officer, Wing Commander Leonard Cheshire. Having experimented with low-level marking, Cheshire was curious to see how effective it was during actual operations. Spearheading twelve Lancasters against the factory, he swooped over the objective and buzzed it three times to alert the French factory workers inside. Then he dropped his flares from between fifty and 100 feet along with a load of incendiaries. The following eleven aircraft each dropped the RAF's new 12,000-lb. bomb atop the conflagration with great accuracy. All but one explosive found its mark. Production at the factory was brought to a near total standstill. But the crowning achievement was the return of all twelve bombers and their crews.

Berlin was hit only once in February. The largest bomber force since the Thousand Bomber raids two years earlier was assembled for the night of February 15. The attack force numbered 826 — 561 Lancasters, 314 Halifaxes and sixteen Mosquitos — and dropped a record quantity of explosives: 2,642 tons. More than 1,110 fires ravaged the city and consumed 1,000 houses and a vast number of the temporary wooden barracks that had been set up. Columns of smoke rose 20,000 feet into the air. Civilian casualties were relatively light. By now, most of the Berlin populace — perhaps influenced by the holocaust in Hamburg — had fled the city. Fighters and flak knocked twenty-six Lancasters and seventeen Halifaxes out of the sky. Harris's final attempt to destroy Berlin would not come until the following month when the Battle of Berlin came to a close.[370]

Until then, Harris struck out at other targets, dispatching between 500 and 900 bombers nightly to level as much urban ground as they possibly could. On 19 February 823 aircraft were sent to Leipzig. Seventy-eight of them — nearly ten per cent — never made it home. Five nights later, British bombers flew in support of an American raid on Schweinfurt and lost thirty-three aircraft in the process. It was part of 'Big Week' — commenced on 20 February — an effort by the American Eighth and Fifteenth Air Forces to wipe out German aircraft factories. Harris participated reluctantly and was quick to turn his attention back to the area-bombing campaign. Nearly 600 aircraft dropped 2,000 tons of bombs on Augsburg the following night. The raid was incontrovertibly successful. The centre of the city was completely obliterated and 90,000 people were left without homes in temperatures as low as eighteen below zero. More than 1,000 fires were left burning. The Germans publicised the raid as an extreme example of Britain's 'terror bombing.'[371]

The final month of the Berlin campaign, March, was Bomber Command's bloodiest. For all intents and purposes, the Battle of Berlin was already over. Harris had been denied his victory by bombing. He turned his attention elsewhere. Twice that month, Frankfurt came under fire. Both raids — on the nights of 18 and 22 March — wrought heavy devastation upon the city. More than 170,000 people were left homeless and more than two dozen Nazi party buildings were destroyed. The total number of sorties Bomber Command flew in the two raids was 1,662, of which fifty-five never returned. It was a casualty rate of about three per cent — a number inconsequential in light of what was to come.

In hindsight, Harris came just short of ruling the Battle of Berlin a failure. He wrote:

> Judged by the standards of our attacks on Hamburg, the Battle of Berlin did not appear to be an overwhelming success. With many times as many sorties, a far greater bomb load, and ten times as many casualties, we appeared to have succeeded in destroying about a third of the acreage destroyed in the attack on Hamburg...[372]

His last major effort against Berlin came on 24 March. To the capital he dispatched 811 bombers. Powerful winds blowing in from the north scattered the bombers en route to the target and made marking difficult for the Pathfinders. Bombing was scattered and damage to industrial complexes was not of major consequence. As always, a substantial amount of housing was wiped out, forcing another 20,000 people onto the streets. The flak was intense and took a heavy toll. The strong winds continued to harass the bombers on their flight home, pushing some over the Ruhr where more aircraft fell to the ground defences. The number lost that night totalled seventy-two, of which night fighters destroyed fourteen. The nights were linked in a seemingly unbreakable chain of horrendous bloodshed.

Throughout the four-month campaign to destroy Berlin, morale amongst British aircrew sank to an all-time low. Not even in the dark days of 1940 and 1941, when Britain stood alone, did airmen find themselves burdened with such a fatalistic attitude. There had always been fear, but never was there such a sense of hopelessness. They had helped Britain conquer the threat of Nazi invasion, fighting, in the words of Churchill, for 'our own British life.' Now, there was just a sense of dread. It was the same feeling from which the Americans suffered in the wake of their appalling losses the year before. The Battle of Berlin saw Bomber Command fly 29,459 sorties — 1,117 of these resulted in loss. Great areas of the German capital had been reduced to jagged piles of rubble, but the Reich's war economy seemed no further from collapse than it had at the beginning of the campaign. In fact, it hit its peak in 1944 with aircraft and weapons production more than doubling. One must then wonder what its rate of production would have been without the continual onslaught of bombs battering Germany's industrial centres.

Black Night

Everything reached its bloody flashpoint on the night of 30 March. The target: Nuremberg. The weather over Germany that night was unseasonably clear, with little wind. The moon shone bright and cast everything in silver light. Under normal circumstances, Bomber Command would have been stood down because of the moon — but met. officers had forecast a high layer of cloud that would protect the bombers on their outward route. This prediction was contradicted later in the day after a Mosquito flew meteorological reconnaissance to the target and back. Though cloud could be expected over Nuremberg, there would probably not be any on the outward journey. 'If the British really came,' states *The Luftwaffe War Diaries*, 'they were in for a bad time.'[373]

Night fighter crews were placed on a state of alert early that evening. At 2300 hours they took to the skies from their bases stretching along the occupied coast and through the shattered heart of Germany. As the fighters winged through the night, a running commentary played in their ears. Ground stations were monitoring the advance of the British bombers. Hundred were approaching, the pilots were warned, at heights ranging from 16,000 to 22,000 feet. The exact number was 795 aircraft: 572 Lancasters, 214 Halifaxes and nine Mosquitoes. The fighters were assembled at radio beacons straddling the route the bombers would take to the target. There they waited, ready to pounce and engage in what would be the most violent air-to-air confrontation between the bombers of the RAF and the Luftwaffe's night forces.

'All around the enemy were going down like swatted flies,' read one Luftwaffe report after the desperate struggle.[374] The fighters swarmed amongst the bomber stream before it even reached the Belgian coast. The light of the moon cast the raging scene in pale colours. Fighters descended from all over the Reich to take part, and for an hour the battle raged. The bombers' guns had always been outclassed by the Luftwaffe's weaponry — including the vicious, up-swinging *Schräge Musik* cannon. Bombers fell in wide spirals spitting out flame and smoke behind them. Others vaporized in sudden, violent flashes. Burning wrecks littered the blacked-out landscape below, marking the bombers' bloody progress. Before they even reached the target, eighty-two British aircraft had been lost.

Strong winds and the brutal engagement had pushed many bombers off course. What many crews thought to be Nuremberg was actually Schweinfurt, which was bombed by 120 aircraft. The bombs that hit Nuremberg did so with little consquence. Heavy winds over the target pushed the Pathfinders and ensuing bombers to the east and many explosives fell in the open countryside to the north of the city. Meanwhile, night fighters continued to ravage the British intruders. Throughout the entire raid, the bombers and their crews were strafed and blasted from all sides. One German pilot, First-Lieutenant Martin Becker, and his crew shot down seven bombers that night. What bombers had managed to survive so far set a desperate course for England and tried to fight their way home. By the time the smell of cordite had faded and the screaming of men and engines had died away, ninety-five bombers had been shot out of the sky. It was Bomber Command's greatest loss of the war, a 'black night' despite the light cast by the moon.

It was a point of transition in the air war. For the Luftwaffe it was the last great victory over British bombers. The onslaught of the P-51 Mustang and the strategic bombing of the United States Army Air Forces would ensure that German pilots and their machines no longer enjoyed dominance over the Continent. It marked the end of Harris's great battles. He had reduced the great cities of Germany to smoking ruins. Hundreds of thousands lay buried amidst the rubble. Millions were left homeless. Amongst the Nazi hierarchy, his name was spoken with vehement hatred.

Vast German resources had been redirected to the cities to counter the threat of bombers from across the Channel. It had been a hard and bloody battle for both sides. Now, Harris's bomber offensive, which had remained largely independent of all other Allied war efforts, was to be consumed by the grandest scheme of all: the Allied invasion of Nazified Europe.

Bomber Command would return to Germany following the American, British and Canadian breakthrough at Normandy. But the scope of the war had changed drastically. Harris stood steadfast in his belief that area bombardment was the only worthwhile means of aerial attack. The final year of the war would witness the full potential of this devastating policy in the destruction of Dresden. But by then, victory was assured and questions were being asked about the necessity of such action.

XIV

The Beginning of the End

Overlord

By January 1944, Harris realised that Overlord was an 'inescapable commitment.' In the wake of the disastrous Nuremberg raid, the cross-Channel
invasion of Occupied Europe was barely three months away — but Harris
still remained convinced the key to Allied victory lay in the smashing of
German cities. The British and Americans had approved the concept of
Overlord in August the year before. Appointed Air Commander-in-Chief
of what would be the Allied Expeditionary Air Force was the head of RAF
Fighter Command, Sir Trafford Leigh-Mallory. Harris was instructed by
Portal towards the end of 1943 to meet with Mallory and plan the deployment of heavy bombers in support of the massive land operation. Harris
was, to say the least, less than enthusiastic about the concept. The ordeal
of Hamburg was proof-positive of Bomber Command's destructive potential, and Harris was convinced that given more time he could secure the
enemy's surrender by December 1944.[375]

The AEAF, well-armed with fighters, reconnaissance planes and
medium- and light-bombers, lacked a heavy bombing capabil-
ity. Eisenhower, who in December 1943 had been appointed Supreme
Commander for the massive operation, made clear his desire to elicit the
support of British and American heavy bombers whenever he deemed
their firepower necessary. Harris — along with Spaatz, his American
counterpart — did not like the idea. Just as Harris wished to continue
his city busting campaign, Spaatz was hesitant to divert his forces from
operations against German airfields and oil refineries. Both commanders,
however, realised that Overlord was an inevitable endeavour and argued

that the role of their bombers should remain strictly strategic. That said, Harris was quick to lay down guidelines according to which his force should operate. Bomber Command, he asserted, thrived on the widespread destruction of large-scale targets. His men could not be expected to suddenly switch operating tactics and bomb precision-based targets in daylight. Bombing would have to be done at night, he informed his superiors, and several hours' notice would be required for all operations. The military chiefs balked.[376]

In January 1944 Portal wrote Harris a diplomatically worded letter underlining the Allies' commitment to Overlord. In the letter, Portal said he was sure Bomber Command would do whatever was deemed necessary to guarantee the success of the invasion. Harris remained sceptical, but whatever concerns he harboured were somewhat alleviated with the eventual appointment of Air Chief Marshal Sir Arthur Tedder as Eisenhower's deputy. Tedder would be responsible for air matters, relegating Mallory to a secondary role. Thus, through Tedder, Harris would answer to Eisenhower. Although Harris maintained a healthy sense of scepticism, he resigned himself to the fact that larger forces were at play. On 14 April Bomber Command was officially diverted to attack targets in preparation of the Allied landings in Normandy. This date, however, is largely inconsequential, for Bomber Command had been blasting such targets for the past month.

On 17 April Bomber Command received the 'The Overlord Directive' from the office of the Supreme Allied Commander, calling for the destruction and disruption 'of the enemy's rail communications, particularly those affecting the enemy's movements toward the "OVERLORD" lodgment area.'[377] From Mallory's office, meanwhile, had come a bombing plan to be carried out in the preparatory phase of Overlord. Known as 'The Transportation Plan,' the bombing campaign would serve both a tactical and strategic role.[378]

In northern France and Western Germany, railway centres would come under heavy fire. Locomotive sheds and service installations would bear the brunt of the heavy bombers' fiery cargo. This would serve a strategic purpose, rendering the installations useless and forcing German traffic onto the roads. To assist the land armies in their advance into enemy territory, the roads would then be blasted, thus cutting off routes to the combat area. This would make up the tactical aspect of the plan. But to ensure tactical success, the strategic component had to be implemented as soon as possible.[379] There was some concern, however, amongst Churchill and his War Cabinet as to the inherent dangers such bombing would pose to French and Belgian civilians. Both Harris and Spaatz, too, were opposed to the new campaign, arguing their bombers could be put to better use. Mallory, tired of excuses and delays, penned a letter to the Air Ministry on 2 March and sought permission to attack — by night and day — a number of railway targets in France and Belgium. The Air Staff agreed to a trial run and gave Mallory permission to dispatch Bomber Command against a number of transportation targets in lightly populated areas.[380] Thus, on the night of 6 March 267 Halifaxes and Mosquitoes flew against French railway targets in Trappes. Visibility was clear and the aiming was sound. Bombs ripped through numerous tracks and rolling stock, and caused major damage without a single bomber lost.

Throughout March, Bomber Command continued its trial run against pinpoint targets. Le Mans and Amiens came under heavy fire with impressive results and zero casualties amongst the raiders. Casualties, too, amongst the civilian population were kept at a minimum. The end-product of Bomber Command's actions was promising, and the Air Ministry took notice. As the month progressed, the Air Ministry cleared other targets for attack. Interspersed with operations against transportation, Bomber Command lashed out against more familiar targets. A raid by 846 aircraft against Frankfurt on the night of 18 March left more than 55,000 people bombed out of their homes and ninety-nine industrial targets destroyed. Twenty-two aircraft succumbed to the city's defences. Attacking the same target four nights later, British bombers left 120,000 people homeless. Great swaths of the city went up in flames. Areas of the metropolis that had stood since the Middle Ages were reduced to ruins.[381] Forty-three of the 816 Lancasters, Halifaxes and Mosquitoes were lost to enemy fire. All the while, Bomber Command continued its campaign against enemy transit.

Between the Trappes operation and the night of 10 April — when 789 Lancasters, Halifaxes and Mosquitoes struck railway targets in Tours, Tergnier, Laon, Aulnoye and Ghent — Bomber Command struck fifteen separate centres of transportation with great success. Flares were dropped with stunning accuracy via the use of Oboe. The night sky above the targets glowed green and red as the bomber crews did their work.[382] Throughout this period of March, April and May, Bomber Command's average front-line strength was 1,360 aircraft, with Lancasters and Halifaxes making up the main bulk of the force, assisted by the Mosquitoes of the No. 8 (Pathfinder) Group. Together, these aircraft were slowly pushing the Stirlings and early model Halifaxes into secondary roles, such as mine-laying duties and flying diversionary raids.[383] At the same time, the Luftwaffe was readjusting its tactics to counter the RAF threat. The shift in targets from mainland Germany to the occupied territories did not go unnoticed. German fighter groups in France, Belgium and Holland were bolstered in strength and designated a first line of defence. The fighter pilots were told they no longer had to lie in wait along the British bombers' outward route. Instead, they were directed to penetrate the British bomber stream miles from the objective. German pilots were aided in their endeavour by the extended daylight hours of early summer. By

May the Luftwaffe's new approach to combatting Bomber Command was generating results. Nearly five per cent of British bombers were being destroyed over German-occupied territories. Over the Nazi homeland, British losses grew to nearly six per cent. A burden to the British was the fact that their transportation targets fell within a limited area of operations.[384] As Harris himself later noted: 'We had to go on attacking targets in the same comparatively small area without much chance of confusing the night-fighter force by widely separated attacks, and in many instances the target indicators dropped by the Pathfinders must have been visible from the enemy airfields.'[385]

By May the railway lines crisscrossing northern France and Belgium were suffering a near-constant ordeal by fire. In some French towns, anti-British slogans began to appear in public places. The British were mindful of the residents in the towns below and, generally, civilian casualties numbered less than 100 during such raids. But there were exceptions. On the night of 9 April 456 residents of Lille were killed when bombs fell outside the target area. In the Belgian town of Ghent the following night, 728 people were either killed or wounded in a raid that mauled the main rail line to Brussels.[386] On 1 May the men and machines of the American Eighth Air Force joined the campaign. All the while, Churchill and his War Cabinet continued to express reservations about 'The Transportation Plan.' They worried what impact civilian casualties inflicted by Allied bombs might have on the local populace, and how that might hamper the Allies once they reestablished themselves on the continent. To placate Churchill, Eisenhower — towards the end of April — erased from his list of targets twenty-seven objectives in heavily populated areas. He reversed his decision on 5 May, however, after extensive conversations with Mallory. Operations which were likely to result in numerous deaths amongst civilians were scheduled closer to D-Day.[387]

Between 6 March and the week of the landings, Bomber Command dropped 45,000 tons of bombs on thirty-seven railways. This was twice the combined tonnage of explosives dropped by the American Eighth on its twenty-six targets and the AEAF on its twenty. By the time the bombers were through, fifty-one railway yards had been demolished. Other railway lines were left so heavily mangled their use by the enemy was considered negligible. Mallory delivered the news at the Air Commander's Conference three days before the landings. 'The Transportation Plan' had run its course, he said. Only if a centre was found to be in heavy use by the Germans would the bombers return.[388] Harris was delighted with the performance of his men, even going so far as to say their extended foray into precision bombing went on to benefit them when they returned to their city busting campaign:

I may as well say outright that Bomber Command's night bombing, from this point onwards, proved to be rather more accurate, much heavier in weight, and more concentrated, than the American daylight attacks, a fact which was clearly recognized by SHAEF when the time came for the bombing of German troop concentrations within a mile or so of our own troops.[389]

Transportation was just one facet of Overlord's preparatory phase. Airfields and radar installations fell within Bomber Command's crosshairs, as did Normandy's coastal batteries. 'Here the main problem was how to give no indication to the enemy of where the actual lading was to be made,' Harris wrote. 'The only way of doing this was by the wildly extravagant method of bombing at least two coastal batteries or defences elsewhere for every one that was attacked on the invasion coast of Normandy.'[390] But both Mallory and Harris were doubtful whether such objectives could be destroyed — especially at night. The fortifications presented targets smaller than the rail depots, and many were protected by several feet of steel-reinforced concrete. Nevertheless, their destruction was deemed pivotal to Overlord's success. A plan for the assault put together by the RAF, Royal Navy and British Army gave top priority to the obliteration of coastal guns in the invasion area. The landing zones bristled with forty-nine batteries, many of which were still under construction. The Joint Fire Plan was issued on 8 April, and deemed twenty-four of the batteries worthy of immediate attack. Eight of the targets were located in the actual landing zones, the remaining sixteen were in 'cover areas.'[391]

Bomber Command's assault against the Atlantic Wall commenced with an attack on the night of 7 May, when fifty-six Halifaxes flew against a coastal gun at St Valery. Unfortunately, the explosives missed their mark. The following night, however, a direct hit was scored on the coastal guns at Morsalines. Raids that same night against batteries at Berneval and Cap Criz Nez proved less successful, and the only good news derived from the operations was that every bomber returned safely. Throughout May, British bombers dropped nearly 7,000 tons of bombs in thirty raids against coastal fortifications. In a change of tactics employed against railway targets, the British carpet-bombed the areas around the batteries, transforming the rolling landscape into a barren wasteland of scorched earth and craters. The approach yielded results. By the end of the month, reconnaissance showed the extent of Bomber Command's impact. Five batteries in the landing zone had been destroyed, and a further six were so mauled it was believed they would prove useless to the Germans when the Allied land assault began.[392]

One costly raid for the British on the night of 3 May also proved devastating to the Germans, when an enemy military camp near the French village of Mailly was brutalized by more than 300 bombers. The onslaught of explosives and incendiaries destroyed thirty-seven tanks and killed more than 200 soldiers, the majority of whom were Panzer NCOs. An additional 102 military vehicles went up in flames and 114 barracks were reduced to splinters. The explosions that ripped through the camp consumed forty-seven transport sheds. But in the midst of the raid, an American forces' broadcast wreaked havoc with the bombers' radio sets and jammed transmissions. Lancasters waiting for their orders to attack the target could not be reached. The delay proved costly. German fighters arrived over the target area and swarmed the raiders. Fighters and bombers exchanged heavy fire in a fierce action that sent forty-two out of 346 Lancasters spiralling to the ground in flames. It was a casualty rate of nearly twelve per cent.

Bomber Command, meanwhile, continued blasting Normandy's coastal batteries, attacking ten such targets between 1 and 5 June. 'On the night of the invasion,' wrote Harris, 'ten batteries in the actual area of the landing had to be attacked, and this took more than 5,000 tons of bombs, by far the greatest weight of bombs dropped by Bomber Command in any single attack up till then.'[393] That same night, sixteen Lancasters from 617 Squadron and six Stirlings from 218 Squadron flew diversionary raids to fool German radar. The bombers flew out over the Channel, dumping large bundles of Window into the blackness. It was an operation complex in technical details and one that had required the participating crews to train for months. The bombers flew in large circular paths that overlapped one another and continually increased in size. As the Lancasters' and Stirlings' circular flight paths grew in circumference, the bombers were brought closer to the enemy coast, as were the scattering clouds of Window. On German radar screens, it appeared as if a massive Allied armada some fourteen miles wide and crossing the Straits of Dover was approaching the French coast between Boulogne and Le Havre, north of the Normandy landing beaches. It was, noted Harris, 'a remarkable feat of navigation' on the part of the bomber crews.[394] Near Boulogne, the night sky exploded in a dazzling display of light as the Germans fell for the feint. A weaving network of searchlights exploded upwards, and the sky was torn apart by anti-aircraft fire. All the while, Stirlings, flying in support of the operation, carried radar-jamming equipment to confound the enemy's early warning system.

Elsewhere on the night of 5 June, thirty-six Halifaxes and Stirlings of No. 3 Group dropped dummy parachutists rigged with explosives to simulate an airborne invasion far removed from the Normandy area. More than 100 additional aircraft flew support operations, patrolling night-fighter approaches and jamming German ground-control radio. All told, Bomber Command flew 1,211 sorties that night — a record number — and lost only eight aircraft.[395] Thus, the stage was set for the Allies' last great endeavour on the bloody road to victory. And as always, Bomber Command would play a vital role.

The Battle for Normandy

Grey troop transports cut through the churning silver of Normandy's coastal waters at 6:31 a.m. on Tuesday 6 June. Seasick and frightened, 156,000 American, British and Canadian troops would eventually storm ashore. Not until August, however, would they battle their way free of Normandy to advance across France and Belgium with Germany in their sights. Bomber Command stoked the flames every night for a week following the landings, blasting railways and roads near the Allied beachhead with 11,800 tons of bombs and flying 3,500 sorties. Rain and heavy cloud hung over the invasion zone for two weeks following the landings and hampered both day and night operations. And although the US Eighth was forced to abort a number of missions due to its inexperience with blind-bombing, British crews were able to continue flying through the use of Oboe, though low cloud cover forced them down to heights of 2,000 to 6,000 feet.[396]

Bright moonlight guided British bombers on the first low-level raid against railways in the Paris area on the night of 7 June. A force of Halifaxes, Lancasters and Mosquitoes numbering 337 slammed targets at Acheres, Juvisy, Massey-Palaiseau and Versailles in two half-hour attacks from 0100 to 0130 and 0200 to 0230. Heavy anti-aircraft fire tore through the attackers as did German night-fighters. Although the targets were accurately bombed, the operation cost the British seventeen Lancasters and eleven Halifaxes. Thirteen of the aircraft lost were destroyed over Massey-Palaiseau, eight of which were knocked from the sky by enemy fighters. The intensity of the battle in the skies grew over the coming week with raids against rail lines running from the east and south of France. Main lines were devoured by fire and a considerable amount of rolling stock was destroyed.[397]

Railways at Acheres, Dreux, Orlans and Versailles were the objectives for the night of 10 June. But German fighters intercepted the attacking bombers to the west and southwest of Paris. The Lancasters and Halifaxes struggled through the maelstrom and successfully bombed their designated targets, but the action cost Bomber Command 18 aircraft. Two nights earlier, on 8 January, the RAF unleashed a new weapon: the 12,000-lb. Tallboy, otherwise known as the 'earthquake' bomb. The device — another product of Barnes Wallis' ingenuity — was designed to slam into the ground and bury itself beneath the earth, destroying its intended target with a subterranean explosion. The weapon's inaugural target was a railway tunnel in Saumur, 125 miles south of Normandy. The plan of attack was devised under great urgency, for it was believed a German panzer unit would soon be transported by train — and through the tunnel — to the combat zone. The tunnel's entrance and exit were designated as target points and marked by three low-flying Mosquitoes. A salvo of fiery red flares were dumped at the tunnel's south end, drawing the attention of the twenty-five Lancasters from 617 Squadron that followed in the Mosquitoes' wake. Eighteen Tallboys found their mark, tearing into the ground and blasting through the tunnel's foundations. One bomb slammed through the tunnel's roof. The blast ripped through the structure and brought down a masive amount of rock and dirt. The tunnel was effectively blocked, and the railway running through it was severed by the massive craters that disfigured the surrounding landscape.[398]

Throughout June, the Command struck railways and communication networks. On the night of 12 June Harris dispatched 671 Lancasters, Halifaxes and Mosquitoes to attack communication networks in Arras, Caen, Cambrai and Poitiers.

Objects of concrete and steel were not Bomber Command's only targets during the battle for Normandy. Bombers had flown in direct support of the Allied armies at Monte Cassino in February and March of 1944, and only hampered ground efforts in a bloody campaign of attrition. But now, it was time to re-examine the possibilities of bomber support. Harris had deep reservations. 'When the use of heavy bombers in the battlefield, very close to our own troops, was first put forward I expressed doubts,' he wrote. 'It seemed to me the army had no idea of the risk that the troops would be running.'[399] Eisenhower and Mallory were eager to implement firepower from above to assist the British Second Army in capturing Caen, a vital objective in the ground campaign and an area of heavily concentrated German armour. Following a request from Montgomery, Bomber Command flew against German troop and vehicle positions near Caen at Aunay-sur-Odon and Evrecy on the night of 14 June. Crews were assisted in their endeavour by clear skies, and accurate bombing was reported. No bombers were lost.

British forces in the final week of June established a bridgehead across the Odon river, south of Caen. But within days, the British Second Army and the Canadian First Army were being thwarted in their advance by a series of heavily fortified villages on the north side of Caen. Montgomery requested the bombing of an area measuring 4,000 by 1,500 yards — an area believed to be bristling with enemy defences. The raid — tasked to 283 Lancasters, Halifaxes and Mosquitoes — was quickly scheduled for the evening of 7 July. The raid was accurately marked by Oboe-equipped Mosquitoes. About two and a half square miles of land was smashed by nearly 2,300 tons of bombs. Great, roiling clouds of dust and debris rose skyward as buildings and roads collapsed under the explosive onslaught. But when the smoke cleared and the dust settled it was discovered the vast majority of enemy positions remained untouched. The northern suburbs of Caen — a major link in the German line — lay in a mangled heap. The bombing, however, although inflicting only minimal casualties amongst the German infantry, was not entirely futile. British and Canadian troops, hampered by the enormous damage done to the roads on which they were travelling, were nevertheless bolstered in spirits by the shattered morale of the German forces who witnessed the bombing.[400]

The British succeeded in conquering all of Caen on their side of the river by 10 July. The following day, Churchill received a message from Montgomery. Heavy air bombardment had weakened German resistance, Montgomery wrote, and rendered much of the area leading up to Caen a desolate wasteland.[401] But plenty of fierce fighting remained.

On the morning of 18 July the British commenced Operation Goodwood. The plan called for British armour to fight its way through a narrow front east of Caen and into Normandy's open country. Montgomery — strongly supported by both Eisenhower and Tedder — again requested air support, calling upon Bomber Command, the American Eighth and the AEAF. British and American heavy bombers were tasked with blasting troop concentrations on the flanks of the British advance, while German ground forces beyond the range of British artillery were targeted for annihilation. Fragmentation bombs were used to shatter enemy defences lying directly in front of the British. Bombs were dropped from 5,000 to 9,000 feet and wreaked heavy damage on the 16th Luftwaffe Field Division and the 21st Panzer Division, which saw an entire company blown to pieces along with fifteen tanks. Of the 6,800 tons of explosives dropped by American and British bombers, more than 5,000 tons were released by Bomber Command.[402] One of Montgomery's staff officers witnessed the attack and watched the bombers as they soared through thick clouds of flak. While he admired the bravery of the British crews, he also felt empathy for the cities that crumbled under the 'Harris technique' of bombardment.[403] For three days, the Germans and British slugged it out. German anti-tank guns on the Bourgebous ridge, which lay beyond the bombers' target area, exacted a heavy toll on the British armour that was now bogged down in swampy soil following a detrimental change in the weather. In the wake of the bombing, Montgomery moved his forces forward six miles, insisting it was part of his grand scheme.

Although Operation Goodwood was ultimately deemed a failure by Allied commanders, German documents eventually seized painted another picture. A communiqué sent to Hitler on 21 July — three days after the bombing — by Von Kluge, Rommel's successor, revealed the German's desperation. 'The psychological effect of such a mass of bombs coming down with all the power of elemental nature on the fighting forces, especially the infantry, is a factor that has to be taken into very serious consideration,' Von Kluge wrote. 'It is immaterial whether such a carpet catches good troops or bad. They are more or less annihilated and their equipment is shattered.'[404]

On one occasion, Harris's worst fears were realised when British bomber crews unintentionally blasted Canadian troops. The incident occurred on 14 August when British crews were dispatched to carpet bomb German positions a mere 2,000 yards in front of the Canadian line. During the assault, Canadian troops — for some reason — lit their yellow recognition flares, which the bomber crews mistook for target indicators. Eighty-eight Canadians were killed in the ensuing carnage. Six days earlier, American bombers accidentally attacked Canadian forces — killing 350 troops — during a raid to support the Canadian advance on Falaise. Such was the still risky business of army-air cooperation.[405] But Bomber Command carried on, smashing synthetic oil plants, Luftwaffe airfields, enemy shipping in occupied ports and German ground forces. 'Between D-Day and the middle of August, Bomber Command dropped 17,560 tons of bombs on German concentrations,' wrote Harris, estimating his force could lay down a barrage at any one time equal in weight to the shells fired from 4,000 artillery pieces.[406]

American forces under the command of General Omar Bradley — benefiting from the struggle around Caen to the east — broke through the German lines on 31 July at Avranches. Paris was liberated on 25 August, and the British Second Army reached Brussels on 3 September after advancing nearly eighty miles in a single day. The Allied charge across France and Belgium was a benefit to Bomber Command. The advance deprived the Germans of their early warning radar on the Brest peninsula and their night-fighter bases in France. In Holland and Belgium, Luftwaffe airfields came under increasing fire. In September the Supreme Headquarters Allied Expeditionary Force relinquished control of Bomber Command, reverting it to the Air Ministry. The question now was what role would Bomber Command play for the remainder of the conflict? The Command had resumed daylight operations over Germany, flying shallow penetration raids against tactical targets. Amidst all this, there was one target requiring Bomber Command's attention by day and night.

Crossbow

Churchill called it 'The Pilotless Bombardment.'[407] In Bethnal Green, the early morning quiet of 13 June was shattered by a massive explosion that killed six people and injured nine others. Three more explosions rocked Greater London that morning, though no further casualties were reported. In a desperate bid of retaliation in the wake of the Allied successes at

Normandy, Hitler had unleashed the V-1 rocket against Britain's battered capital. On 15 June the rocket onslaught began when more than 200 'Flying Bombs' slammed into London in a twenty-four-hour period. More than 3,000 V-1s screamed across the skies of southern England, detonating in the streets of London over the next five weeks. Packed with a ton of explosive, they rocketed towards their target at up to 400 mph. Amongst the weary London populace, the unique sound of the V-1's engine earned the rocket the nicknames 'doodlebug' and 'buzz bomb.'[408] The new bombardment inflicted a heavy toll on Londoners, both mentally and physically, Churchill noted in his memoirs. Returning home from a day at the office or factory, one never knew if they would find their house still standing and their family still alive. Women, at home with the children, saw their husbands off to work each morning and wondered if they would ever see them again.[409]

Bomber Command was immediately thrown against the V-weapon launch sites in an operation dubbed 'Crossbow.' The US Eighth and the AEAF had bombed such targets in the Pas de Calais and Cherbourg areas in the months prior to Bomber Command's assault. The carnage wreaked in these raids forced the Germans to build smaller, more concealed facilities to launch the rockets. These new sites — or 'modified launch sites' with catapult mechanisms to fling the rockets skyward — were Bomber Command's prime objectives, along with the quarries and limestone caves where the rockets were stored. In the final two weeks of June, British crews would fly 4,057 sorties against Hitler's V-weapons, releasing 15,907 tons of bombs. The Pas de Calais region was reduced to a tortured landscape of moon-like craters as Harris threw men and machines against Crossbow objectives by day and night. The targets, however, were 'small, easily constructed, and extremely... unrewarding for air attacks.'[410] Throughout July 24,292 tons of bombs slammed into the launch sites and storage areas. The campaign continued into August.[411]

British bombers ravaged storage depots and weapons dumps with 1,000-pound explosives and the devastating 'earthquake' bomb. On the ground, as Allied troops advanced, the launch sites fell to their guns. Back in Britain, anti-aircraft defences were being redeployed along the coast and fighters were scrambling to knock the 'Flying Bombs' out of the sky before they reached London. It was a massive undertaking, involving 1,000 anti-aircraft guns and more than 20,000 men and woman of Anti-Aircraft Command. All the while, Bomber Command prosecuted its campaign with vigour, leaving churning palls of smoke rising from Fôret de Nieppe, St-Leu-d'Esserent and Bois de Cassan. But as the Allied advance continued to gain momentum, pressure was eased on Harris and his force to wreck the flying-bomb sites. From mid-June to mid-August, nearly 60,000 tons of bombs were dropped by Bomber Command in the course of 16,000 sorties, during which 131 bombers were lost. On 28 August ninety-four 'Flying Bombs' rocketed across the English coast en route for London. All but two were destroyed by British anti-aircraft fire, RAF fighters and air-raid balloons. The last V-1 streaked towards Britain on 2 September. By then, Churchill declared, the weapon had been 'mastered.'[412]

Bomber Command's campaign against the launch sites achieved questionable results. The frenzied launching of V-1s well into August suggested the bomber crews had failed in their task. But as Harris noted:

> The launching sites were small and very well concealed, and more than half the operations against them were carried out when they were covered by low cloud; nevertheless, nearly all of them were knocked out. Unfortunately, as one went down another sprang up, for they were very cheap and quick to build.[413]

Of greater impact against Germany's V-weapon programme was the British raid on Peenemunde in August the previous year. The smashing of the research facility had forced the Germans to scatter their manufacturing operations and delayed the weapon's launch against Britain.[414] It was the Allied ground advance that would eventually lay the launch sites to waste. Together, the V-1s — then the V-2 rockets, which were launched in September — killed 5,864 people throughout London and Southern England. In the meantime, Bomber Command brought its fury to bear elsewhere.

Left mainly intact by the Germans, the vital port of Antwerp fell to the Allies on 4 September. It was the closest port to the front, but its usefulness was compromised by German positions along the Scheldte estuary. Targeted for destruction was the island fortress of Walcheren, a mass of land below sea level — surrounded by a seawall measuring 200 feet thick at its base — dominating the approach to the port. But before Allied bombers could slam the island, the powers-that-be sought to knock Germany out of the war with a crossing at the Rhine. The end result of Operation Market Garden was a vicious clash of arms at Arnhem and an infamous defeat for the British. In the wake of this failure, Bomber Command was dispatched to clear the Antwerp approaches.

The target for the British bombers was Walcheren's seawall on which the Germans had placed a number of coastal batteries. Harris was tasked with the destruction of these guns and the breaching of the seawall, which would result in the swamping of the island and the drowning of enemy defences farther inland. On 3 October eight waves of bombers — 252 Lancasters and seven Mosquitoes — attacked the seawall on the island's western tip, battering it with high explosives. The wall crumbled under the onslaught, and soon the onrushing waves were taking a toll, eating away at the damaged wall and widening the breach to some 100 yards. Four batteries were swallowed by the ocean. Another seven were swallowed following another series of raids. Defences farther inland, out of reach of the water, were blasted in the final weeks of October. Bomber Command dropped 9,000 tons of bombs on Walcheren in the course of 2,000 sorties. Only eleven bombers were lost. On 1 November British and Canadian troops stormed the island and commenced a fierce, week-long struggle against the die-hard defenders. The campaign devastated the island, smashing homes and flooding fertile land. 'The wholesale destruction of property, in my view, is always justified if it is calculated to save casualties,' Harris later wrote.[415] Even after the Allies captured Walcheren, the Scheldte had to be cleared of mines. Allied ships entered the port of Antwerp on 26 November.[416]

Stoking the Fire

While Harris did what he could to assist the land forces, he also stoked the long-burning fires in Germany. On the night of 18 August Bremen's city centre was devoured by flames that quickly spread to the north-western suburbs and the city's port. While just 1,100 tons of bombs were dropped by 274 Lancasters, Halifaxes and Mosquitoes, the human toll on the ground was heavy. People choked on fumes and burned to death in the city's air-raid shelters. At least 1,058 bodies were discovered in the wake of the raid. An additional 375 people were reported missing. Nearly 9,000 homes were obliterated and, in the port, eighteen ships were blasted out of the water. Anti-aircraft fire claimed only one Lancaster. Eleven nights later in Stettin, fifty-five factories were blown apart and more than 2,000 tons of shipping were sunk by 402 Lancasters. Casualties on the ground numbered 2,067. Night fighters and anti-aircraft guns knocked twenty-two Lancasters from the sky. The following week, V-2 rocket stores and airfields were pummeled. And, on 6 September Emden went up in a stormy conflagration.

Darmstadt fell to Bomber Command on the night of 11 September. The city of 120,000 had thus far escaped major damage. But following the 11 September raid, it was left a smoldering heap with more than 12,000 people dead amidst its ruins and up to 70,000 of its residents homeless. The city centre went up in a cauldron of flame that engulfed the suburbs to the south and east, wiping out virtually every building. The city's air raid sirens began wailing shortly before 11:30 p.m. and sent people scurrying for the cover of their cellars. Unlike the strong-points of Nazi power, Darmstadt had no deep public shelters.[417] Somewhere in the darkness above, 240 Lancasters, Halifaxes and Mosquitoes were closing in, carrying maximum loads of incendiary clusters and 4,000-lb. blast bombs. The approach to the city was visually unstimulating, for the target lacked the great sweeping belts of search lights and the formidable armoury of anti-aircraft guns employed by the likes of Hamburg, Nuremberg or Berlin. At fifteen minutes to midnight, the city's western sky lit up in a crimson glow as the first marker flares were dropped.

In their cellars, families huddled together as the city's meagre flak defences opened fire. Target indicators, dropped by 83 and 97 Squadrons, continued to fall. The sky burned green as backup flares were dropped to reinforce the primary markers. This raid, the people of Darmstadt knew, would be different. At four minutes to midnight, the main bombing force received its orders to attack. Streets caved in and buildings disintegrated, and the civil defences collapsed under the weight of the British onslaught. In crowded cellars, temperatures rose and walls began to crumble. Re-called one woman:

> There was a dreadful crash, the walls shook, we heard masonry cracking and collapsing, and the crackle of flames. Plaster began to fall and we all thought the ceiling would collapse… About thirty seconds after, there was a terrible explosion, the cellar-door flew open, and I saw, bathed in a brilliant light, the staircase to the cellar collapsing and a river of fire pouring down. I shouted 'Let's get out!' but the Hauptmann gripped me: 'Stay here, they are still overhead.' At that moment, the house opposite was hit. The armoured plate in front of our cellar flew up in the air, and a tongue of fire about fifteen feet long shot through at us.

> Cupboards and other furniture burst and fell onto us. The terrible pressure hurled us against the wall. Now somebody shouted: 'Get out and hold hands!'… More bombs were already falling in the gar-den. We crouched low, each one of us beating out the small flames flickering on the clothes of the one in front. Phosphorous clung to the trees and dripped down on us… the heat was terrible. Burning people raced past like live torches, and I listened to their unforget-table final screams.[418]

For fifty-one minutes, the bombs continued to fall. A 4,000-lb. blast-bomb detonated in a graveyard, churning up the earth and throwing corpses everywhere. The city had become a burning, apocalyptic landscape lit-tered with dead bodies.[419] Railway communications that passed through the city had brought the bombers here. The operation ultimately cost the British twelve of the 226 Lancasters dispatched on the operation. Darmstadt's ordeal has, through the years, been overshadowed by the likes of Hamburg and the February 1945 destruction of Dresden. Whether or not Darmstadt was a vital centre of communications remains a disputed point to this day. The greater truth lies in the city's destruction; by 1944 Bomber Command was a devastating weapon of war that found 'many of the larger cities were no longer worth bombing.'[420]

A fortnight later, a directive crossed Harris's desk instructing him to lash out against the petroleum industry, German rail and waterborne transportation systems, enemy armour and motor vehicles. Buried at the bottom of the directive was an order to bomb cities — but only when attacks on petroleum, transportation and armour were not possible. 'When weather or tactical conditions are unsuitable for operations against specific primary objectives,' the directive stated, 'attacks should be delivered on important industrial areas, using blind bombing technique if necessary.'[421] The directive was not to Harris's liking, and he made his displeasure known. The order was reinforced via a directive dated 1 November 1944. Again, he revealed his discontent with a note he scribbled at the top of the directive: 'Here we go round the mulberry bush.'[422] So there would be no question as to who wrote the remark, Harris slapped his initials — ATH — underneath it. Nevertheless, the bomber war had entered its final phase. Harris obeyed his masters, bombing oil facilities at Sterkrade and Scholven, Wanne-Eickel and Homberg, Gelsenkirchen and Dortmund. But only six per cent of Bomber Command's efforts in October were directed at oil targets.[423]

Harris remained intent on bombing Germany into submission, and his faith in the bomber as a means to end the war remained unyielding. There was still urban ground to lay flat. On 13 October another directive reached Harris at High Wycombe — one that this time veered somewhat more towards his liking. Operation 'Hurricane' was conceived to show Germany the true extent of the Allied air forces' 'overwhelming superiority' in north-west Europe. The directive instructed British and American forces to 'apply within the shortest practical period the maximum effort of the Royal Air Force Bomber Command and the VIIIth United States Bomber Command against objectives in the densely populated Ruhr.'[424] The Americans would bomb targets from the current list of synthetic-oil plants, while 'the targets for RAF Bomber Command are to be areas selected from the undamaged parts of the major industrial cities of the Ruhr.'[425] Both the American and British bomber commands were instructed to direct a 'maximum night and day bombing effort' against the Ruhr. The new orders, however, were not to be carried out 'to the prejudice of any operations which can be delivered effectively on oil targets in Germany generally.'[426]

Harris had already commenced such an effort on the night of 6 October — one week prior to the 'Hurricane' directive, initiating what some would dub the 'Second Battle of the Ruhr.' The targets were Dortmund and Bremen. More than 500 bombers blasted the former, losing only one per cent of their number. On the ground, the industrial and transportation centres of the city went up in flames. But the real damage that night fell upon Bremen, targeted by 246 Lancasters and seven Mosquitoes from 1 and 5 Groups. This was the last of Bomber Command's thirty-two major operations against the city.[427] The moon that night was three-quarters full and Bremen, according to one report out of the city, lay spread out beneath the bombers like a fat bull's eye.[428] What remained of Bremen was soon burning as 1,021 tons of explosives — of which 868 tons were incendiaries — fell across the shattered metropolis. A raging conflagration lit up the city centre and spread to the surrounding suburbs, most of which already lay in ruins. Nearly 5,000 houses were blown apart, along with five churches, eighteen schools and sixteen public buildings. Heavily damaged were Bremen's two Focke-Wulf factories, the Siemens Schuckert electrical plant and the AG Weser shipyard. More than 37,000 people were left homeless. The number of dead was mercifully low at sixty-five, suggesting many of the city's residents had deserted. Bomber Command lost five Lancasters, and the city of Bremen was left burning.

Officially adhering to the Hurricane directive, Harris mounted an operation of Herculean proportions against Duisburg — a major inland port where the waters of the Ruhr and Rhine meet — on 14 October. The heavy bomber crews had been on stand down for two days, but were now dispatched on a daylight operation. Detailed for the raid were 1,013 Lancasters, Halifaxes and Mosquitoes, which were escorted to their objective by machines of RAF Fighter Command. Over the target, 957 of the raiders unleashed 3,574 tons of high explosives. Roads crumbled and roofs disintegrated, and then came the fires as 820 tons of incendiaries ignited the beleaguered port and swamped the anti-aircraft defences. As Duisburg buckled under the massive bombardment, more than 1,000 American B-17s and B-24s hit the Cologne area. American casualties were light with five bombers and one fighter lost. At Duisburg, the British lost fourteen Lancasters and Halifaxes, but returned that night with 1,005 aircraft. Over a two-hour period, the massive force attacked in two separate waves, dropping 4,040 tons of high explosives and 500 tons of incendiaries, crippling the city's mine and steel operations. Elsewhere that night, 240 Lancasters and Mosquitoes wiped out Brunswick and left 80,000 of its residents bombed-out.

Harris was eager to remove any healthy flesh that still clung to the dying patient. Throughout October, he targeted Hannover, Stuttgart, Essen, Nuremberg and Cologne. On 25 October 771 bombers hit Essen and destroyed the Krupps pig-iron plant, reducing the city's war-production industry to near ruin. Still mindful of the emphasis placed on Germany's oil industry, Harris — throughout November — attacked plants in Gelsenkirchen, Dortmund, Harburg, Castrop-Rauxel and Sterkrade in twenty-two operations, fourteen of which were by day.[429] And it was in

November that Bomber Command finally claimed victory over an old adversary: the *Tirpitz.*

Sink the Tirpitz

The *Tirpitz* had cast a long shadow over Churchill's war. In September 1944 the battleship, anchored in Norway's Alten Fjord, was out of range of bombers operating from Britain. Nevertheless, at Churchill's bidding, Harris took on the task of securing the vessel's destruction. On the evening of 11 September Nos 9 and 617 Squadrons were dispatched to a hastily prepared airbase in Russia at Yagdonik, near Archangel. The outward trek proved to be an arduous journey. Strong winds and heavy rains lashed the aircraft and thick cloud all but blinded the pilots. Once in Russian airspace, the crews' problems only intensified when it was discovered the landing-beacon system employed by the Russians was different to that used by the British. On landing — during which six bombers were severely damaged, but no crew members were injured — the force scattered itself over six airfields. Noted a report filed by No. 5 Group: 'It reflects considerable credit on the navigators that they reached the vicinity of Archangel, let alone find one particular airfield.'[430]

On 15 September after time had been allowed to repair the damaged bombers, the aircraft — armed with 20 x 12,000-lb. 'Tallboys' — were ready for action. At 0630 hours, the bombers took off from their airfields at Yagdonik and set a low-level course for Alten Fjord. It was hoped that by attacking from the east, the crews would achieve tactical surprise and avoid the battleship's smokescreen. At 1100 hours the bombers reached their objective, rocketing over *Tirpitz* in four waves of five. Although the weather was clear, the target was shrouded beneath a swirling grey cloud. Enemy fighters were noticeably absent and flak caused only minor damage to two bombers. As the Lancasters passed over their target, they dropped seventeen 'Tallboys.' The bombs sent massive plumes of water up on either side of the ship. One bomb found its mark and slammed into the ship's forward starboard side, wrenching open a massive hole through which 2,000 tons of water poured into the ship's structure.[431]

The bombers returned to their Russian base, then made the trip back to England on 26 September. On the night of 16 October, the severely damaged *Tirpitz* was moved to Tromso — an anchorage farther south and just in range of Lancasters operating from their English airfields. Another attack followed on 29 October but was thwarted by poor weather. The roundtrip for the bombers, operating from forward bases in the northern reaches of Scotland, was still a daunting 2,252 miles. To make the journey, the Lancasters of Nos 9 and 617 Squadrons were heavily modified. They were fitted with Merlin Mark XXIV engines and paddle-bladed propellers for extra power on takeoff. Additional fuel tanks were also fitted. To lessen the weight, their mid-upper turrets were removed. On 12 November as part of Operation Catechism, the men and machines of Nos 9 and 617 Squadrons were again dispatched to sink the *Tirpitz*. The bombers left in the early hours from airfields in Lossiemouth, Milltown and Kinloss. They set a low-level course for the Norwegian border, changing track en route towards Russia. They rendezvoused at a lake at latitude 68.20 north, longitude 1900 east and proceeded from there towards Tromso. Clouds hung low over the water, but dissipated as the bombers closed in on the fjord.[432]

The crew of the *Tirpitz* had been warned of the approaching bombers and cleared the decks for action at 0815 hours. When the thirty-one bombers passed over the target at 0941 hours, the *Tirpitz* opened with a thunderous volley from her main armaments. Anti-aircraft batteries along the shore also threw fire into the sky, but to little effect. The battleship proved to be an easy target as there was no smokescreen to camouflage it. Attacking from heights of 12,000 to 16,000 feet, the Lancasters rocked the *Tirpitz* with 29 x 12,000-lb. 'Tallboys.' Two bombs slammed into her structure, the first smashing her amidships. The second bomb ripped into her aft and to port of 'C' turret, and set the ship aflame. A swirling column of smoke rose above the ship, and a jet of white steam leapt some 200 feet into the air. A third bomb found its mark and rocked the ship with a massive explosion. The ship's port side disintegrated in a 120-foot hole that stretched from deck to keel. As the last bomber turned for home, the ship had already begun to capsize. Shortly thereafter, the *Tirpitz* rolled over 140 degrees and lodged her superstructure in the muddy sea bottom. On board, 1,000 of her 1,900 crew were either killed or wounded. As for the British, flak inflicted heavy damage on one Lancaster, which landed safely in Sweden without any casualties amongst its crew.[433]

In the wake of the operation, Harris received congratulations from His Majesty the King and Churchill, as well as Portal. On the battlefront, the demise of the *Tirpitz* meant the Royal Navy could now send its heavy warships to fight in the Pacific.[434]

And still Bomber Command continued to grow. Seven new Lancaster squadrons had joined the ranks of Bomber Command in October. Four more squadrons joined the air battle over the next two months. At the end of December 1944, Harris had at his disposal fifty-three operational Lancaster squadrons, seventeen Halifax III squadrons, three squadrons of Halifax VII bombers and ten Mosquito squadrons. By the beginning of 1945, Harris had an average of 1,348 heavy bombers and 138 light bombers ready for operations at any time.[435] It was with this arsenal that Bomber Command entered the final months of the war.

XV

The Final Act

The Ardennes

In the early morning hours of 16 December 1944 under the command of Field Marshal von Runstedt, ten Panzer and fourteen infantry divisions slammed the Allied lines on a forty-mile front from the south of Aachen to the north-east of Luxembourg. It was the commencement of Hitler's last great gamble, a desperate bid to seize the Allied points of supply at Antwerp and Brussels, and drive a wedge between the British and American armies. Two days later, the American Eighth launched operations against railways behind the enemy front. On 19 December Bomber Command joined the fray and bombed a railway junction on the Mosel river north-east of Luxembourg. Heavy fog hampered the operation and only thirty-two of the 150 Lancasters detailed for the raid dropped their bombs. Despite this, the damage done made an impression on Eisenhower, thus ensuring heavy bombers played a pivotal role in the Battle of the Bulge.[436]

Fog continued to hang heavy over the battlefield from 20 to 22 December and brought Allied air assaults to a near halt. The American Eighth was grounded, but Bomber Command — because of its ever-evolving navigational technology — was able to continue operations. Guiding Bomber Command through the swirling haze was a radar aid dubbed GH. Similar in concept to Oboe, GH relied on radio signals that were transmitted from the aircraft, received by two ground stations back in England and relayed back to the bomber. Measuring how much time elapsed between the bomber's emission of the signal and the return transmission, a navigator could determine his distance from the receiving stations and pinpoint his exact location. Development of the system began in 1942 at the Telecommunications Research Establishment. By October 1944 Bomber Command had sixty aircraft equipped with the sets, allowing them to blast precise targets through inclement weather within a 250-mile range of ground stations established in France and Belgium. The fact that 100 aircraft at a time could use GH only added to the weapon's potency.[437]

The focus of Bomber Command's attention was the rail system that passed through the Rhine and pumped reinforcements into the German front. The railways crossed bridges and tributaries, cutting through Frankfurt and Cologne. On the night of 21 December more than 200 Lancasters, Halifaxes and Mosquitoes took off in bad weather to attack railway targets in Cologne and Bonn. Skies over the targets were tempered by storm clouds. At Cologne, the Nippes marshalling yards were the target. Crews bombed through thick cloud. Only a few explosives found their mark, wiping out forty railway wagons, a repair shop and a number of railway lines. Over Bonn, crews bombed on the glow of ground markers that coloured the clouds red and green. Only light damage was done. Bad weather the following night continued to challenge the bomber crews. Over Bingen and Coblenz, cloud shrouded the targeted railway yards. Coblenz got off easy, but at Bingen, the bombers hit their mark hard. Wagons were blown off the tracks and railway lines were torn apart, ending the movement of reinforcements and supplies through Bingen to the Ardennes front.[438]

The skies above the battlefield cleared on 23 December and propelled the Luftwaffe into action. Bomber Command was dispatched on a daylight operation against the Gremberg railway yards in Cologne. The attacking force was small, consisting of twenty-seven Lancasters and three Mosquitoes split into three formations. For the British, the raid would prove to be a bloody endeavour. Rocketing over the French coast, two Lancasters crews were lost in a fiery mid-air collision. It was a portent of things to come. The cloud cover that crews had been told to expect over the target dissipated as the bombers approached. Leading each of the three formations was an Oboe-equipped Lancaster and — as a reserve — an Oboe-equipped Mosquito. Operating in unexpectedly clear skies, the bombers broke formation to bomb visually and make themselves less vulnerable to the clouds of flak exploding around them. Flying on his 110th operation, Squadron Leader R A M Palmer, DFC, of No. 582, Squadron never received the order to break formation. Although his aircraft was already damaged by flak, he continued on his straight Oboe approach as shrapnel relentlessly bit into the bomber. The plane was knocked from the sky, but not before its bombs were released on target. Although the tail gunner managed to escape the spiralling Lancaster, the rest of the crew was killed. Palmer was posthumously awarded the Victoria Cross.[439]

Flak was not the only problem for the British in the skies above Cologne that day. German fighters, originally dispatched to intercept a large contingent of American bombers attacking marshalling yards behind the Ardennes front, engaged the British instead. Flak and cannon fire took a heavy toll, sending a Lancaster and a Mosquito to the ground in a fiery display. Over Belgium, a Lancaster crew was forced to abandon its heavily damaged aircraft, bringing the number of bombers lost that day to six out of the thirty. The Luftwaffe's spirited response to the raid prompted Allied air commanders to order attacks on enemy airfields near the Ardennes battlefront the following day, Christmas Eve. More than 300 machines of Bomber Command blasted airfields at Düsseldorf and Essen. Raids continued that night as Hangelar airfield at Bonn was bombarded by 104 Lancasters. That same night, 102 Lancasters and Mosquitoes returned to the Nippes marshalling yards at Cologne. An ammunition train took a direct hit and went up in a dazzling conflagration. A nearby airfield was heavily damaged and a number of railway lines were severed, knocking the yard out of commission.[440]

On the ground, tough American resistance and damage to German transit lines had thwarted the Wehrmacht advance. The day after Christmas, Bomber Command was asked to lend direct support to American ground forces. In the northern sector of the battlefront, the 6th SS Panzer Army was fighting its way towards the town of St. Vith, a vital road junction that offered routes to all the main sectors of battle. For the operation, all bomber groups were scoured for the most experienced crews. Nearly 300 aircraft took part in the raid and dropped 1,138 tons of high explosive on the town. Choked with debris and cratered under the heavy onslaught, the main routes of transport through the town were ravaged. Three days passed before clean-up efforts got underway — but such work had little impact. It was not until 3 February 1945, more than a week after Allied troops entered the town, that the main roads would be cleared. During the Ardennes offensive, the St Vith operation proved to be the most effective air raid against a major transit route.[441]

Bomber Command continued raiding tactical targets. In the latter half of December, Harris's men dropped 5,950 tons of bombs on lines of communication and rail routes to the front. This forced the Germans to transport armoured and motorised units by main roads, thus consuming rapidly diminishing stocks of fuel. Roads were soon choked with traffic, which delayed the delivery of supplies and reinforcements to the enemy battle area. Damage to railway lines and the threat of bombardment by day also meant the use of some lines ceased, while others could only carry troops to within 100 miles of their intended destination. Germany's last great offensive action was crumbling into ruin. As the last full year of war gave way to 1945, railway traffic through the Cologne-Coblenz-Trier area had virtually come to a halt. Elsewhere, tragedy was imminent. Nestled at the mouth of the Gironde river, near Bordeaux, the French town of Royan was about to become a casualty of war. The events leading to the catastrophe remain a matter of debate.

Retreating from the advancing Allied armies, the Germans had left behind in Royan a garrison to prevent Allied forces from using the port at Bordeaux. Along the western seaboard of France, the Germans had dug in similar detachments at St Nazaire and Lorient. In the town of Cognac on 10 December 1944, General de Larminat, commander of the French Army in the West, met with General Royce, commander of the First TAF and the French Western Air Force. The topic of discussion was the determined enemy garrison in Royan. The men conversed over dinner and — supposedly — liberal amounts of alcohol. During the course of the meal, Royce suggested that night-bombing training units of the American Eighth should be employed to dislodge the Royan garrison. The French, open to the idea, offered their assurances that the town's civilians would be evacuated within five days. Those civilians that remained, the French said, would likely be German collaborators. The idea was forwarded to Supreme Headquarters Allied Expeditionary Force, which, in turn, delegated the operation to Bomber Command.[442]

On 3 January 1945 the order came down from on high to destroy the town, which was believed to be occupied by German troops only.[443] The following night, the meteorological forecast for western Germany predicted stormy weather. Conditions over the west coast of France and the Royan target area, however, were clear. Attempts were made by SHAEF to verify the town had indeed been evacuated. Signals sent to the French Western Air Force Commander and French headquarters that evening went unanswered. Consequently, it led to the presumption that the town had been evacuated — a presumption that would prove fatal. At 0400 hours on 5 January 347 Lancasters and seven Mosquitoes, flying in two waves, commenced their attack on the town. Royan, in the ninety minutes that followed, was decimated. Its ancient architecture and the serenity of its waterside setting gave way to a maelstrom of fire. Passing overhead, the bombers dropped 1,576 tons of high explosives. Amongst the deadly cargo dropped on the town were 285 of Bomber Command's 4,000-lb. blast bombs. What Allied commanders failed to realise at the moment the first bomb fell was that 2,000 of the town's residents were still at home.[444]

Prior to the raid, 12,000 men of the French Resistance had been tasked with softening up Royan's German garrison. Their efforts, however, were hampered by a lack of heavy field artillery. Before striking back, the German commander of the town gave Royan's residents a chance to evacuate. Instead, the residents opted to remain with their homes and possessions. They would pay for the decision in blood. On the night of the raid, nearly ninety per cent of the town went up in flames, killing 800 civilians and inflicting a further 200 casualties. The number of Germans killed was no more than fifty.[445] What followed was a barrage of recriminations and accusations, and an investigation demanded by Sir Charles Portal. Bomber Command was cleared of any wrongdoing, and bombardment of French towns was prohibited unless directly approved by the French. Harris, for his part, said he used a strong concentration of high explosive because he'd been told a German garrison was stubbornly entrenched in the town. One French general, in the wake of the operation, committed suicide. A bitter taste would linger in the mouths of French officials for many years to come.[446] But whatever controversies hung over the destruction of Royan, they paled in comparison to those born in the fires of Dresden.

Thunderclap

From the Operations Record Book of No. 83 Squadron Pathfinder Force:

> Orders for operations came through early and the Squadron detailed fourteen crews. Squadron briefing was held at 14:45 the target being Dresden. Take off was soon after five o'clock in to a lovely sunny evening.[447]

Dresden. The name has become synonymous with the brutality of war, relegating the veterans of Bomber Command in the minds of many to war criminals. It has cast a long crimson stain over the post-war reputation of Sir Arthur Harris and overshadowed the sacrifices made by the young airmen who flew for him.

By the beginning of February 1945, Russian troops had fought their way to within fifty miles of Berlin. The Red Army's advance had prompted the British Joint Intelligence Committee on 25 January to review the possibility of assisting the Russian advance through heavy bombing. The committee was convinced the impact of the Russian offensive against Germany necessitated an urgent review of the employment of British and American bomber forces. In its deliberations, the committee opined that Anglo-American bombers should blast tank factories and devastate Berlin with a series of heavy attacks. It was believed that raiding the German capital would wreak havoc with German troop movements to the east and disorganise the administrative machinery of the Reich. Civilians fleeing the bombed ruins of Berlin and those escaping westward away from the Russians 'would be bound to create great confusion, interfere with the orderly movement of troops to the front and hamper the German military and administrative machine,' reported the committee.[448] There was also some hope that such a destructive raid would cause the final collapse of the Nazi regime.

The plan was discussed under the codename Thunderclap and prompted vigorous discussion amongst the commanders of the Allied air war. The idea of a sustained campaign against Berlin, however, was not a plan that filled Portal with any sense of enthusiasm. Casualties amongst the aircrews, he feared, would be horrendous, and he doubted — quite correctly — whether such attacks would bring about a German surrender. Oil, Portal said, was to remain the top priority for the western bomber commands. With this in mind, Portal suggested an alternative to the 'heavy and sustained attacks on Berlin'[449] called for in Thunderclap. Noted Portal:

> Subject to the overriding claims of oil and such other agreed targets as the rocket and jet engine factories, submarine building yards for marginal effort etc., we should use available effort in one big attack on Berlin and attacks on Dresden, Leipzig, Chemnitz, or any other cities where a severe blitz will not only cause confusion tin the evacuation from the East but will also hamper the movements of troops from the West.[450]

Thunderclap was not a new concept. The plan had originally been discussed in August 1944 and called for British and American bombers to drop more than 25,000 tons of explosive and incendiaries on Berlin over a four-day period. Even then, the scheme was met with reservations. Now, on 27 January Portal instructed Air Marshal Bottomley to convince Sir Arthur Tedder and General Spaatz to go along with his alternative plan. Both commanders were in line with the scheme. That same day, Bottomley contacted Harris and ordered him to attack the cities mentioned in Portal's minute as soon as weather and moon conditions allowed. Churchill, never far from the action and always quick with a minute of his own, expressed his interest in the Eastern Front on 26 January, when he wrote to the Secretary of State for Air: 'Berlin, and no doubt other large cities in Eastern Germany, should now be considered especially attractive targets.'[451] The Prime Minister was quickly assured that such cities were in the process of being targeted with a minimum diversion from oil operations. But because of moon conditions, Bomber Command would not be able to commence raids in eastern Germany until 4 February.[452]

At the end of January a list of priorities was assembled dictating how the western air forces should respond to the fighting in the east. Oil, as always, remained the most important objective. But ranked second in importance were the raids on Berlin, Dresden and the other previously mentioned cities. As was noted:

A series of heavy attacks by night upon these administrative and control centres is likely to cause considerable delays in the deployment of troops at the front, and may well result in establishing a state of chaos in some or all of these centres... The justification for continuance of such attacks would be largely reduced if the enemy succeeded in stabilizing his eastern front. Successful attacks of this nature delivered at once, however, might well prevent him from achieving this aim.[453]

Communications came next, followed by jet-aircraft factories and lines of communication in southern Germany. Tank factories and submarine yards rounded off the list, which was dispatched to the Chiefs of Staff on 2 February. As Harris later wrote: 'The attack on Dresden was at the time considered a military necessity by much more important people than myself.'[454]

The way was clearing for 8,500 British and American airmen to fly against Dresden — but doubts lingered surrounding the necessity of the operation. Harris, for one, was concerned with the distance crews would have to fly in winter weather. Some bombers would be in the sky for nearly ten hours. There was little intelligence available on Dresden, and not much was known about the city's defences. Harris and his staff at High Wycombe believed there were more vital targets to strike. Meanwhile, meeting with Allied leaders in Yalta, the Red Army Deputy Chief of Staff, General Antonov, expressed his country's desire for the British and Americans to prevent the Germans from transporting more troops to the Eastern Front. When Anglo-American plans for attacks on Berlin, Dresden, Leipzig and Chemnitz were presented, the Russians voiced their approval. Dresden's fate was sealed in part by the immense damage British and American bombers had done to Berlin. The USAAF had raided the capital as recently as 3 February when 1,000 B-17s blasted railways and government buildings. Orders were thus sent to Harris and Spaatz calling for their forces to bomb the second-priority target — Dresden — at the earliest opportunity.[455]

On 13 February battle orders went out.

'A Very Important Rail Centre'

The opening blows of the Dresden assault were to be delivered by the US Eighth, but bad weather that fateful morning kept the Americans grounded. The RAF's met. officers, however, forecast a five-hour period free of cloud over the city that night. Thus, it fell upon the British to commence

Thunderclap. No. 5 Group was detailed to raid the city first. The intent of the initial low-level attack was to set the city ablaze. A larger force of bombers from Nos 1, 3, 6 and 8 groups would follow three hours later and feed the inferno. Across England, the orders were received. At RAF Conningsby, the intelligence officer for No. 97 Squadron made note of the fact that Dresden was being raided to assist the Russians:

> Rain during the morning prevented early flying, but operations were laid to attack Dresden, a very important rail centre for the supplying of German armies at the Russian front.[456]

Aircrew members heard similar sentiments when they reported for their briefing late that afternoon and early that evening. Zero-hour for No. 5 Group was set for 2215. Each aircraft would carry in its belly 8,000 pounds of incendiaries and a 4,000-lb. 'Cookie.' The second force would commence its attack three hours later. It was made clear the intent of the operation was to burn Dresden.[457] But to the young men who sat there, listening to their orders, it was just another operation. What made them uneasy was the distance, for the capital of Saxony lay some 900 miles away. Crews were told diversionary raids would be flown to keep the night-fighters busy. Just before the first bombs were scheduled to land on Dresden, 368 Halifaxes, Lancasters and Mosquitoes would blast the Braunkohle-Benzin synthetic-oil plant at Bohlen. Dresden's ordeal was now just hours away.

The city, by all accounts, was an architectural marvel, drawing comparisons to the artistic centres of Italy. But after 13 February Dresden would never be the same, and its name would forever be associated with the fiery holocaust soon to be unleashed. By 1800 hours 244 Lancasters were winging their way through the dark skies over England, cutting through the black at heights ranging from 17,000 to 19,000 feet. They soared across the English Channel and flew over the Pas de Calais at 220 mph. Over the city of Aachen, the bombers swerved to the east into enemy airspace. They skirted the fierce defences of the Ruhr, keeping the valley's formidable firepower to the north.[458]

At 9:51 p.m. the air raid sirens in Dresden began to wail. A few minutes before 2215 hours, the first target indicators began to fall, bathing the sky in shades of green and white. Nine Mosquitoes followed, cutting a swatch across the city at 3,000 feet and marked the aiming points with red target indicators. One squadron marking the target areas was No. 83 Pathfinder Squadron. Reported one of the squadron's Lancaster crews: 'Route to target was free of trouble. Just before we commenced to run exactly on time, it was noticed that approximately 3 sticks of flares were starting to go down. H-15 one Red T.I. seen bursting at 5,000 feet. Marking completed quickly and Main Force called in to bomb.'[459] The flares fell in tightly concentrated areas, flooding the cityscape in crimson. The colour seeped up through the clouds, the tops of which levelled out at 6,000 to 8,000 feet. At 2212 hours the main force was signalled to come in and blast the city. Receiving the message 'Attack Red R.I.s as planned,' the attack force commenced its run.

'The higher aircraft were to come down below the base of the medium cloud,' notes the Operation Records Book for No. 44 Squadron, which dispatched fourteen aircraft to the city. 'The glow of red T.I.s was quickly supplemented by the glow from fires, and many good fires could be seen through gaps by aircraft which had left the target area.'[460] All fourteen crews successfully bombed the target — and within minutes, the city was burning. 'There was a fairly large area of glow,' reported one crew. 'Green T.I.s were seen beyond the reds. Fires seen astern for a long time and several explosions.'[461] It was not long before the sky was bathed in the glow of flames. Seventeen Lancasters from No. 49 Squadron bombed from heights of 12,000 to 13,700 feet. 'Crews attacking at beginning of attack had no difficulty in running up on glow of markers,' report squadron records. 'But as fires spread, glow of markers was indistinguishable, and it is likely that in early stages this bombing was reasonably confined to sectors, but later became scattered.'[462] Massive explosions were seen erupting skyward less than two minutes after the bombing began. All crews from both squadrons would return to base safely and report the operation to be a success.

The pounding lasted fifteen minutes. Between 10:13 p.m. and 10:28 p.m., some 881 tons of bombs ripped through the centre of Dresden. Nearly sixty per cent of the weight dropped was high explosive.[463] In the city, people huddled in shelters and basements, cringing against the fearful cannonade. Roofs were ripped off buildings and walls crumpled like paper. Doors vaporised in clouds of splinters and roads were gashed wide open. From above, 172 x 4,000-lb. 'Cookies' and 25 x 2,000-lb. air mines slammed into the city. A maelstrom of 1,000-lb. and 500-lb. high explosives tumbled through the darkness along with 205,068 four-pound sticks of incendiaries.[464] The emergency services were paralysed as roads disintegrated into rubble. Flames leapt from building to building and tree to tree. People stumbled about the streets in blind confusion wrapped in wet blankets in a useless attempt to fend off the heat. Burning buildings collapsed on fleeing masses and smouldering corpses littered the roadways. Some people were vaporized, while others died slow suffocating deaths, choking on scolding air and thick clouds of ash and dust. Cries for help and screams for loved ones were lost in the roar of the firestorm.[465]

As the bombers winged their way back to England, Dresden glowed like a beacon in the darkness. From 100 miles away, the city was a stark red stain on the horizon. By midnight, the city centre was consumed by a raging conflagration. Fire-fighting efforts proved useless. Twisting clouds of hot embers whipped through burning air that choked and strangled panic-stricken residents. Skin blistered and lungs were seared as the firestorm tightened its merciless grip on the city. Much more was still to come, for the second wave of British bombers — numbering 550 — was on its way. They were in the sky by 10 p.m. and crossed the French coast near Boulogne. A formidable force, the bomber stream measured more than 120 miles in length. Unlike the first wave, the second contingent of bombers maintained a steady outward track with few diversionary changes in direction.[466] At 1:07 a.m. the city's air raid sirens screamed again. Fourteen minutes later, the second wave of bombing began.[467]

Explosives fell from 20,000 feet into the frenzy of blazing light below. Target markers dropped by sixty Lancasters of 8 Pathfinder Group were quickly obscured by the spreading flames, prompting crews to aim for the centre of the already burning fires. The flames devoured everything. Like Hamburg, roadways turned to rivers of tar and convection currents sucked people into the flames. Emergency crews and evacuees choked to death in the streets as ancient Dresden collapsed around them. Wild animals escaped from the zoo and sought shelter from the maelstrom only to roast alive in their bid for safety. For twenty-three minutes, the Lancasters circled above and dropped 1,800 tons of mostly high explosives.[468] Then, with bombs gone, they turned for home. Dresden — now a fiery hell — could be seen burning from 200 miles away. And as that second wave of British bombers made their way for home in the pre-dawn darkness, American crews in England were readying themselves for their turn.

When 311 B-17s arrived over the city shortly after noon on 14 February, the city was a smoking heap. Thick, grey smoke hung over Dresden's skeletal remains and blocked out the sun. The firestorm was over, but 1,000 fires still burned throughout the city.[469] When the Americans arrived on target that Ash Wednesday, there was little left to bomb. The attack lasted thirteen minutes as the American force dumped 136,800 incendiaries and nearly 2,000 x 500-lb. bombs on the city from heights of nearly 30,000 feet.[470] There was little more the Americans could do that the British hadn't already done. More than 400 B-17s had actually been detailed for the raid, but a number of them — through errors of navigation — wound up bombing Prague.[471] The following day, 15 February, 210 B-17s returned to the ravaged city and blasted its marshalling yards. The stigma of Dresden, however, would attach itself almost solely to the British.

According to reports out of Dresden following the raids, nearly three-quarters of the city centre's nine square miles were obliterated. Of the city's 220,000 houses, more than 86,000 were either completely destroyed or heavily damaged. Assessing the number of dead proved to be challenging. Estimates ranged wildly into the hundreds of thousands. German propaganda played up the carnage as a clear example of Allied brutality, citing the fiery deaths of 400,000 people. Disposing of the bodies became a major problem in the wake of the raids. Flame throwers were used to torch corpses found in cellars and bomb craters. Numerous funeral pyres

— stacked high with up to 500 bodies — were built in the streets and set alight immediately following the raid.[472] Remains of those killed were still being found years after the bombing. Today, the estimated number of dead hovers somewhere between 25,000 and 40,000.[473] From a strategic point of view, the destruction of Dresden prevented the city from ever becoming a control centre for German forces on the Eastern Front — but the end results remain questionable. The attack did little to weaken German resistance in the East. The Red Army did not capture the city until 8 May. Perhaps the greatest impact of the Dresden raid was on the post-war opinion of Bomber Command itself, for the city would become the barometer by which the actions of Harris's crews were judged.

Even Churchill sought to distance himself from Dresden's ordeal with a 28 March minute to his Chiefs of Staff, suggesting the policy of bombing German cities 'simply for the sake of increasing the terror, though under other pretexts, should be reviewed.' If bombing on such a scale continued, Churchill wrote, the Allies would be left in control of nothing 'but an utterly ruined land' once Germany surrendered. Churchill continued: 'The destruction of Dresden remains a serious query against the conduct of Allied bombing. I am of the opinion that military objectives must henceforward be more strictly studied in our own interests rather than that of the enemy.'[474] In his criticism of the Dresden raid, Churchill seemed to forget he had approved the bombing of cities in eastern Germany to assist the Russians. It was a clear example of how Churchill the war leader differed from Churchill the politician. Although the Prime Minister ultimately withdrew the minute, his feelings on the matter were clear. Already, there were public murmurings surrounding the raid. On the evening of 16 February, news of the bombing broke over the wire via an Associated Press dispatch from SHAEF headquarters in Paris. The story said leaders in the Allied air war had finally made the long-delayed decision to adopt 'terror bombing' against the German population as a means of hastening Hitler's downfall.[475] The story cleared Allied censors and was released to the world. It was, notes historian Frederick Taylor, one of the biggest propaganda blunders of the war.[476]

And indeed, sixty years on, the fallout still lingers.

Cities would continue to burn, but not to Dresden's extent. The day following Churchill's minute of 28 March, Harris was asked to respond. As he had always done, Harris defended the policy of area bombardment. It was because of the destruction of German cities that Allied troops were able to advance swiftly into Germany, he said, adding he was not convinced the bombing of oil facilities and lines of communication were an expedient to victory. Destroying German cities, Harris continued, had shortened the war and softened the enemy — lack of hard evidence supporting such a theory notwithstanding. Harris argued the bombing of German cities should continue until all hardened resistance had crumbled.[477] The following week, the Air Staff established four guiding principles to govern the policy of area bombardment. Such attacks would be permitted in populated areas 'behind the fronts containing reserves and maintenance organization in the event of stiffening resistance on the western or eastern fronts.'[478] If weather conditions did not allow precision bombing and time was of the essence, vital targets — such as communications — could be attacked through area bombardment. Towns housing evacuees of the German High Command from Berlin could be blasted on a widespread scale. Finally, Bomber Command could employ the use of carpet-bombing against naval towns, such as Kiel, if the resulting devastation meant the destruction of German naval capabilities.[479] On 6 April the Air Ministry informed a bristling Harris of these new guidelines.

XVI

Final Victory

On the Precipice

Harris saw the writing on the wall. The war was not yet over, but already the fires of public miscontent with Bomber Command's actions were burning brightly. Night after night for three years, he had sent thousands of young men out to die while implementing British strategic policy. Now, writing his response to Churchill's 28 March memorandum concerning the 'terror bombing' of Germany, Harris was incensed. He wrote:

> To suggest that we have bombed German cities 'simply for the sake of increasing the terror though under other pretexts' and to speak of our offensive as including 'mere acts of wanton destruction' is both an insult to the bombing policy of the Air Ministry and to the manner in which that policy has been executed by Bomber Command.

His assessment of Germany was blunt:

> I do not personally regard the whole of the remaining cities of Germany as worth the bones of one British Grenadier.[480]

And so Harris was left to stand alone in his defence of Bomber Command's offensive. Nevertheless, he had to admit it was becoming increasingly difficult to find targets he considered worthy of his men's attention. Starting on the night of 20 February, Mosquitoes slammed Berlin for thirty-six consecutive nights.[481] On 1 March Harris dispatched his forces against Mannheim in what would be the last large-scale area bombardment of the city. It was a daylight operation flown by 478 Lancasters, Halifaxes and Mosquitoes. The intent was to smash any built-up areas that remained untouched. This was followed the next day by two daylight raids on Cologne by nearly 900 bombers. American troops entered Cologne four days later to find the city in skeletal ruins. In its final assault on Essen on 11 March, Bomber Command carried out its largest daylight operation of the war. More than 4,600 tons of bombs were dropped by 1,079 aircraft, under the cover of eighteen Mustang squadrons. There was little left to bomb, but heavy damage was done to the city's central station marshalling yard, which was rendered ninety per cent unserviceable. Seven Spitfire squadrons operating from continental airfields covered the bombers' withdrawal. Only three Lancasters were lost. Essen, which in the early stages of the war had proven to be one of Bomber Command's toughest targets, was now completely shattered. Mass evacuations had reduced the city's pre-war population of 648,000 to 310,000. Air raids had claimed the lives of 7,000 Essen residents.[482]

Throughout March Bomber Command's heaviest raids were directed against the Ruhr and carried out by day. The last major night operation flown by the Command was against Pforzheim — south of Karlsruhe — on the evening of 23 February. Briefing air commanders on the attack at a SHAEF conference, Harris reported 'the whole place had been burned out.'[483] According to Harris, the town boasted numerous workshops used in the manufacturing of precision instruments. In less than thirty minutes, 367 bombers dropped 1,825 tons of bombs. More than 17,000 people died in the fiery onslaught, according to one city report.[484] More than eighty per cent of the city's built-up area was laid to waste. It was the greatest proportion of damage done by Bomber Command in a single raid and cost the British twelve Lancasters.[485] Nuremberg, always a hard option, claimed twenty-four Lancasters on the night of 16 March when nightfighters infiltrated the bomber stream. The raid by 231 aircraft knocked the city's gasworks out of commission for the remainder of the war. Hamburg was blasted three more times in March. On the last day of the month, flying against Germany's second city, Bomber Command suffered its last double-digit aircraft loss of the war. Attacking U-boat plants at the Blohm & Voss shipyards, eight Lancasters and three Halifaxes were blasted from the sky by Luftwaffe dayfighters. On 8 April American bombers attacked the city's shipyards. The assault was followed several hours later by another pounding from Bomber Command. It was the RAF's last assault on the city.[486] Railways, bridges and canals were bombed in a final effort to isolate the Ruhr. Like its cities, German resistance was crumbling. Encountering weak opposition to the east of the river, the Allies had crossed the Rhine by the end of March. German forces in the west retreated into the shattered remnants of the Ruhr, where more than 300,000 troops surrendered to the advancing British and American armies on 18 April. At the same time, the Americans and Russians were preparing to meet at the Elbe, and the British moved north to capture German ports. The face of the war had changed drastically. There was no longer a need for the Anglo-American bomber forces to target Germany's industrial and metropolitan centres. If anything, there was now a need to preserve what little was left standing to assist occupation forces in the future rebuilding of Germany.[487] Harris, however, remained unconvinced.

Mosquitoes continued ravaging Berlin throughout April, dropping 1,273 tons of bombs on the city in the course of fifteen raids.[488] At Kiel on the night of 9 April Lancasters and Mosquitoes bombed the harbor and sank the pocket battleship *Admiral Scheer*. The warships *Admiral Hipper* and *Emden* were severely damaged. Potsdam went up in flames on the night of 14 April. It was Bomber Command's final major operation against a German metropolis. A force of 599 Lancasters and Mosquitoes targeted the city centre, blasting military barracks and railways. The bombardment took place just days after the Air Ministry announced its news guidelines governing area attacks. Less than pleased with the Potsdam operation, Churchill fired off a minute to the Chief of the Air Staff demanding, 'What was the point of going and blowing down Potsdam?'[489] The city, the Prime Minister was told, served as a centre of communications leading west from Berlin and that Luftwaffe operational headquarters had been evacuated to Potsdam.[490]

Against Berlin, the RAF ceased operations on 20 April, when seventy-six Mosquitoes made six separate attacks on the city. Mosquito XVI ML929 of No. 109 Squadron dropped the last bomb at 2:14 a.m. British time.[491] What remained of the ravaged capital was left to the Red Army, which was rapidly closing in. Two days later — at the behest of the 21st Army Group — 195 Lancasters blasted Bremen as a prelude to an assault by the British XXX Corps. Through 10/10th cloud cover, explosives were dropped on the Borgward motor transport works and the Lloyd dynamo works in the southeast part of the city. Mosquitoes swooped in low that evening and blasted a number of military camps and barracks. For five more days, the British kept up the pressure with an unrelenting artillery bombardment, attacks from RAF fighter-bombers and the final infantry and armour advance. Bremen — the first major German port to be captured — fell to the British on 26 April with the surrender of 6,000 German troops.[492]

By now, the strategic bomber offensive was as good as over. Germany was a mangled heap, though few targets still remained. Against an oil refinery in the Norwegian town of Tonsberg on the night of 25 April, 107 Lancasters carried out the final heavy bomber assault of the war. The last of the RAF's lost 3,341 Lancasters was knocked out of the sky over Sweden, where its crew survived the crash and was interned until the end of the war.[493] On the morning of the Tonsberg raid, Bomber Command sighted Berchtesgaden — Hitler's retreat in the Bavarian Alps — in its crosshairs. Earlier in the month, Harris had suggested that the 'Eagle's Nest' be wiped out. Nearly 400 Lancasters and Mosquitoes — under the cover of ninety-eight Mustangs of the US Eighth and thirteen Mustang squadrons of Fighter Command — thundered over the snow-frosted peaks. A swirling ground fog shrouded the chalet and prevented visual targeting. Lancasters from Nos 9 and 617 Squadron bombarded the mark with their 12,000-lb. 'Tallboys.' The monstrous blasts echoed off the mountainous slopes, but Hitler's retreat remained unmolested. Lancasters and Mosquitoes of Nos. 1, 5 and 8 Groups fared better against the nearby barrack blocks and an SS residence. Guns entrenched in hillside positions threw up a storm of flak, which claimed two Lancasters. It was hoped Hitler would die in the raid. Instead, he was far removed from the serene tranquillity of the mountains and facing his last desperate days under the brutalised streets of Berlin.[494]

Reaping the Whirlwind

Hitler's Thousand-Year Reich was fast approaching its violent end. In the final days of conflict, Bomber Command would fly not missions of devastation, but operations with a humanitarian objective. On 26 April forty-two bombers of No 5 Group flew to Brussels and retrieved 999 liberated British prisoners of war. It was the beginning of Operation Exodus, during which the aircraft of Bomber Command — which had wreaked such devastation against Nazi Germany — brought 75,000 Allied repatriates home by 6 June.[495] Bomber Command also began flying operations over the Netherlands, dropping food to the people of Holland. Five years of occupation had brought the Dutch population to the brink of starvation. On 29 April 239 Lancasters from Nos 1 and 3 Groups dropped more than 500 tons of food over Rotterdam, The Hague and Leiden, commencing Operation Manna.[496]

The noise of the engines brought people out into the streets, where they turned their gaze skyward as the bombers thundered overhead. Between the day of the first drop and the general German capitulation on 8 May, Bomber Command flew mercy operations every day except for one, when it was grounded by bad weather. Designated as dropping zones were Valkenburg airfield at Leiden, Kralingsche Plas and Waalburg airfield at Rotterdam, and Gouda airfield and the racecourse at The Hague. The drops became major events, with the Dutch population turning out in massive numbers. They cheered and waved Union Jacks as the food was dropped from bombers flying no higher than 500 feet. The rations were placed in double sacks. When they hit the ground, the outer sack burst, but the inner sack remained intact. Pilots would reduce their airspeed to 150 mph to prevent the sacks from slamming into a bomber's tail plane. Lancasters, assisted by Mosquitoes, flew 3,156 successful ration sorties and dropped 6,684 tons of food. On 1 May, the US Eighth joined the operation. The American drop zones were at Amsterdam, Vogelensang, Alkmaar, Hilversum and Utrecht. In six days, American B-17s and Liberators dropped 4,180 tons of food.[497]

The last aircraft of Bomber Command lost during the war went down on the night of 2 May in an operation against ships at Kiel. Flying in support of the main assault force of more than 120 Mosquitoes, two Halifaxes of No. 199 Squadron flying counter-measures collided. Each bomber had eight men on board and each was carrying 4 x 500-lb. bombs. The burning wreckage fell just south of Kiel. Only three of the sixteen men survived.[498] On 3 May, warning of a ceasefire reached High Wycombe. The following day, at Montgomery's tactical headquarters on Lüneberg Heath, German officers signed a document of surrender for all German forces in Denmark, Holland and north-west Germany. On 7 May German plenipotentiaries at Eisenhower's headquarters accepted unconditional surrender for German forces on all fronts. With representatives from Great Britain, Russia and France watching, the final act of surrender was signed at 0241 hours. From the Air Ministry, the final signal of war to Bomber Command read: 'All German land and sea and air forces will cease active operations at 0001/B hours on May 9.[499]

The war in Europe was over.

In the fierce fighting that began on the beaches of Normandy and continued for eleven harsh months, the British Army had lost nearly 40,000 men in the campaign to liberate north-west Europe. In the killing skies above, Bomber Command had lost roughly 10,000 men and 2,128 aircraft during the same period. Now, many Bomber Command squadrons were assigned to Tiger Force for the British bombardment of Japan. The dropping of the atomic bombs in August, however, rendered the plan unnecessary.[500] On 10 May — a day after the guns in Europe fell silent — Harris issued a special Order of the Day to those who had served the Command.

It read, in part:

> To all of you I would say how proud I am to have served in Bomber Command for 4½ years and to have been your Commander-in-Chief through more than three years of your saga. Your task in the German war is now completed. Famously you fought. Well have you served your country and her Allies.[501]

It had been a saga of extreme violence and unfathomable courage. In his war memoirs, Churchill recounts a visit he made to Peckham, South London, where a bomb, dropped the previous night, had completely destroyed thirty houses in a lower-class neighbourhood. Where families had once lived, there now stood mountains of shattered brick and smoking timber. Craters had torn the street wide open. The crowd present, Churchill wrote, was in a furious mood. They screamed for vengeance and urged Churchill to submit the Germans to the same suffering. The war leader took their wishes to heart and made sure the 'debt was repaid… twentyfold' in the nightly onslaught of British bombs, which grew increasingly destructive as the war dragged on. 'Alas,' wrote Churchill, 'for poor humanity!'[502]

More than fifty years on, Bomber Command and its devastating offensive against Nazi Germany is still the subject of much debate and conjecture. Some post-war critics continue to equate the men of Bomber Command and the man who ultimately led them, Sir Arthur Harris, with war criminals. But to do so is to resort to cheap metaphor and betrays an ignorance of the complexities of that gruelling campaign. The number of German dead on the ground range from 300,000 to 600,000. The bombing of British cities took the lives of 60,500 people. Each night, the men of Bomber Command took to the skies knowing their chances of survival were one in ten. Night fighters, flak and sub-zero temperatures all took their toll, but their sacrifice has been forever obscured by the story of Dresden and the 'killing of women and children.' After any event, it is easy to sit back and wax righteous about what could have been done as an alternative. By June 1940 the might of the Nazi war machine had subjugated most of Europe. Britain, its army hurled into the sea at Dunkirk, stood alone. America remained neutral, veiled behind a curtain of isolationism. The bomber represented Britain's one means of striking back. To this day, those who served the Allied cause in Bomber Command remain without a campaign medal. That such an immense sacrifice should go unheeded is abysmal. In its war against Nazi Germany, Bomber Command lost 8,953 aircraft. Of the roughly 125,000 airmen who flew with Bomber Command, 73,741 became casualties — 55,500 of which were fatalities. Nearly sixty per cent of Bomber Command aircrew became a statistic.[503]

Just as the number 6 million remains an ugly monument to the evils of the Holocaust and the vile mechanization of the death camps, the number of dead on both sides still stands as a horrific testament to the brutality of the air offensive, to the sacrifice demanded and paid in the killing skies.

Bibliography and Sources

Published Sources

Air Ministry, *Bomber Command Handbook,* HMSO, 1941.
Alanbrooke, Field Marshal Lord, *War Diaries 1939-45,* University of California Press, 1998.
Arnold-Foster, Mark, *The World at War,* Methuen, 1981.
Barker, Ralph, *The RAF at War,* Time-Life Books, 1981.
Bekker, Cajus, *The Luftwaffe War Diaries: The German Air Force in World War II,* Birlinn, 2001.
Bennett, Air Vice-Marshal D C T, *Pathfinders,* Muller, 1958,
Brickhill, Paul, *The Dam Busters,* Pan, 1954.
Busch, Fritz-Otto, *The Drama of the Scharnhorst,* Wordsworth Editions, 2001.
Churchill, W S, *The Second World War,* vols I-VI, Cassell, 1948-54.
Cooper, Alan, *Air Battle of the Ruhr,* Air Life Publishing, 2000.
Deighton, Len, *Blitzkrieg: From the Rise of Hitler to the Fall of Dunkirk,* Cape, 1979.
_____ *Bomber,* Cape, 1970.
_____ *Fighter: The True Story of the Battle of Britain,* Cape, 1977.
Delve, Ken and Jacobs, Peter, *The Six-Year Offensive: Bomber Command in World War II,* Arms and Armour Press, 1992.
Gibson, Guy, *Enemy Coast Ahead,* Crecy Publishing, 2001.
Goulding, A G, *Uncommon Valour: The Story of Bomber Command 1939-45,* Air Data Publications, 1996.
Harris, Marshal of the RAF Sir Arthur, *Bomber Offensive,* Greenhill Books, 1990.
Hastings, Max, *Bomber Command,* Michael Joseph, 1979.
Holmes Richard, *Battlefields of the Second World War,* BBC Worldwide, 2001.
Jackson, Robert, *Before the Storm: The Story of Bomber Command 1939-42,* Cassell, 2001.
Knell Hermann, *To Destroy a City: Strategic Bombing and its Human Consequences in World War II,* De Capo Press, 2003.
Manchester, William, *The Last Lion: Alone,* LittleBrown, 1988.

Middlebrook, Martin, *The Battle of Hamburg: The Firestorm Raid*, Cassell, 2000.
_____ *The Berlin Raids: RAF Bomber Command, Winter 1943-44*, Cassell, 2000.
Middlebrook Martin and Everitt, Chris, *The Bomber Command War Diaries: An Operational Refernce Book, 1949-1945*, Midland Publishing, 1996.
Neillands Robin, *The Bomber War: Arthur Harris and the Allied Bomber Offensive, 1939-1945*, John Murray, 2001.
Nesbit, Conyers Roy, *An Illustrated History of the RAF*, Bramley Books, 1990.
Nichol, Joh and Rennell, Tony, *Tail-End Charlies: The Last Battles of the Bomber War 1944-45*, Penguin, 2004.
Overy, Richard, *Bomber Command 1039-45*, HarperCollins, 1997.
Probert, Henry, *Bomber Harris: His Life and Times*, Greenhill, 2001.
Richards, Denis, *The Hardest Victory: RAF Bomber Command in the Second World War*, Penguin, 2001.
Saward, Group Captain Dudley, *The Bomber's Eye*, Cassell, 1959.
_____ *'Bomber' Harris: The Authorized Biography*, Sphere, 1985.
Speer, Albert, *Inside the Third Reich*, Weidenfeld & Nicholson, 1970.
Taylor, Frederick, *Dresden: Tuesday, February 13, 1945*, HarperCollins, 2004.
Taylor, James and Davison, Martin, *Bomber Crew*, Hodder & Stoughton, 2004.
Terraine, John, *The Right of Line: The Royal Air Force in the European War, 1939-1945*, Wordsworth Editions, 1997.
Various, *Britain at War*, Eyre & Spottiswoode, 1943.
Webster, C and Frankland, N, *The Strategic Air Offensive Against Germany 1939-45* [Official History], HMSO, 1961.
Ziegler, Paul, *London at War*, Alfred A Knopf, 1995.

PRO Sources

In writing this book, I relied on the following documents at the National Archives, Kew, the details of specific operations. The materials listed can be found in class Air 27.

Operation Records Book (ORB), No. 7 Squadron: 23 July 1941
—11 Aug. 1942
ORB, No. 9 Squadron: 4 Sept. 1939
—18 Dec. 1939
ORB, No. 35 Squadron: 23 July 1941
—18 Nov. 1932
ORB, No. 44 Squadron: 12 April 1942
ORB, No. 49 Squadron: 12 Aug. 1940
—1 Oct. 1942
ORB, No. 50 Squadron: 3 March 1942
ORB, No. 58 Squadron: 16 April 1940
ORB No. 75 (NZ) Squadron: 7 July 1941
ORB, No. 76 Squadron: 23 July 1941
ORB, No. 82 Squadron: 13 Aug. 1940
ORB, No. 83 Squadron: 12 Aug. 1940
ORB, No. 97 Squadron: 12 April 1942
ORB, No. 99 Squadron: 14 Dec. 1939

ORB, No. 105 Squadron: 4 July 1940
—19 Sept. 1942
—25 Sept. 1942
—30 Jan. 1943
ORB No. 107 Squadron: 7 April 1940
—17 April 1940
ORB, No. 115 Squadron: 9 April 1940
ORB No. 139 Squadron: 3 Sept. 1939
—30 Jan. 1943
ORB, No. 149 Squadron: 18 Dec. 1939
ORB, No. 487 Squadron: 3 May 1943

Aside from memorandums quoted in the text from Air 8 and Air 14, combat reports from Air 50 were also consulted in the reconstruction of several air battles.

Air Historical Branch Papers

The following AHB papers were consulted and relied heavily upon in the writing of this book.

PRO Air 41/21: The Campaign in France and the Low Counties, Sept. 1949-June 1941.
PRO Air 41/24: The Liberation of North West Europe, vol. 3: The Landings in Normandy.
PRO Air 41/39: The RAF in the Bombing Offensive Against Germany, vol. 1: Pre-War Evolution of Bomber Command, 1917-1939.
PRO Air 41/40: The RAF in the Bombing Offensive Against Germany, vol. 2: Restricted Bombing, Sept. 1939-May 1941.
PRO Air 41/41: The RAF in the Bombing Offensive Against Germany, vol. 3: Area Bombing and Makeshift Force, June 1941-Feb. 1942.
PRO Air 41/42: The RAF in the Bombing Offensive Against Germany, vol. 4: A Period of Expansion and Experiment, March 1942-Jan. 1943.
PRO Air 41/43: The RAF in the Bombing Offensive Against Germany, vol. 5: The Full Offensive, Feb. 1943-May 1944.
PRO Air 41/56: The RAF in the Bombing Offensive Against Germany, vol. 6: The Final Phase, March 1944-May 1945.

Imperial War Museum

Numerous private diaries, letters and logbooks archived at the Imperial War Museum were reviewed in preparation for this book. Extracts that appear in this text from those documents do so with kind permission. Among some of the documents consulted were:

Hull, G J — Con Shelf
Dobson, J P/RAFVR — 92/2/1
Hobbs, G H — 92/10/1
Field Flying Officer D R — 92/9/1
Dye B G — 85/6/1

Endnotes

[1] IWM Archives: Papers of Captain John Dobson.

[2] IWM Archives: Papers of Pilot Officer Michael Andrew Scott.

[3] Air Ministry's Bomber Command Handbook, p. 94.

[4] Ibid, p. 95

[5] Ibid

[6] Description taken from Operation Records Book of No. 214 Squadron, relating to crash involving the author's grandfather. A copy of the report was found in his logbook.

[7] From an unpublished memoir by Airgunner Jack Catford, given to the author by Catford.

[8] IWM Archives: Papers of Captain John Dobson, op. cit.

[9] Catford, op. cit.

[10] Bomber Command Handbook, op. cit., p. 97

[11] PRO Air 27/No. 139 Squadron, 3 Sept. 1939.

[12] Richards, The Hardest Victory, pp. 13-14.

[13] PRO Air 14/225, Air Staff, 27 Sept. 1938

[14] PRO Air 14/225, Air Staff, 9 Dec. 1937; Overy, Bomber Command 1939-45, p. 24.

[15] Webster and Frankland, op. cit., p. 97.

[16] Air Historical Branch Papers Quoted in Terraine, The Right of Line, p. 80

[17] PRO Air 8/283 Air Ministry 'Instructions Governing Naval and Air Bombardment', 22 Aug. 1939.

[18] Richards, op. cit., p. 2.

[19] Webster and Frankland, The Strategic Air Offensive Against Germany 1939-45, vol. I, p. 97.

[20] Air Ministry's Bomber Command Handbook, p. 22.

[21] Operation details in PRO Air 27/110 Squadron, 4 Sept. 1939; Bekker, The Luftwaffe War Diaries, p. 62.

[22] PRO Air 27/No. 99 Squadron, 4 Sept. 1939.

[23] Terraine, op. cit., 100.

[24] Harris, Bomber Offensive, p. 36

[25] Bomber Command Handbook, op. cit., p. 33

[26] Ibid, p. 34.

[27] Terraine, op. cit., p. 111.

[28] PRO Air 27/No. 99 Squadron, 14 Dec. 1939.

[29] Ibid.

[30] Ibid.

[31] Ibid.

[32] Ibid.

[33] Ibid.

[34] Quoted in Webster and Frankland, op. cit., p. 194.

[35] Ibid, pp. 194-199.

[36] Harris, op. cit., p. 35.

[37] Memo quoted in Terraine, op. cit., p. 87.

[38] Ibid.

[39] Harris, op. cit., p. 34.

[40] PRO Air 27/No. 37 Squadron, 18. Dec. 1939.

[41] Bekker, op. cit., p. 73.

[42] PRO Air 27/No. 149 Squadron, 18 Dec. 1939.

[43] Bekker, op. cit., p. 74.

[44] PRO Air 27/No. 149 Squadron, 18 Dec. 1939.

[45] Details of damage to bomber and crew's rescue found in Terraine, op. cit., pg. 197.

[46] Webster and Frankland, op. cit., p. 187.

[47] Quoted in Bekker, op. cit., p. 77.

[48] Quoted in Webster and Frankland, op. cit., p. 199.

[49] IWM Archives: Private papers of Pilot Officer Michael Andrew Scott.

[50] Terraine, The Right of Line, p. 112.

[51] Richards, The Hardest Victory, p. 32.

[52] Air Ministry's Bomber Command Handbook, p. 36.

[53] PRO Air 27/No. 107 Squadron, 7 Apr. 1940.

[54] Ibid.

[55] Deighton, Fighter, p. 78.

[56] Bekker, The Luftwaffe War Diaries, p. 79.

[57] Bomber Command Handbook, op. cit., p. 36.

[58] Middlebrook and Everitt, The Bomber Command War Diaries, p. 33.

[59] Ibid.

[60] Gibson, Enemy Coast Ahead, p. 58.

[61] Harris, Bomber Offensive, p. 39.

[62] Gibson, op. cit., p. 58.

[63] Bomber Command Handbook, op. cit., p. 58.

[64] Letters provided to author by airman's family.

[65] Richards, op. cit., p. 41.

[66] Ibid, p. 90.

[67] Bomber Command Handbook, op. cit., p. 38.

[68] PRO Air 27/No. 107 Squadron, 17 Apr. 1940.

[69] Ibid.

[70] Terraine, op. cit., p. 118.

[71] Richards, op. cit., p. 39.

[72] Churchill, The Second World War, vol. 1, pp. 525, 527.

[73] Bekker, The Luftwaffe War Diaries, p. 101.

[74] Air Ministry's Bomber Command Handbook, p. 42.

[75] Terraine, The Right of Line, p. 127.

[76] PRO Air 14/21: AHB: Campaign in France and the Low Countries, p. 203.

[77] Jackson, Before the Storm, p. 103.

[78] PRO Air 14/21, op. cit., p. 204.

[79] Ibid; Barker, The RAF at War, pp. 34-5

[80] Ibid; Ibid.

[81] Ibid; Ibid.

[82] PRO Air 14/21, op. cit., p. 204.

[83] Richards, The Hardest Victory, p. 46.

[84] Bomber Command Handbook, op. cit., pp. 50; PRO Air 41/21, op. cit., pp. 221-2.

[85] Churchill, op. cit., pp. 206-7.

[86] Details of raid found in Middlebrook and Everitt, The Bomber Command War Diaries, p. 43.

[87] Bomber Command Handbook, op. cit., p. 51; PRO Air 41/21, op. cit., pp. 254-5.

[88] Hastings, Bomber Command, p. 61.

[89] Bomber Command Handbook, op. cit., pp. 52-3; casualty figures from Middlebrook and Everitt, op. cit., p. 49.

[90] PRO Air 41/21, op. cit., p. 379; Richards, op. cit., p. 52.

[91] Terraine, op. cit., p. 163.

[92] Bomber Command Handbook, op. cit., p. 163.

[93] Ibid.

[94] Churchill, The Second World War, vol. II, Appendix A, p. 505.

[95] Air Ministry's Bomber Command Handbook, p. 65.

[96] Richards, The Hardest Victory, p. 57.

[97] Bomber Command Handbook, op. cit., p. 68.

[98] Gibson, Enemy Coast Ahead, p. 86.

[99] Ibid.

[100] Hastings, Bomber Command, p. 95.

[101] Churchill, op. cit., p. 88.

[102] Bekker, The Luftwaffe War Diaries, pg. 152.

[103] Ibid.

[104] Hastings, op. cit., p. 62.

[105] Churchill, p. 281.

[106] Ibid, p. 342.

[107] Deighton, Fighter, p. 212.

[108] Quoted in Bekker, op. cit., p. 170.

[109] Bomber Command Handbook, op. cit., p. 68.

[110] Ibid.

[111] Ibid, p. 69.

[112] London Gazette, 1 Oct. 1940; Richards, op. cit., p. 67.

[113] Quoted in Bekker, op. cit., p. 174.

[114] Ibid, p. 175.
[115] Ibid. p. 176.
[116] Barker, The RAF at War, p. 85.
[117] Bomber Command Handbook, op. cit., p. 71.
[118] Quoted from 'Women of London' in Britain at War, p. 280.
[119] Quoted in Webster and Frankland, The Strategic Air Offensive Against Germany 1939-45, vol. IV, p. 129.
[120] Quoted in Churchill, Appendix A, p. 535.
[121] Ibid.
[122] Middlebrook and Everitt, The Bomber Command War Diaries, p. 104.
[123] Bekker, op. cit., p. 180.
[124] Richards, op. cit., p. 77.
[125] Quoted in Webster and Frankland, The Strategic Air Offensive Against Germany 1939-45, vol. IV, pp. 132-2.
[126] Ibid, vol. 1, p. 159.
[127] Terraine, The Right of Line, p. 277.
[128] Barker, The RAF at War, p. 90.
[129] Quoted in Webster and Frankland, op. cit., vol. IV, p. 133.
[130] Ibid.
[131] Churchill, The Second World War, vol. IV, Appendix C, p. 588.
[132] Air Ministry's Bomber Command Handbook, op. cit., pp. 77-8.
[133] London Gazette, 22 July 1941.
[134] Bomber Command Handbook, op. cit., pp. 77-8.
[135] Richards, The Hardest Victory, p. 93.
[136] Delve and Jacobs, The Six Year Offensive, p. 67.
[137] Webster and Frankland, op. cit., vol. IV, pp. 201-2.
[138] Ibid.
[139] Air Ministry's Bomber Command Handbook, p. 83.
[140] Ibid, pp. 83, 86.
[141] Ibid, pp. 86-7.
[142] Reproduced in Webster and Frankland, The Strategic Air Offensive Against Germany, vol. IV< pp. 135-6.
[143] Richards, The Hardest Victory, p. 87; Middlebrook and Everitt, The Bomber Command War Diaries, pp. 174, 175.
[144] PRO Air 27/No. 7 Squadron, 23 July 1941.
[145] PRO Air 27/No. 35 Squadron, 24 July 1941.
[146] Ibid.
[147] Ibid; PRO Air 27/No. 76 Squadron, 24 July 1941; Terraine, The Right of Line, p. 279.
[148] Terraine, op. cit., p. 279.
[149] Terraine, op. cit., pp. 279-80.
[150] Richards, op. cit., p. 88.
[151] Bekker, The Luftwaffe War Diaries, p. 203.
[152] Bekker, op. cit., p. 204.
[153] Bekker, op. cit., p. 203.
[154] Hastings, Bomber Command, p. 235.
[155] Bekker, op. cit., p. 209.

[156] PRO Air 27/No. 75 Squadron, 7 July 1941.
[157] Ibid.
[158] Middlebrook and Everitt, op. cit., p. 209.
[159] Ibid.
[160] Diary provided by family to author.
[161] Churchill, The Second World War, vol. III, Appendix G, p. 635.
[162] Bomber Command Handbook, op. cit., p. 102.
[163] Taken from descriptions of various raids provided by crews in the Operations Record Book for No. 214 Squadron.
[164] Terraine, op. cit., p. 271.
[165] Webster and Frankland, op. cit., p. 250.
[166] Details provided to author in interview.
[167] Reproduced in Webster and Frankland, op. cit., p. 205.
[168] Webster and Frankland, op. cit., pp. 182-3.
[169] Webster and Frankland, op. cit., vol. I, pp. 177-182.
[170] Quoted in Webster and Frankland, op. cit., pp. 182-3.
[171] Memorandum quoted in Webster and Frankland, op. cit., p. 183.
[172] Terraine, op. cit., p. 296.
[173] Reproduced in Webster and Frankland, op. cit., pp. 184-5.
[174] Webster and Frankland, op. cit., pp. 179-80.
[175] IWM Private papers of Captain John Dobson.
[176] Jackson, Before the Storm, p. 163.
[177] Reproduced in Churchill, op. cit., p. 650.
[178] Reproduced in Webster and Frankland, op. cit., p. 186.
[179] Jackson, op. cit., p. 161.
[180] Saward, 'Bomber' Harris, p. xx.
[181] Bekker, The Luftwaffe War Diaries, p. 306.
[182] Churchill, The Second World War, vol. II, p. 104.
[183] Interview with author.
[184] Quoted in Webster and Frankland, The Strategic Air Offensive Against Germany 1939-45, vol. I, p. 322.
[185] Reproduced in Webster and Frankland, op. cit., vol. IV, pp. 143-5.
[186] Ibid.
[187] Ibid.
[188] Hastings, p. 123.
[189] Reproduced in Webster and Frankland, op. cit., vol. I, p. 324.
[190] Harris, Bomber Offensive, p. 79.
[191] Ibid, p. 73.
[192] Richards, The Hardest Victory, p. 305.
[193] Alanbrooke, War Diaries 1949-45, p. 460.
[194] Quoted in Webster and Frankland, op. cit., vol. I, p. 324.
[195] Ibid, p. 329.
[196] Middlebrook and Everitt, The Bomber Command War Diaries, p. 242.
[197] Ibid.
[198] Harris, op. cit., p. 83.
[199] Middlebrook and Everitt, op. cit., p. 245.
[200] Webster and Frankland, op. cit., p. 386.

[201] Harris, op. cit., p. 105.

[202] Webster and Frankland, op. cit., vol. I, p. 392.

[203] Harris, op. cit., p. 105.

[204] Saward, op. cit., p. 164.

[205] Ibid, p. 165.

[206] Harris, op. cit., p. 83.

[207] PRO Air 27/No. 44 Squadron, 17 April 1942.

[208] PRO Air 27/No. 97 Squadron, 17 April 1942.

[209] PRO Air 27/No. 44 Squadron, 17 April 1942.

[210] Ibid.

[211] Ibid.

[212] Ibid.

[213] Webster and Frankland, op. cit., vol. I, p. 443.

[214] Gibson, Enemy Coast Ahead, p. 151.

[215] Saward, op. cit., p. 175.

[216] Harris, op. cit., p. 108.

[217] Bennett, Pathfinder, p. 103.

[218] Ibid.

[219] Ibid.

[220] Ibid.

[221] Ibid.

[222] Ibid.

[223] Ibid, p. 115.

[224] Reproduced in Webster and Frankland, The Strategic Bomber Offensive Against Germany 1939-45, vol. I, pp. 180-1.

[225] Ibid, pp. 331-2.

[226] Ibid, p. 337.

[227] Ibid, p. 338.

[228] Reproduced in Webster and Frankland, op. cit., vol. IV, p. 238.

[229] Speer, Inside the Third Reich, p. 382.

[230] PRO Air 14/276.

[231] Webster and Frankland, op. cit., vol. I, p. 404.

[232] Middlebrook and Everitt, The Bomber Command War Diaries, p. 271.

[233] Harris, Bomber Offensive, p. 110.

[234] Ibid.

[235] Reproduced in Webster and Frankland, op. cit., vol. I, p. 406.

[236] Probert, Bomber Harris: His Life and Times, p. 199.

[237] Ibid.

[238] Saward, The Bomber's Eye, p. 126.

[239] Terraine, The Right of Line, p. 485.

[240] Richards, The Hardest Victory, p. 127.

[241] Bekker, The Luftwaffe War Diaries, p. 306.

[242] London Gazette, 23 Oct. 1942.

[243] Letter to Harris quoted in Saward, op. cit., p. 146.

[244] Speer, Op. cit., p. 382.

[245] Harris, op. cit., p. 113.

[246] Conversation detailed in Bennett, Pathfinders, p. 147.

[247] Ibid.

[248] Quoted in Cooper, Air Battle of the Ruhr, p. 19.

[249] Letter provided to author by family.

[250] Harris, op. cit., p. 122.

[251] PRO Air 27/No. 7 Squadron, 24 Aug. 1942.

[252] Hastings, Bomber Command, p. 167.

[253] Middlebrook and Everitt, The Bomber Command War Diaries, p. 297.

[254] Harris, Bomber Offensive, p. 128.

[255] Reproduced in Webster and Frankland, The Strategic Air Offensive Against Germany 1939-45, vol. IV, p. 234.

[256] Letter to Harris, quoted in Saward, Bomber Harris, pg. 151-2.

[257] Harris, op. cit., p. 129.

[258] Richards, The Hardest Victory, p. 51.

[259] Bennett, Pathfinders, p. 117.

[260] Ibid, p. 118.

[261] Ibid.

[262] Ibid, p. 126.

[263] Hastings, op. cit., p. 280.

[264] Middlebrook and Everitt, op. cit., p. 306.

[265] Bennett, op. cit., p. 129.

[266] PRO Air 27/No. 105 Squadron, 19 Sept. 1942.

[267] Bennett, op. cit., p. 132.

[268] Terraine, The Right of Line, p. 496.

[269] PRO Air 27/No. 49 Squadron, 17 Oct. 1942; Middlebrook and Everitt, op. cit., p. 317.

[270] Webster and Frankland, op. cit., vol. I, pp. 446-7.

[271] Middlebrook and Everitt, op. cit., p. 315.

[272] Harris, op. cit., p. 140.

[273] London Gazette, 15 Jan. 1943.

[274] Gibson, Enemy Coast Ahead, p. 179.

[275] IWM: Personal papers of D. R. Field.

[276] From the Bomber Command Quarterly Review reproduced in Delve and Jacobs, The Six Year Offensive, p. 114.

[277] Middlebrook and Everitt, The Bomber Command War Diaries, p. 340; Richards, The Hardest Victory, p. 157.

[278] Jackson, Before the Storm, p. 209.

[279] Reproduced in Churchill, The Second World War, vol. IV, p. 282.

[280] Ibid, p. 281.

[281] Middlebrook and Everitt, op. cit., p. 349.

[282] Ibid, p. 353.

[283] Bennett, Pathfinders, p. 136.

[284] Middlebrook and Everitt, op. cit., p. 335.

[285] Ibid, p. 336.

[286] Harris, Bomber Offensive, p. 144.

[287] Reproduced in Webster and Frankland, The Strategic Air Offensive Against Germany 1939-45, vol. IV, pp. 152-3.

[288] Harris, op. cit., p. 137.

[289] PRO Air 14/739a.

[290] Saward, 'Bomber' Harris, pp. 175-6.

[291] Bekker, The Luftwaffe War Diaries, p. 307.

[292] Reproduced in Webster and Frankland, op. cit., vol. IV, pp. 153-4.

[293] Ibid.

[294] Harris, Bomber Offensive, p. 144.

[295] Ibid.

[296] PRO Air 41/42: AHB: OBOE and the Battle of the Ruhr, pp. 37-8; Webster and Frankland, The Strategic Air Offensive Against Nazi Germany 1939-45, vol. II, pp. 114-18; Hastings, Bomber Command, p. 197; Richards, The Hardest Victory, p. 168.

[297] Middlebrook and Everitt, The Bomber Command War Diaries, p. 365.

[298] Saward, 'Bomber' Harris, pp. 253-4.

[299] Webster and Frankland, op. cit., vol. I, pp. 201-2.

[300] PRO Air 41/42, op. cit., pp. 38-40; Middlebrook and Everitt, op. cit., see 'The Battle of the Ruhr.'

[301] Quoted in Saward, op. cit., p. 245.

[302] Richards, op. cit., p. 170.

[303] Churchill, The Second World War, vol. V, p. 403.

[304] Details of campaign provided by PRO 41/42, op. cit., pp. 35-44; Middlebrook and Everitt, op. cit., see 'The Battle of the Ruhr.'

[305] Speer, Inside the Third Reich, p. 381.

[306] Ibid, p. 383.

[307] PRO Air 27/No. 487 Squadron, 3 May 1943.

[308] PRO Air 41/42, op. cit., pp. 41-2.

[309] Operation Chastise Battle Order, PRO Air 2/8395.

[310] Speer, op. cit., p. 381.

[311] PRO Air 41/42: AHB: Operation Chastise – The Dams Raid, p. 45.

[312] Ibid, p. 47.

[313] Ibid, pp. 47-7.

[314] Operation Chastise Battle Order, PRO Air 2/8395.

[315] PRO 41/42: AHB: Operation Chastise – The Dams Raid, op. cit., pp. 48-9; also Brickhill, The Dam Busters, pp. 80-1.

[316] [317] PRO 41/42: AHB: Operation Chastise – The Dams Raid, op. cit., pp. 48-9; Gibson, Enemy Coast Ahead, p. 247.

[318] PRO 41/42: AHB: Operation Chastise – The Dams Raid, op. cit., ibid; Gibson, op. cit., pp. 249-50.

[319] PRO 41/42: AHB: Operation Chastise – The Dams Raid, ibid; Gibson, ibid; Brickhill, op. cit., pp. 89-96.

[320] PRO 41/42: AHB: Operation Chastise – The Dams Raid, op. cit., pp. 48-51; Middlebrook and Everitt, op. cit., pp. 386, 388.

[321] Speer, op. cit., p. 384.

[322] Richards, op. cit., p. 178.

[323] PRO Air 41/42: AHB: Oboe ... op. cit., pp. 42-4; Middlebrook and Everitt, op. cit., see 'The Battle of the Ruhr.'

[324] Terraine, The Right of Line, p. 543.

[325] Webster and Frankland, op. cit., vol. II, pp. 17-19.

[326] Reproduced in Webster and Frankland, op. cit., vol. II, pp. 273-283.
[327] Harris, op. cit., p. 144.
[328] Ibid, p. 147.
[329] Ibid, p. 148.
[330] Hastings, op. cit., p. 205.
[331] PRO Air 41/42: AHB: The Devastation of Hamburg, p. 85; PRO Air 25/257.
[332] Middlebrook, The Battle of Hamburg, pp. 83-4.
[333] PRO PRO Air 41/42: AHB: The Devastation of Hamburg, op. cit., pp. 86-8.
[334] Bekker, The Luftwaffe War Diaries, p. 310.
[335] Ibid.
[336] PRO Air 41/42: AHB: The Devastation of Hamburg, op. cit., pp. 88-9; Middlebrook and Everitt, The Bomber Command War Diaries, pp. 410-15.
[337] PRO Air 41/42: AHB: The Devastation of Hamburg, op. cit., pp. 89-91; Middlebrook, The Battle of Hamburg, pp. 263-4.
[338] Reproduced in Webster and Frankland, The Strategic Air Offensive Against Germany 1939-45, vol. IV, pp. 310-15.
[339] Middlebrook and Everitt, The Bomber Command War Diaries, op. cit., p. 413.
[340] Speer, Inside the Third Reich, pp. 388-9.
[341] Ibid, p. 389.
[342] Terraine, The Right of Line, p. 547.
[343] PRO Air 41/42: AHB: The Devastation of Hamburg, op. cit., pp. 89-92.; Middlebrook and Everitt, The Bomber Command War Diaries, pp. 414-15.
[344] Harris, Bomber Offensive, p. 176.
[345] Middlebrook and Everitt, op. cit., p. 439.
[346] Speer, Inside the Third Reich, p. 391.
[347] Reproduced in PRO Air 41/43: AHB: The Battle of Berlin, p. 121.
[348] Bekker, The Luftwaffe War Diaries, p. 333.
[349] Details in letter from Flt Officer Hart in letter to author.
[350] Middlebrook and Everitt, The Bomber Command War Diaries, p. 425; Middlebrook, The Berlin Raids, p. 26.
[351] Harris, Bomber Offensive, p. 246.
[352] Terraine, The Right of Line, p. 550.
[353] Richards, The Hardest Victory, p. 204.
[354] PRO Air 41/43: AHB: The Battle of Berlin, op. cit., p. 122.
[355] Harris, op. cit., p. 176.
[356] Terraine, op. cit., pp. 548, 549.
[357] Speer, op. cit., p. 394.
[358] PRO Air 41/43: AHB: The Battle of Berlin, op. cit., p. 124; Middlebrook, The Berlin Raids, op. cit., p. 26; Middlebrook and Everitt, op. cit., p. 453.
[359] Harris, op. cit., pp. 186-7.
[360] PRO Air 41/43: AHB: The Battle of Berlin, op. cit., p. 124; Bekker, op. cit., p. 334.
[361] PRO Air 41/43: AHB: The Battle of Berlin, op. cit., p. 127.
[362] Quoted in PRO Air 41/43: AHB: The Battle of Berlin, op. cit., p. 125.

[363] Middlebrook, The Berlin Raids, op. cit., p. 118; Harris quoted in Hastings, Bomber Command, pp. 244, 245.

[364] Harris, op. cit., p. 186.

[365] PRO Air 41/43: AHB: The Battle of Berlin, op. cit., p. 125.

[366] Ibid, p. 123; Harris, op. cit., p. 187.

[367] PRO Air 41/43: AHB: The Battle of Berlin, op. cit., p. 126; Bekker, opo. Cit., p. 338.

[368] Webster and Frankland, op. cit., vol. II, p. 56.

[369] PRO Air 41/43: AHB: The Battle of Berlin, op. cit., pp. 126-7; Middlebrook, The Berlin Raids, op. cit., p. 221.

[370] PRO Air 41/43: AHB: The Battle of Berlin, op. cit., p. 127; quoted in Middlebrook and Everitt, op. cit., p. 468.

[371] PRO Air 41/43: AHB: The Battle of Berlin, op. cit., p. 127.

[372] Middlebrook and Everitt, The Bomber Command War Diaries, op. cit., p. 476.

[373] Harris, op. cit., p. 187.

[374] Bekker, op. cit., p. 335.

[375] Ibid, p. 339.

[376] Probert, Bomber Harris: His Life and Times, p. 289.

[377] Richards, The Hardest Victory, p. 222.

[378] Reproduced in Webster and Frankland, The Strategic Air Offensive Against Germany 1939-45, vol. IV, pp. 167-8.

[379] Middlebrook and Everitt, The Bomber Command War Diaries, p. 489.

[380] PRO Air 41/56: AHB: The Role of Bomber Command in the Preparations for Overlord, p. 38.

[381] Ibid.

[382] See Frankfurt records referenced in Middlebrook and Everitt, op. cit., p. 483.

[383] PRO Air 41/56: AHB: The Role of Bomber Command in the Preparations for Overlord, op. cit., p. 39.

[384] Ibid, p. 27.

[385] Ibid, pp. 27-9.

[386] Harris, Bomber Offensive, p. 204.

[387] PRO Air 41/56: AHB: The Role of Bomber Command in the Preparations for Overlord, op. cit., p. 41; Middlebrook and Everitt, op. cit., pp. 492-3.

[388] PRO Air 41/56: AHB: The Role of Bomber Command in the Preparations for Overlord, p. 42.

[389] Ibid; Richards, op. cit., p. 227.

[390] Harris, op. cit., p. 203.

[391] Ibid, p. 205.

[392] PRO Air 41/56: AHB: The Role of Bomber Command in the Preparations for Overlord, op. cit., p. 47-8.

[393] Ibid.

[394] Harris, op. cit., pp. 47-8.

[395] Ibid, p. 206; PRO Air 41/56: AHB: Bomber Operations from 6 June to 15 September 1944, p. 84.

[396] Middlebrook and Everitt, op. cit., p. 523.

[397] PRO Air 41/56: AHB: PRO Air 41/56: AHB: Bomber Operations from 6 June to 15 September 1944, op. cit., p. 81.

[398] Ibid, pp. 81-2; Middlebrook and Everitt, op. cit., p. 539.

[399] PRO Air 41/56: AHB: Bomber Operations from 6 June to 15 September 1944, op. cit., p. 82.

[400] Harris, op. cit., p. 213.

[401] PRO Air 41/56: AHB: Bomber Operations from 6 June to 15 September 1944, op. cit., p. 86; Churchill, The Second World War, vol. VI, p. 23; Middlebrook and Everitt, op. cit., p. 539.

[402] Churchill, op. cit., p. 23.

[403] PRO Air 41/56: AHB: Bomber Operations from 6 June to 15 September 1944, op. cit., p. 87; Middlebrook and Everitt, op. cit., p. 539.

[404] Nichol and Rennell, Tail-End Charlies, p. 217.

[405] Quoted in Richards, op. cit., p. 238.

[406] PRO Air 41/56: AHB: Bomber Operations from 6 June to 15 September 1944, op. cit., p. 88.

[407] Harris, op. cit., p. 212.

[408] Churchill, op. cit., p. 48.

[409] Ibid, p. 39.

[410] Ibid.

[411] Harris, op. cit., p. 216.

[412] PRO Air 41/56: AHB: Crossbow Operations, 16/17 June to 1 September, p. 91.

[413] Churchill, op. cit., p. 48; PRO Air 41/56: AHB: Crossbow Operations, 16/17 June to 1 September, op. cit., p. 91; Richards, op. cit., p. 242.

[414] Harris, op. cit., p. 237.

[415] PRO Air 41/56: AHB: Crossbow Operations, 16/17 June to 1 September, op. cit., p. 92.

[416] Harris, op. cit., p. 237.

[417] Ibid.

[418] Hastings, Bomber Command, p. 309.

[419] Quoted in Hastings, op. cit., pp. 311-12.

[420] Hastings, op. cit., p. 315. Overall details taken from this account.

[421] Middlebrook and Everitt, op. cit., p. 581.

[422] Reproduced in Webster and Frankland, op. cit., pp. 172-3.

[423] Ibid, p. 177.

[424] Richards, op. cit., p. 257.

[425] Reproduced in Webster and Frankland, op. cit., pp. 174-5.

[426] Ibid.

[427] Ibid.

[428] Middlebrook and Everitt, op. cit., p. 595.

[429] Ibid, p. 596.

[430] Richards, op. cit., p. 259.

[431] PRO Air 41/56: AHB: The Attack on the Tirpitz, p. 103.

[432] Ibid.

[433] PRO Air 41/56: AHB: Naval Targets: The Sinking of the Tirpitz, p. 91.

[434] Ibid.

[435] Churchill, op. cit., vol. V, p. 276.
[436] PRO Air 41/56: AHB: Growth of the Heavy Bomber Force, p. 167
[437] PRO Air 41/56: AHB: The Battle of the Ardennes, pp. 183-4.
[438] Harris, Bomber Offensive, p. 225; Richards, The Hardest Victory, p. 255.
[439] PRO Air 41/56: AHB: The Battle of the Ardennes, op. cit., pp. 184-5; Middlebrook and Everitt, The Bomber Command War Diaries, p. 635-6.
[440] Middlebrook and Everitt, op. cit., p. 636.
[441] PRO Air 41/56: AHB: The Battle of the Ardennes, op. cit., p. 185.
[442] Ibid, p. 186.
[443] PRO Air 51/56: AHB: The Bombing of Royan, p. 189.
[444] Middlebrook and Everitt, op. cit., p. 647 (see 4/5 January 1945).
[445] PRO Air 41/56: AHB: The Bombing of Royan, op. cit., p. 189.
[446] Ibid, pp. 188, 189; Middlebrook and Everitt, op. cit., pp. 647, 648.
[447] Ibid, p. 189; ibid, p. 648.
[448] PRO Air 27/No. 83 PFF Squadron, 13 February 1945.
[449] Quoted in Webster and Frankland, The Strategic Air Offensive Against Germany 1939-45, vol. III, p. 100.
[450] Ibid, p. 98.
[451] PRO Air 41/56: AHB: Effect of the Russian Offensive on Bombing Policy: decision to bomb cities in Eastern Germany, reproduced on p. 99.
[452] Ibid, p. 200.
[453] Ibid.
[454] Ibid.
[455] Harris, op. cit., p. 242.
[456] Probert, Bomber Harris: His Life and Times, p. 319.
[457] PRO Air 27/No. 97 Squadron, 13 February 1945.
[458] Nichol and Rennell, Tail-End Charlies, p. 300.
[459] Route details in Taylor, Dresden: Tuesday, February 13, 1945, pp. 3-4.
[460] PRO Air 27/ No. 83 PFF Squadron, 13 February 1945.
[461] PRO Air 27/No. 44 Squadron, 13 February 1945.
[462] Ibid.
[463] PRO Air 27/No. 49 Squadron, 13 February 1945.
[464] Taylor, op. cit., p. 257.
[465] Ibid.
[466] Details provided in letter reproduced in Taylor, op. cit., p. 269.
[467] Taylor, op. cit., p. 274-5.
[468] Ibid.
[469] PRO Air 41/56: AHB: Raids on Area Targets, p. 224; Taylor, op. cit., pp. 278-84; Middlebrook and Everitt, op. cit., p. 663.
[470] Taylor, op. cit., p. 322.
[471] Ibid.
[472] Richards, op. cit., p. 272.
[473] PRO Air 41/56: AHB: Raids on Area Targets, op. cit., p. 224.
[474] Knell, To Destroy a City, p. 254; Taylor, op. cit., p. 354.
[475] Minute reproduced in Webster and Frankland, op. cit., p. 112.
[476] Taylor, op. cit., p. 361.
[477] Ibid, p. 362.

[478] PRO Air 41/56: AHB: The End of Area Bombing, p. 204.

[479] Ibid.

[480] Ibid, pp. 204, 205.

[481] Memorandum quoted in its entirety in Hastings, Bomber Command, Appendix C, pp. 368-70.

[482] PRO Air 41/56: AHB: Mosquito Attacks on Berlin, p. 227.

[483] PRO Air 41/56: AHB: Raids on Area Targets, pp. 225-6; Middlebrook and Everitt, The Bomber Command War Diaries, p. 678.

[484] PRO Air 41/56: AHB: Raids on Area Targets, op. cit., p. 225.

[485] Middlebrook and Everitt, op. cit., p. 669.

[486] Ibid.

[487] Ibid, pp. 690, 692

[488] PRO Air 41/56: AHB: The Fourth Directive to the Strategic Air Forces, p. 205.

[489] PRO Air 41/56: AHB: Mosquito Attacks on Berlin, op. cit., p. 227.

[490] PRO Air 41/56: AHB: Raids on Area Targets, op. cit., p. 226.

[491] Ibid, pp. 226-7.

[492] Middlebrook and Everitt, op. cit., p. 698.

[493] PRO Air 41/56: AHB: The Bombing of Heligoland and Wangerooge and the Fall of Bremen, pp. 237-8; Middlebrook and Everitt, op. cit., p. 699.

[494] Middlebrook and Everitt, op. cit., p. 701.

[495] PRO Air 41/56: AHB: The Bombing of Berchtesgaden, p. 238.

[496] PRO Air 41/56: AHB: Operation Exodus, p. 244.

[497] PRO Air 41/56: AHB: Operation Manna, p. 243.

[498] Ibid, pp. 243-4.

[499] Middlebrook and Everitt, op. cit., p. 702-3.

[500] PRO Air 41/56: AHB: The End of the Year in Europe, p. 244; Middlebrook and Everitt, op. cit., p. 703.

[501] PRO Air 51/56: AHB: The End of the War in Europe, op. cit., p. 244; Middlebrook and Everitt, op. cit., p. 703.

[502] Quoted in Probert, Bomber Harris: His Life and Times, p. 344.

[503] Churchill, The Second World War, vol. II, p. 308.

[504] Fatality figures from Middlebrook and Everitt, op. cit., p. 708 (see 'Aircrew Casualties').

Index